From Their Lips

Gorgias Handbooks

53

Gorgias Handbooks provides students and scholars with reference books, textbooks and introductions to different topics or fields of study. In this series, Gorgias welcomes books that are able to communicate information, ideas and concepts effectively and concisely, with useful reference bibliographies for further study.

From Their Lips

Voices of Early Christian Women

VK McCarty

GORGIAS PRESS

2021

Gorgias Press LLC, 954 River Road, Piscataway, NJ, 08854, USA

www.gorgiaspress.com

2021 Copyright © by Gorgias Press LLC

2021

ISBN 978-1-4632-4255-8   **ISSN 1935-6838**

Library of Congress Cataloging-in-Publication Data

A Cataloging-in-Publication Record is available at the Library of Congress.

Printed in the United States of America

The Word of the Father is formed by the word of a mother, and the Creator is created by the voice of a creature. And just as when God said, "Let there be light," "at once there was light," so, as soon as the Virgin spoke, the true light dawned.[1]

This book is dedicated to the memory of my parents, June McAlister Long & Charles Osner Long, MD; so glad I can still hear you

---

[1] Nicholas Cabasilas, "Homily on the Annunciation" 10:40-41, J. Sanidopoulos, trans., "Homélies Mariales Byzantines (II)," Martin Jugie, ed., in *Patrologia Orientalis* XIX, R. Graffin, F. Nau, eds (Paris: Firmin-Didot, 1920), pp. 484-495.

TABLE OF CONTENTS

ACKNOWLEDGEMENTS

This book could not have been made without the support, generosity, and mentorship of several people while I was researching the individual chapters over the last several years. Among them, I am indebted to the Very Rev. John McGuckin and the Rev. Howard T.W. Stowe for opening the way to this theological chapter of my life; to Dr. Brice C. Jones and Dr. Tuomas Rasimus, for shepherding this book through the publication process at Gorgias Press, and also to the Sophia Institute and the Institute for Studies in Eastern Christianity, to the Rev. Dr. John T. Koenig, the Rev. Dr. Ellen Barrett, the Rev. Dr. Janet Wootton, the Rev. William Forrest, OSB, the Rev. Clark Berge, SSF, Barbara Pizio, the Sisters of the Community of the Holy Spirit, and all the friends who feed me. And last of all, I need to thank two friends for their compassionate generosity and guiding support—Dr. Conrad Fischer and the Rev. Dr. Sergey Trostyanskiy.

ABBREVIATIONS

AB	Analecta Bollandiana
ACCS	Ancient Christian Commentary on Scripture
An Res	De Anima Et Resurrectione
AP	Apophthegmatum Patrum
ASBMH	American Society of Byzantine Music and Hymnology
ATR	Anglican Theological Review
BMFO	Byzantine Monastic Foundation Documents
BZ	Byzantinische Zeitschrift
Byz	Byzantion
CH	Church History
CSCO	Corpus Scriptorum Christianorum Orientalium
CSEL	Corpus Scriptorum Ecclesiasticorum Latinorum
De Obit. Theo	Ambrose, De Obitu Theodosii
DOP	Dumbarton Oaks Papers
Ecclec. Hist.	Eusebius, Ecclesiastical History
GNO	Gregorii Nysseni Opera
ER	The Ecclesiastical Review
HTR	The Harvard Theological Review
Hist. Ecclec.	Socrates, Historia Ecclesiasticus
JAAR	Journal of the American Academy of Religion
JECS	Journal of Early Christian Studies
JEH	Journal of Ecclesiastical History
JMH	Journal for Medieval History
JTS	Journal of Theological Studies
JSNT	Journal for the Study of the New Testament

Kr	S. Gregorii Episcopi Nysseni de Anima et Resurrectione cum Sorore Sua Macrina Dialogus, J.G. Krabinger, ed.
Lampe	A Patristic Greek Lexicon, Lampe, ed.
Laus. Hist.	Palladius, Lausiac History
NPNF	Nicene and Post-Nicene Fathers
NTS	New Testament Studies
NT	Novum Testamentum
PG	Patrologiae Cursus Completus. Series Graeca
PL	Patrologiae Cursus Completus. Series Latina
REB	Revue des Études Byzantines
RIC	Patrick M. Bruun, The Roman Imperial Counage, VII, Constantine & Licinius
SC	Sources Chrétiennes
SH	Subsidia Hagiographica
SOC	Scriptores Originum Constantinopolitanarum
SVTQ	St. Vladimir's Theological Quarterly
ThDNT	Theological Dictionary of the New Testament
TS	Theological Studies
VB	Vox Benedictina
VC	Eusebius, Vita Constantinii
VS	Vita Syncletica
VSM	Vita Sancta Macrinae

FOREWORD

V.K. McCarty's lovely book on the lives and intellectual significance of a carefully selected group of ancient and medieval Christian women is a delightful addition to the comparatively scarce
literature on a very important subject. In Antiquity, women, with
few exceptions, did not break through the literary glass ceiling,
and given the massively prevailing patriarchal consensus, the result was that a deep Greek and Roman silence descended upon
them. They are hardly seen, even more rarely noticed, and when
they do form a subject of ancient historical scrutiny, it is through
the resolving lens of the interests of a tiny group of élite male
commentators. Only in this way are women allowed to appear on
stage. Only through this channel are they given a voice. V.K.
McCarty goes out of her way here to find the "lost recordings"
that have greater authenticity.

A modern generation of (mainly) women scholar-historians
has made great strides in the last fifty years to change the way
women's lives in Antiquity have been read: but often their work
has been meant for the more rarefied rooms in the Academy. This
new study, elegantly written, with an eye for the telling detail as
well as a firm grasp of the historical overview, is approachable by
a much wider audience. It comes out from a passion to ask: Why
do these women's lives matter to the Church? to Christian life? to
the history of spirituality? As such, this book will instruct and inspire a new generation to look back to the early days of the Christian movement and find there genuinely appealing and encouraging examples, not merely patriarchalism dressed up.

V.K. McCarty's book makes for a consistently lively and en-
grossing journey through ancient and medieval Christian times,

and her patient scholarship and deep background reading is apparent everywhere, generously presented to allow further individual research for anyone who wishes to take the stories onward. This would make a perfect book for universities and Christian reading circles across a very wide range of denominations—since these are stories of heroic fidelity and belief that belong to all.

V.Rev'd Prof John A. McGuckin,

Oxford University, Faculty of Theology; Emeritus Prof of Byzantine Christian Studies, Columbia University, and Union Theological Seminary.

INTRODUCTION

The female voice of Orthodox Christianity is all around us, familiar in prayer from the close harmony of the chanted Liturgy, and surrounding the faithful in the cloud of treble voices among the Church's saints. This volume provides a narrative of remarkable Early Christians by exploring the lives of a dozen or so female leaders, many of them venerated as saints; people whose courage and mission exemplify the role of women in the life of the developing Church. In the first centuries of Church history, including the earliest chapters of the rise of Christian monasticism, their participation was in some ways made possible by the expansion of the Gospel within the environment of the family home, an arena where women could operate without violating societal norms for proper behavior.

To the extent that the contribution of women to the Early Church has tended to be minimized and under-reported, this book is offered to fill in the niche of knowledge about women's share in the development of Early Christianity, with lively *vitas* illustrating the ministry and life-stories of several of our Christian fore-mothers, based on traditional ancient sources. Each one provides something of a "textual ikon" crafted from the wisdom of the Church Fathers, and together they create for the reader elements of an embodied "Matrology."[1]

In our own time, it has been encouraging to hear that Patriarch Kirill of Moscow, on the Feast of Princess Olga (July 24),

---

[1] *Pace*, Andrew Kadel's helpful reference resource, *Matrology: A Bibliography of Writings by Christian Women from the First to the Fifteenth Centuries* (New York: Continuum, 1995).

highlighted the importance of the role of Orthodox women in the continuing Christianization of our world. "I encourage you to remember her remarkable example," he said, "and to pass on the greatest unshakable values of human existence imprinted in the Christian message to each subsequent generation; so that until the end of time faith in Christ, crucified and risen, the Savior of the world, remains in the hearts of people."[2] His message rings true, not only for the ministry of the parent and the priest's spouse, but also for women theologians and iconographers, for women scholars and grad school administrators, for women who are Church diplomats and certified chaplains, for women parish counselors and those who have been given a formal Blessing to preach the Gospel during the Liturgy.[3] There are important and sometimes overlooked foundational roots for the ministry of all these women which are deeply grounded in the early centuries of Christianity, and several of them are explored in this book.

The first section, "Early Voices, Early Women's Ministry," opens in first-century Philippi, where the memory of the Gospel of Jesus Christ is so immediate and transformative in the hearts and minds of His followers that Lydia, a purple-fabric dealer ("Lydia: Speaking up to the Apostles"), is witnessed in the Acts of the Apostles at the very moment of evangelization by the Apostle Paul himself. She is reported to have experienced a transformative life-change; for "the Lord opened her heart" (Acts 16:14).[4] In response to this divine action, she is remembered being baptized with all the people in her household and speaking up so

---

[2] "Patriarch Kirill Highlights the Important Role of Orthodox Women in the Christianization of Society," *Orthodox Life* (July 29, 2019) Julia Frolova, trans.; available at: pravmir.com. (accessed 1/6/2020).

[3] Examples of women who have been given a formal Blessing to preach during the Liturgy: Sr. Rebecca Cown at New Skete and Mother Raphaela Wilkinson, of the Holy Myrrhbearers. See P. Bouteneff, "Invisible Leaders of the Orthodox Church;" available at: https://www.aphaiaresources.com/2016/09/05/invisible-leaders-in-the-orthodox-church/

[4] Unless otherwise noted, all Scripture is quoted in the NRSV; *The New Oxford Annotated Bible: New Revised Standard Version: with the Apocrypha*; 4th edition, Michael D. Coogan, ed. (Oxford; New York: Oxford University Press, 2010).

persuasively to Paul that she is quoted in the text—a valuable and rare marker of memory in Scripture, especially for women. Even though Acts is written in narrative form, the challenging issue of Lydia's possible historicity is enhanced by her story being embedded in the first "we" section with its keen sense of eye-witness immediacy (Acts 16:10-17).

When Paul encountered Lydia among the women gathered at the Jewish place of prayer just outside the city gate,[5] she may have been leading the group in prayer, there by the river. Her persistent offer of hospitality indicates her substantial socio-economic status; she was capable of providing table fellowship, and probably housing to Paul and his cohort of missionaries, as well as the new believers in Jesus whom his ministry was succeeding in winning.

The development of the Church made possible new roles for women: for example, they could function as missionaries and ministers, and the hospitality which they offered in their homes made possible the evolution of house churches as an early environment for the Church, at a time when the structure of table fellowship celebrated in the Spirit of Jesus Christ was in its earliest stages of formation. Indeed, Jaroslav Pelikan has pointed out that it is unavoidably clear, both from the original words in the second chapter of Joel and from quotation of them in the sermon of Peter at Pentecost that it was to be "sons and daughters," both men and women on whom God "will pour out my Spirit" and who "shall prophesy" (Acts 2:17-18).[6]

By the end of the chapter in Acts, the expanding assemblage of followers of the Way meeting in Lydia's home—in an example of the early development of the house church—are addressed as

---

[5] Although there is scant indication of a formal pattern of worship or organization, evidence suggests that Jews prior to the end of the first century were involved in informal gatherings for the purpose of "fresh appropriation of the Torah, for the strengthening of group identity, and for heightening devotion to the God of Israel." Robert Clark Kee, "The Transformation of the Synagogue after 70 C.E.: Its Importance for Early Christianity," *New Testament Studies* 36 (1990), p. 14.

[6] Jaroslav Pelikan, *Acts* (Grand Rapids, MI: Brazos, 2005), p. 206.

multiple "brethren" (Acts 16:40), when Paul bids them farewell and his band of evangelizing co-workers depart for further church-building in Thessalonica. Furthermore, as with Prisca (Acts 18:2-3, 18, 26), Chloe (1Cor. 1:11) and Nympha (Col. 4:15), "these Christians of means must have exercised some leadership in the house churches that they hosted."[7] The Acts of the Apostles presents the house church functioning as the locus of the Christian community; "as the creative hub of God's redemptive work...these churches were banquet communities, celebrating the abundance of God in Christ which is continually opening up doors for repentance."[8]

The Protomartyr Thekla[9] as well ("The Voice of St. Thekla: 'Inwardly Tuned by God'") hears the Gospel directly from St. Paul during his missionary visit to Iconium, which is likely referenced in Acts 13:51. Both this and Paul's ministry in Philippi took place during the principle period of his apostolic work, his Aegean Mission, one which has arguably made "the most lasting impact on Christian development and thought."[10] His compelling interpretation of the Beatitudes of Jesus (Mt. 5:3-12), which he commingles with a charge to holy chastity, stirs the heart of young Thekla who longs to "be made worthy to stand in the presence of Paul and hear the word of Christ." Her story is known to us from the *Acts of Paul and Thecla*,[11] one of the apocryphal texts which was circulating with robust popularity alongside the authorized

---

[7] John Koenig, *New Testament Hospitality: Partnership with Strangers as Promise and Mission* (Eugene, OR: Wipf and Stock Publishers, 2001), p. 65.

[8] Koenig, *New Testament Hospitality*, p. 106.

[9] Thekla's divine visions during her martyrdom have been regarded as equivalent to the Lord appearing to St. Stephen before he was stoned, as described in Acts 7:55-56; and as a result, both Stephen and Thekla are characterized as Proto-Martyrs by the Orthodox Church.

[10] James D.G. Dunn, *The Acts of the Apostles* (Valley Forge, PA: Trinity Press International, 1996), p. 213.

[11] "Praxeis Paulou kai Thekles" in *Acta Apostolorum*, R.A. Lipsius, M.Bonnet, eds (Hildesheim: Georg Olms, 1958), pp. 235-272; for English, "The Acts of Paul," *New Testament Apocrypha*, revised ed., W. Schneemelcher, ed., R. McL. Wilson (Louisville, KY: Westminster/John Knox Press), 2:213-270.

books of Scripture in the late second century, at a time when the canon of the New Testament was still in a dynamic process of being formally codified.

The tale of Thekla's miraculous deliverance from martyrdom, and her preaching ministry which it inspired, captivated Early Christian thought in the first centuries of the Jesus movement, a time when the ecclesiological development of the Church lacked as yet formal organization, and can now be seen as remarkably fluid and collaborative. Even though Thekla's hagiographic account[12] did not gain canonical status, it may nevertheless quite accurately reflect the radical experience of many second-century women who ventured away from the safety and societal sanction of the family hearth to follow the Gospel taught by Paul—and found themselves, like Thekla, in "violent confrontation with society."[13]

As is demonstrated in the chapter, the *Acts of Paul and Thecla* is a tale of high adventure and divine intervention, and it reveals to the listener the incarnational tension at work between the ascetic and emotional aspects of Thekla's experience in the ancient document. Several Fathers of the Church took note as well, and Thekla is praised: in the *Symposium* by Methodius;[14] by Gregory of Nyssa, as the secret soul-name of his sister, Macrina, in the *Vita Macrinae*; by Gregory Nazianzus who regards her as apostle-martyr in his *Oration Against Julian*; by John Chrysostom in his Homily on Acts 25; in the *Panegyric to Thecla* by Pseudo-Chrysostom; and, by Ambrose in the *De Virginibus*. Furthermore, the fifth-century *Life and Miracles of Thekla* offers a fuller version of the story,

---

[12] While texts may fluidly vary from biography to hagiography and back, hagiography can be generally distinguished from biography by its principle intention to reflect a biography of God—the nature and loving action of God—through the life of the saint.

[13] Margaret Y. MacDonald, "Rereading Paul: Early Interpreters of Paul on Women and Gender," in Ross Shepard Kraemer, Mary Rose D'Angelo, eds, *Women and Christian Origins* (New York: Oxford Press, 1999), p. 249.

[14] Note that the title of the chapter on Thekla references Methodius, *Symposium* 8, Proem. 3-5, where he describes Thekla as a "cithera, inwardly tuned and prepared to speak carefully and nobly," the Gospel of Jesus Christ.

as well as describing the growth of the cult of Thekla in the following years.[15]

Just as with the story of her sister in faith, Lydia, the gracious offer of hospitality by a local queen ("Queen Tryphaena: The Lord's Refuge in Hospitality") was not only crucial to safety and comfort for Thekla; but, during her preaching career, it was critical to her ministry. In fact, hospitality was key to the mission of Paul's evangelization enterprise, based as it was on the extensive network of households which supported the "sending" (propempein) and "receiving" (prosdechesthai) of co-workers. It is good to be mindful, especially outside the arena of these chapters specifically focused on women, that any description of itinerant preachers presupposes an equal complement of householders opening their homes to the progress of the Gospel.

While Thekla survived to preach the Gospel of Paul, and the irony that neither of her martyrdoms actually killed her is not lost on the modern ear, no such fortunate nuance assisted the martyr Perpetua ("Perpetua's Story in Her Own Words: Hope Facing Martyrdom"), whose last days are vividly described in her own words in the confession sections of The Passion of Perpetua and Felicity,[16] making this the earliest surviving example of autobiography in Latin—and furthermore, written by a woman.

Perpetua was arrested and condemned ad bestias, probably as part of the Roman games arranged in the Carthage Amphitheatre[17] to celebrate the birthday of Caesar Geta in 203 C.E.[18] This sentence from the Roman governor meant that Perpetua was

---

[15] "Thaumata tes Hagias kai Proto-martyros Theklas," in Gilbert Dragon, Vie et miracles de Sainte Thecle: Texte Grec, Tradution et Commentaire (Bruxelles: Societé des Bollandistes, 1978); for selected English translation, see: Scott F. Johnson, The Life and Miracles of Thekla: A Literary Study (Washington, D.C.: Center for Hellenic Studies, 2006).

[16] Passion de Perpétue et de Félicité suivi des Actes, J. Amat, ed. "Sources Chrétiennes," no. 417 (Paris: Les Éditions du Cerf, 1996); for English translation, Thomas J. Heffernan, The Passion of Perpetua and Felicity (Oxford: Oxford University Press, 2012).

[17] The Carthage Amphitheater still exists; it is a popular pilgrimage destination and has been developed into an UNESCO World Heritage site.

[18] See Heffernan, Passion, pp. 68-77.

imprisoned, humiliatingly displayed, tortured and finally attacked by wild beasts and fatally knifed down by gladiators. Yet shot through her ordeal for the sake of Christ are Perpetua's abrupt and startling mystical visions, where she is granted uplifting images welcoming her into a higher realm, which help distract from the grisly rituals of the Roman games at hand. While not included in the Canon of the New Testament, *The Passion of Perpetua and Felicity* nevertheless circulated among sacred texts and was immensely popular in the early centuries after Christ.

Even with the Deutero-Pauline injunctions (1 Tim. 2:11-12) condemning women speaking and teaching in full force by the late fourth or early fifth centuries,[19] certain significant women's voices and life-stories were nevertheless persistently valued and written down, often by men. Thus, even while rare, several Early Christian women make distinct contributions to Early Christianity and Early Christian thought, their fascinating *vitas* and their textual evidence indelibly ringing out from the traditional volumes of the Greek Fathers, the *Patrologia Graeca*. Among them is the Empress Helena Augusta ("St. Helena: Becoming a Christian Roman Empress"), who takes the stage of history in her old age at the very threshold of the lengthy arc of Byzantine history, examined in the second section of the book, "The Long Byzantine Hymn of Praise."

Before her compelling legend took hold and credited her with the discovery of the True Cross for a score of generations, she was praised by Church historian Eusebius quite soon after her death in his *Vita Constantinii*.[20] There, among the other *Greek Fathers*, he lauds her as the Emperor's "God-loved mother," repeatedly describing her generous commissions in Jerusalem and throughout the eastern provinces of the Roman Empire, which she visited "in the magnitude of imperial authority," supervising building projects at the holy sites associated with the life and

---

[19] V.A. Karras, "The Liturgical Functions of Consecrated Women in the Byzantine Church," *Theological Studies* 66 (2005), p. 97.
[20] Eusebius, *Vita Constantinii*, PG 20.909-1232; for English, Averil Cameron, Stuart G. Hall, trans., *Eusebius: Life of Constantine* (Oxford: Clarendon Press, 1999).

Passion of Jesus Christ. In the process, Christian pilgrimage, as we know it today, was born; for her prayerful presence in the area helped facilitate as well its transformation in identity into the Christian Holy Land.

Even among other Early Christian women present in the *Patrologia Graeca*, the Desert Mother Syncletica ("Divine Fire: The Mystic St. Syncletica Speaks") stands as an extraordinary figure; for her Sayings (*Apophthegmata*) have survived in two volumes of the *Greek Fathers*. Eighty-one of her teachings are gathered together in her *Vita* in PG 28,[21] and a smaller selection appear among the "Sayings of the Desert Fathers" (*Apophthegmata Patrum*) in PG 65,[22] where she joins two other female elders from the Desert Tradition, Mother Theodora and Mother Sarah.

Famous for deploying the image of "Divine Fire," Amma Syncletica's disciples found her teachings sounding an exhortation to those striving for spiritual union with God's love and divine archetypal beauty, calling them to pursue deep contemplation and spiritual enlightenment, by means of humble askesis and practical study with her. "The humility of Christ," she is remembered saying, "is a difficult treasure to acquire, yet necessary to be saved. It is the one virtue the Devil cannot mimic. So, even as it strips down, it clothes in salvation."[23]

While some female spiritual elders, like Amma Syncletica, are remembered venturing into the desert, in order to pursue following a call to life completely devoted to Christ, some women,

---

[21] "Vita et Gesta Sanctae Seataeque Magistrate Syncleticae," PG 28.1487-1558; for English: Pseudo-Athanasius, *The Life and Regimen of the Blessed and Holy Syncletica: Part One: The Translation*, Elizabeth Bongie, trans. (Toronto: Peregrina Publishing Co., 2003).

[22] Sayings of Syncletica, "Apophthegmata Patrum Graecorum" (Alphabetical Collection), PG 65.71-412; supplemented by J.-C. Guy, *Recherches sur la Tradition Grecque des Apophthegmata Patrum*, Subsidia Hagiographica 36 (Brussels: 1962); for English: *Give Me a Word: The Alphabetical Sayings of the Desert Fathers*, John Wortley, trans. (Crestwood, NY: St. Vladimir's Seminary Press, 2014).

[23] Saying 56, *The Life & Regimen of the Blessed & Holy Syncletica by Pseudo-Athanasius; Part One: English Translation*, Elizabeth Bryson Bongie, trans. (Toronto: Peregrina Publishing Co., 2003).

such as the Cappadocian theologian,[24] Macrina the Younger ("St. Macrina: Teaching Gregory of Nyssa on the Progress of the Soul"), were able to spearhead establishing the ascetical arena of prayer and repentance within their residential environment; and as a result, they became foundational leaders in an integral part of the early development of Christian monasticism.

After the cathartic, and perhaps jarring, experience for Gregory of Nyssa of being called to his sister's death-bed very soon after his brother, Basil the Great, had also died, Gregory poured out his observations of his last visit with her in quoted dialogue form, harvesting from his storehouse of her teaching, during the poignant days soon after she died. Here, returning to the monastery his sister founded at Annesa, their family's country estate, his examination of Macrina's life-long exemplary spiritual transformation, by which she eventually led her family toward an ascetical life, illuminates both *On the Soul and Resurrection*[25] and his *vita*[26] of his elder sister. The remembered voice of her theological teachings is ever-present throughout his writing: "The divine life will always be activated through love," she said, "and knows no limit to the activity of love;"[27] and her monastic life highlighted

---

[24] Jaroslav Pelikan defends Macrina the Younger as the "fourth Cappadocian." He observes that "not only was she a Christian role model by her profound and ascetic spirituality, but at the death of their parents she became the educator of the entire family, and that in both Christianity and Classical culture." Jaroslav Pelikan, *Christianity and Classical Culture: The Metamorphosis of Natural Theology in the Christian Encounter with Hellenism* (New Haven, CT: Yale University Press, 1995), p. 8.

[25] *S. Gregorii Episcopi Nysseni de Anima et Resurrectione cum Sorore Sua Macrina Dialogus*, J. G. Krabinger, ed. (Leipzig: Gustav Wittig, 1837); for English, Anna M. Silvas, *Macrina the Younger, Philosopher of God* (Turnhout, Belgium: Brepols Publishers, 2008).

[26] *Vita Sanctae Macrinae*, Virginia Woods Calahan, ed., in *Ascetica*, VIII,1, *Gregorii Nysseni Opera*, Werner Jaeger, gen. ed. (Leiden: Brill, 1958-1996); for English, Anna M. Silvas, *Macrina the Younger, Philosopher of God* (Turnhout, Belgium: Brepols Publishers, 2008).

[27] An Res 6.31-32.

by "meditation on divine things, unceasing prayer, and uninterrupted hymnody,"[28] remained a role model for the rest of his life.

For many of us, one of the abiding and pleasurable memories
of experiencing Orthodox Liturgy is the distinctive ancient musical harmony of female voices chanting the prayers, repeating the
praise due to the glory of God Almighty again and again, so that
it seems to resonate throughout the body of the faithful, standing
at worship. Thus, in an example from the first Christian millennium, certain women were appointed in the Patriarchate of Jerusalem to chant the Liturgy of the Hours on Holy Saturday morning
while cleaning and preparing the lamps inside the Church of the
Holy Sepulchre, liturgically embodying the historical Myrrhbearers who came back to the tomb of Jesus early on the third day
and first experienced the Resurrection.

When their service was completed, the Patriarch extin-
guished the lamps and locked the great doors until the Paschal
Vigil. Later, "the *typikon* mentions that the Myrrhbearers remained behind and re-entered the Holy Sepulchre in order to
cense and anoint it."[29] When the Patriarch and Archdeacon en-
tered the Church on Easter Morning, the Myrrhbearers were
"standing before the Holy Sepulchre," and at the "Rejoice! Christ
is risen!" they prostrated and rising up, censed the Patriarch,
chanting the "Many Years!" hymn (*Polychronion*).[30] These
Myrrhbearers (*Myrophoroi*) appear to have served the Byzantine
Church from the fifth to the ninth centuries and their chanted
prayer was part of the Holy Week observances.

In focusing on turn-of-the-fifth-century Constantinople, the
Deaconess Olympias ("The Deaconess Olympias: Soulmate of St.
John Chrysostom") may have been among the treble voices heard
chanting in the Cathedral when John Chrysostom was brought in
abruptly and consecrated as the new Bishop of Constantinople.
Frail, aristocratic virgin heiress that she was, Bishop John Chrysostom likely heard her singing at prayer before they even spoke

---

[28] VSM 13.5.
[29] Karras, "Liturgical Functions," p. 111. See original text in Papadopoulos-Karameus, *Analekta* 189, 1.11-14.
[30] See Papadopoulos-Karameus, *Analekta* 190-191.

to one another. It was certainly known that she "would not budge from the church."[31] Olympias has a fascinating tale to tell, because she was desired by the Emperor Theodosius, who sought her hand when she was widowed, as a still-young bride for his kinsman. As with many daughters from Byzantine nobility, Olympias was strategically offered by her father in the élite marriage market at an early age; and soon thereafter, ended up handsomely endowed financially as a widow, when barely out of her teens.

Instead of taking up the tiara and pearled *pendilia* of a Byzantine courtier, however, Olympias was instead "seized by Christ's flame,"[32] experiencing a call to an ascetical life for the sake of her soul. Nevertheless, by managing to maneuver out of the Emperor's schemes, she was forced to endure heavy political consequences for snubbing the imperial favor: her fortune and vast estates was temporarily sequestered and she was inhibited from visiting the Cathedral's clerics—evidence, of course, that this was indeed what she had been doing. In fact, Palladius reports that she "addressed priests reverently and honoured Bishops."[33]

The *Vita of Olympias*[34] describes the spiritual community she founded for educated ascetic women, one which grew to include 250 women who followed her pious example as Abbess in a life of prayer and charitable acts; its "prestige location and noble profile may have shaped it into a female institution like none other."[35] John Chrysostom's correspondence with Olympias[36]

---

[31] Palladius, Bishop of Aspuna, *Dialogue on the Life of St. John Chrysostom*, Robert T. Meter, trans. (New York: Newman Press, 1985), p. 66.

[32] John Chrysostom, "Homily XIII on Ephesians 4:17-19," NPNF XIII.115.

[33] Palladius, Bishop of Aspuna, *The Lausiac History*, translated and annotated by Robert T. Meyer (New York: Paulist Press, 1964) 56.137.

[34] "Vita Sanctae Olympiadis," Hippolyte Delehaye, ed. *Analecta Bollandiana* 15 (1896), pp. 400-423; for English, see Elizabeth A. Clark, "The Life of Olympias," in *Jerome, Chrysostom, and Friends: Essays and Translations* (New York: Edwin Mellen Press, 1979), pp. 127-142.

[35] Peter Hatlie, *The Monks and Monasteries of Constantinople, ca. 350-850* (Cambridge: Cambridge University Press, 2007), p. 98.

[36] John Chrysostom, *Lettres à Olympias*, Anne-Marie Malingrey, trans.; Sources Chrétiennes, v. 13 (Paris: Éditions du CERF, 1947); for English,

provides tantalizing evidence of her voice responding to him in letters now lost, and he expresses gratitude in his letters for the therapeutic consolation of a lady of "such intelligence and wealth of piety."[37]

Letters from another prominent Church Father, St. Theodore the Studite (759-826), also help us remember the ninth-century hymnographer, Kassia ("The Hymnographer Kassia: Chanting the Incarnation"), whose life is described in no less than four different volumes of the *Patralogia Graeca*.[38] Best known among her large *oeuvre* of published compositions is the beloved *sticheron doxastikon*,[39] "Lord, the Women Fallen into Many Sins," chanted as part of the Holy Wednesday Vespers, which is sung on Tuesday evening; and the *sticheron doxastikon* "On the Birth of Christ," which is chanted during the Vespers service on the Vigil of the Feast of the Nativity.

The survival and acknowledgement of Kassia's hymns and other compositions are due in great part to her deep association with Abbot Theodore and his Stoudian monks in Constantinople, during the time when they were working to organize and unify the Orthodox Liturgy. By including her work in the monthly *Menaion* and the Lenten *Triodion*, a few of Kassia's works have become

---

see "Letters of St. Chrysostom to Olympias," in *Saint Chrysostom: On the Priesthood; Ascetic Treatises; Select Homilies and Letters; Homilies on the Statues*; NPNF IX.284-304.

[37] Letter VIII(II), Malingrey, p. 141.

[38] Beside the *Patria* of Constantinople, *Scriptores Originum Constantinopolitanarum* (Leipzig, 1907), p. 276, John Zonaris, *Epitome Historiarum*, Book XIII-XVIII (Bonn: Weber, 1897), and Michael Glykas, *Chronographia* (Bonn: Weber, 1836), Kassia is mentioned in at least the four following volumes of the *Patralogia Graeca*: St. Theodore the Stoudite's three surviving letters to her (Letters 205, 413, 541) in Volume 99.903-1669, Symeon the Logothete, *Chronographia*, in Volume 109.685C; George the Monk, *Chronikon* 4.264 in Volume 110.1008B, and Leo the Grammarian, *Chronographia*, in Volume 108.1046.

[39] In Byzantine music, a *sticheron* is a lengthy verse chanted in various parts of the morning and evening Orthodox Office. The term d*oxastikon* applies to a *sticheron* which glorifies or commemorates Jesus Christ or a saint.

authorized for worship in regularly scheduled Orthodox services to this day.

A popular tradition is widely reported about Kassia participating in Empress Euphrosyne's bride show for her stepson, the young Emperor Theophilus, where the well-educated Byzantine poet is remembered speaking up to the Emperor; though her wry remark may have lost her his marital favor.[40] But this imperial rebuke likely opened the way for Kassia's family to found a monastic foundation with their daughter leading it as Abbess, where she was able to continue in her creative work with her spiritual father and the Stoudian monks. Kassia's leadership and hymnographic contributions were a significant component of what has been deemed "by far the most productive and sophisticated experiment in monastic culture ever to date."[41]

The final section, "New Theklas and New Helenas," steps back from the single-*vita* approach and explores the Christian virtue of *philanthropia* ("Empresses Speak of *Philanthropy*: Following the Command of Christ"), as it was taught to and embodied by several Byzantine empresses and princesses. It provides an introductory *catena* of Patristic teachings grounding philanthropic action in Christ's own ministry, which charged imperial noblewomen to emulate the transactional aspect of God's love of mankind by their prominent acts of generosity for the needy. As Shewring charmingly renders Gregory of Nazianzus:

> Give to the poor, they before God can plead,
> And win, and richly give, the grace we need...
> Honour in him God's handiwork expressed;
> Reverence in it the rites that serve a guest.[42]

---

[40] To the emperor's sly remark, upon encountering Kassia as one of the maidens presented to him during his bride show: "*Ek gynaikós tá cheírō,*" (Through a woman [came forth] the baser [things]), meaning Eve, she is reported to have cleverly quipped, "*Kaí ek gynaikós tá kreíttō.*" (Yet through a woman [came forth] the better [things]), meaning Mary the Theotokas.

[41] Hatlie, *Monks and Monasteries of Constantinople*, p. 450.

[42] Gregory Nazianzen, "Verses Against the Rich," (Moral Poems XXVIII), quoted in *Rich and Poor in Christian Tradition*, p. 49.

The women in the Imperial Court attending the Liturgy heard the exhortations to philanthropy throughout the services and the Patriarchal Homilies; and in times of catastrophe, litanies rang out invoking the *philanthropia* of God and galvanizing the humanitarian efforts of, for example, Empress Irene after the earthquake of 740. Thus, women operating near the imperial throne were hailed as a "new Helena" when they emulated her pious generosity through commissioned monuments and church-building; and later, in monastic *typyka,* founding empresses were able to leave their voice in the formal record of posterity.

On balance, it is hoped that the examination of the Early Christian women's lives in this volume will bring them into sharper focus, and nurture an environment which will, as former Archbishop Rowan Williams has encouraged, "genuinely make women's voices audible worldwide, looking for the ways in which attitudes can be changed and looking, too, for the ways in which all this can be experienced as good news for men."[43] For where two or three are gathered in the name of Christ, one of them is probably a woman. When two or three Orthodox gather, two of them are likely to be women. This volume—which includes a trio of abbesses and a pair of blushing fiancés, a purple-fabric dealer and a desert mother; a queen, an empress dowager, and a Byzantine emperor's daughter—is meant to encourage visibility of some of our ancient women elders from the early history of Christianity who contributed to the sacred heritage of the Church we enjoy today.

V.K. McCarty,
Feast of the Epiphany, 2021

---

[43] Rowan Williams, "Tackling Violence, Building Peace," Inaugural Parliamentary Lecture, marking the launch of Christian Aid Week, 12 May 2014.

I.
EARLY VOICES,
EARLY WOMEN'S MINISTRY

CHAPTER I.1
LYDIA: SPEAKING UP
TO THE APOSTLES

The generous openness and support of Lydia,
a gentile devotee of Jewish worship,
is a model for the Christian household.[1]

The story of Lydia's persuasive dialogue with the Apostle Paul in Acts 16 reflects an affirmation of divine power; for she is witnessed at the very moment of conversion. As an early believer in the emerging Church, she demonstrates a distinctive exercise of the *charismata*[2] Paul describes in Rom. 12:6-8, namely spiritual generosity and leadership. Additionally, the occasion of Lydia's remembered words in Scripture stands at the threshold between two periods of the Primitive Church: an earlier time when devotion to Jewish practice still influenced the lives of the believers, and the continuing development of the gentile Church. This chapter examining the brief texts which preserve the memory of Lydia sheds light on the lives of the women at work in the Pauline ministry.

One of the happy surprises awaiting those who study the New Testament is the discovery that St. Paul, who is often criticized for his attitude toward women, is actually revealed in Luke's narrative describing him, and in his own writings, to be

---

[1] Raymond E. Brown, *An Introduction to the New Testament* (New York: Doubleday, 1997), p. 310.

[2] The Greek term for "a gift of grace," meaning the blessings bestowed on every Christian for the fulfillment of vocation.

significantly appreciative of the contribution to his ministry made by the women co-workers in his life. Several of these women were collaborative associates with him, and their lives in their own right affected the shaping of Early Christianity.[3] Their contribution was made possible, to some extent, by the expansion of the Gospel within the environment of the first-century family home and workshop, arenas where women could operate without violating societal norms for proper behavior.

The author of Luke/Acts appears to have made a special point of celebrating the ministry of women throughout his two-volume work, and "of hearing and recording also treble voices."[4] The Spirit-driven progress of the Gospel message can be seen here, with the sort of erratic, synergistic detail often characterizing the gift of human growth. Acts was written bearing witness to an age in which the young Church "possessed the Spirit and was triumphantly engaging in a world mission to the Gentiles,"[5] and Paul as well, acknowledges a "genuine pneumatic endowment" in the women with whom he is reported interacting.[6]

In patriarchal society, where it was often assumed that women were properly to be considered an invisible component and were therefore, as John McGuckin observes, significantly under-reported,[7] it is remarkable that Luke chooses to include so many details involving women. The interwoven appearances of so many women in Luke/Acts, sometimes serving in leading roles, creates a robust witness, and shows them making distinct contributions during the early centuries of Christianity. By the very fact that Luke portrays women exercising a variety of responsibilities, "he shows how the Gospel liberates and creates new possibilities

---

[3] Florence M. Gillman, *Women Who Knew Paul* (Collegeville, MN: Liturgical Press, 1992), p. 12.

[4] Jaroslav Pelikan, *Acts* (Grand Rapids, MI: Brazos, 2005), p. 205.

[5] Robert Jewett, *A Chronology of Paul's Life* (Philadelphia: Fortress Press, 1979), p. 8.

[6] Albrecht Oepke, *ThDNT*, v.1, p. 787.

[7] John Anthony McGuckin, *The Westminster Handbook to Patristic Theology* (Louisville, KY: Westminster John Knox Press, 2004), pp. 365-366.

for women."[8] Thus, the development of the Church made possible new roles for women, some with leadership responsibilities.[9]

Women could function as missionaries and ministers, for example, and the hospitality which they offered in their homes made possible the development of house churches as an early environment for the church at a time when the structure of table fellowship celebrated in the Spirit of Jesus Christ was in its earliest stages of formation. Indeed, Jaroslav Pelikan has pointed out that "it is unavoidably clear, both from the original words in the second chapter of Joel and from quotation of them in the sermon of Peter at Pentecost that it was to be 'sons and daughters,' both men and women on whom God 'will pour out my Spirit' and who 'shall prophesy' (Acts 2:17-18)."[10]

Luke, using the high Hellenistic phrase, notes that "not a few leading women" were brought to belief in Jesus Christ and responded in faith with generosity and missionary fervor (Acts 17:4). The witness of Lydia helps to illustrate the vision of the Christian community for Paul and women's potential roles within it. The story recorded in Acts 16 takes place during the principle period of Paul's apostolic work, his Aegean Mission, one which was significantly influential to Christian development and thought. Both Paul and Luke portray women during this time as prominently receptive to the Gospel and among the earliest of those baptized in Europe. They were inspired by the Spirit of God to open their homes, facilitating the creation of house churches. Women like Lydia are remembered giving collaborative support to Paul in his evangelistic work. In his letters and also in Acts, the

---

[8] Ben Witherington, *The Acts of the Apostles: A Socio-Rhetorical Commentary* (Grand Rapids, MI: William B. Eerdmans Publishing Company, 1998), p. 156.

[9] "No less than nine women were at one time or other members of what we might call Paul's mission team—that is nearly twenty percent, a notable statistic in a male-dominated society." James D. G. Dunn, *Beginning from Jerusalem* (Grand Rapids, MI: William B. Eerdmans Pub. Co., 2009), p. 634.

[10] Pelikan, *Acts*, p. 206.

support of women is "integral to the expansion of Paul's mission."[11]

Furthermore, Luke and Paul both offer a picture of men and women contributing to the expansion of Early Christianity by working in partnership. Of course, these very partnerships put the women at risk, for this was a time when "childbirth took as many women's lives as the battlefield took soldiers."[12] One-third of those surviving infancy were dead by age six, and half of children died by age ten. Over half of these survivors died by age sixteen and by age twenty-six three-quarters of them had perished.[13] If they managed to survive the perils of childbirth, many young brides outlived their older husbands and became widows at an early age. Lydia was likely married at some time in her life and could have borne children; the fact that none are named could indicate that they did not survive until the time of Paul's missionary work.

While there are commentators who do not support the idea of Lydia as a real historical person,[14] several others—Brown, Witherington and Cohick among them—maintain the basic assumption that the story of Lydia reflects an actual person. "She was not invented by Luke to serve his theological agenda."[15] Yet, it may also be true that Luke has used his source material

---

[11] Margaret Y. MacDonald, "Rereading Paul: Early Interpreters of Paul on Women and Gender," in *Women and Christian Origins*, Ross Shepherd Kraemer, Mary Rose D'Angelo, eds (New York: Oxford University Press, 1999), p. 237.

[12] Lynn H. Cohick, *Women in the World of the Earliest Christians: Illuminating Ancient Ways of Life* (Grand Rapids, MI: Baker Academic, 2009), p. 160.

[13] Richard S. Ascough, *Lydia: Paul's Cosmopolitan Hostess* (Collegeville, MN: Liturgical Press, 2008), p. 44.

[14] L. Michael White, "Visualizing the 'Real' World of Acts 16: Toward Construction of a Social Index," in *The Social World of the First Christians: Essays in Honor of Wayne A. Meeks* (Minneapolis, MN: Fortress Press, 1995.), p. 246. See also Matthews, *First Converts* (Stanford, CA: Stanford University Press, 2001), p. 93.

[15] Cohick, *Women in the World of the Earliest Christians*, p. 188. See also Witherington, *Women in the Earliest Churches*, pp. 147-149.

concerning the traditions about Lydia in the service of his overall story about the reception of the Gospel as it spread throughout the Roman Empire. With Lydia especially, "we must hold these two—historical detail and theological emphasis—in creative tension,"[16] and evaluate historical probability with caution.[17]

While Lydia is a remarkable New Testament character, she is also in some ways emblematic of the situation of the Early Church, especially with regard to the evidence of her mobility, her conversion experience, and the possibility of new roles for women. The scriptural witness clearly implies that Lydia, being from Thyatira, experienced considerable travel in her lifetime, reflective of the particular mobility characteristic among Early Christians. The spread of the Early Church, like that of Greek culture, was made possible in part by the excellent system of Roman roads throughout the empire; so that travel within the Roman Empire, whether for business or ministry, could be contemplated and accomplished with a confidence and certainty which were unknown in the centuries after.[18] This dynamic mobility of people, enabling them to move from one location to another, is clearly attested in Acts as well as Paul's letters.

The Greek philosopher Epictetus boasted that "Caesar has obtained for us a profound peace. There are neither wars nor battles, nor great robberies nor piracies, but we may travel at all hours, and sail from east to west."[19] While the Roman Empire's excellent road-works made travel possible for both Lydia and Paul, the available night-time accommodations were dismal and dangerous places to seek rest, many being nothing more than brothels. "The moral dangers at the inns made hospitality an important virtue in Early Christianity."[20] Therefore, from the earliest development of the Church, the spread of the Gospel was

---

[16] Cohick, *Women in the World of the Earliest Christians*, p. 188.

[17] Richard A. Pervo, *Acts: A Commentary* (Minneapolis, MN: Fortress Press, 2009), p. 15

[18] Abraham J. Malherbe, *Social Aspects of Early Christianity* (Philadelphia: Fortress, 1983), p. 63.

[19] *Discourses* 3.13.9; Everett Ferguson, *Backgrounds of Early Christianity* (Grand Rapids, MI: Eerdmans, 2003), p. 86.

[20] Ferguson, *Backgrounds of Early Christianity*, p. 89.

intimately dependent on the faithful offer of a safe resting place and refreshment and, as a result, a valued role traditionally connected with women.

Paul is described accepting lodging and table fellowship from those who came to the faith from his teaching as a regular aspect of his ministry. Luke often focuses on new believers who were relatively wealthy and inspired by the message of the Spirit to finance the cause, some by providing hospitality in their residential estates, so that itinerant preachers could be sent out from a stable missionary home base. These benefactors included women who were attested as heads of households, and Lydia is among them (Acts 16:14-15). The home was "the basic cell of organization in the Pauline mission; it was the arena of celebration, teaching, and probably often of conversion."[21] Hospitality was key to the mission, based as it was on an extensive network of households which supported the "sending" (*propempein*) and "receiving" (*prosdechesthai*) of co-workers. Therefore, any description of itinerant evangelists presupposes an equal complement of householders opening their homes to the progress of the Gospel.

Luke appears to take special care to demonstrate to his audience that where the Gospel went, women, often prominent, were "some of the first, foremost, and most faithful converts to the Christian faith, and that their conversion led to their assuming new roles in the service of the Gospel."[22] Women are attested in Scripture serving the early communities of believers through responsibilities that normally would not have been available to them, and Luke emphasizes the viability of women taking on various tasks of ministry for the community. As Paul himself, after all, preached to the Galatians, in the new religion, "There is no longer male and female; for all of you are one in Christ Jesus" (Gal. 3:28). When the work of the Holy Spirit is discerned and faithfully described, both men and women are called to action. Not surprisingly then, an acknowledged and necessary

---

[21] MacDonald, "Rereading Paul: Early Interpreters of Paul on Women and Gender," p. 241.

[22] Ben Witherington, *Women in the Earliest Churches* (Cambridge: Cambridge University Press, 1988), p. 157.

component of sending out preachers for the progress of the Gospel is providing hospitality for their needs.

The ministry of hospitality offered by women is reflected in the life of Jesus as well; the itinerant ministry of Christ is described in connection with the generosity of believers around him. Significant among them were Mary and her sister Martha, whose determined style of hospitality was incorporated into one of his familiar teachings (Lk. 10:38-42). Luke describes women who were present with "the twelve" as they were "proclaiming and bringing the good news of the kingdom of God" (Lk. 8:1-3). They are acknowledged as offering Jesus and the Apostles hospitality; they were women "who provided for them from their resources."

The missionary charge of Jesus in his teaching, imploring the Apostles to rely on hospitality freely given (Lk. 9:2-5, 10:1-16), establishes the practice from which the "house church" emerged. Luke demonstrates that women in the memory of the Early Church who offered the hospitality of their home aided both the intensity and the extensive growth of the Christian community. This explains why prominent women are cited "whenever house churches are mentioned in the New Testament.[23]

Since Lydia's story cannot be confirmed and contextualized by comparing it with another scriptural source, it is difficult to establish that Lydia was a real person. Still, her story in the Acts of the Apostles functions as an effective window illuminating the development of the Early Church. Contrasting with Paul's own letters, which naturally offer a more diffused, impressionistic picture of what happened, Luke presents an active narrative in Acts, rich with vivid details, indicating clearly that the work of God in the Holy Spirit empowers men and women alike. Luke's description in Acts 2:42-47 is useful for describing the action of the Spirit at work in the lives of the early believers. These verses offer a rich glimpse of those responding to the action of God with awe, praise and acts of generosity. Here divine support for the growth of new members "who were being saved" is met with cooperative pooling

---

[23] Witherington, *Women in the Earliest Churches*, p. 145.

of resources and acts of hospitality which further inspire "glad and generous hearts" during table fellowship.

The link between leadership and household created a special significance for the roles of women. The fact that the seminal groups of believers functioned in much the same way as an extended household, the domain traditionally associated with women, undoubtedly facilitated the involvement of women in Pauline Christianity. Since much of their leadership would have been exercised in a household setting, "the house base of the movement may have enabled women to turn community leadership into an extension of their roles as household managers."[24] The private home offered a place of privacy, intimacy and stability, providing an economic infrastructure for the Early Christian community, a headquarters for missionary work, a framework for authority and leadership, and "a definite role for women."[25]

The house church functioned as the locus of the Christian community. Luke presents the house church as "the creative hub of God's redemptive work…these churches are banquet communities, celebrating the abundance of God in Christ which is continually opening up doors for repentance."[26] The individual house church as well as the whole church (*ekklesia*) in a town "counted women as well as men, persons of high and low social status, and persons of different nationalities among its membership and leadership. Those who joined the Early Christian missionary movement joined it as equals."[27]

The very fact, then, that women—that is, half the human race—are absent from so many historical narrations in Scripture

---

[24] Margaret Y. MacDonald, "Reading Real Women through the Undisputed Letters of Paul," in *Women and Christian Origins*, Ross Shepherd Kraemer, Mary Rose D'Angelo, eds (New York: Oxford University Press, 1999), p. 203.

[25] Vincent Branick, *The House Church in the Writings of Paul* (Wilmington, DE: Michael Glazier, 1989), p. 15.

[26] John Koenig, *New Testament Hospitality: Partnership with Strangers as Promise and Mission* (Philadelphia: Fortress Press, 1985), p. 106.

[27] Elisabeth Schüssler Fiorenza, "Missionaries, Apostles, Coworkers: Romans 16 and the Reconstruction of Women's Early Christian History," *Word & World* 6:4 (1986), p. 432.

demonstrates that "both the ancient literary sources and contemporary historiography are not the mirrors or windows they claim to be."[28] More recent historians of Early Christianity are gaining a greater appreciation of how the simple arrangements and primary functions of everyday life in the home and workshop were likely quite significant for the expansion of the movement.

When the Apostle Paul, with his pious background as a Jewish Pharisee, encountered Lydia among the women of Philippi gathered by the river, this colorful character was likely startlingly different than the women familiar to him from his home synagogue family. Taking into account Lydia's cultural background, her level of independence and her occupation, consider how she might have been dressed and groomed. Before speaking to her, Paul may have heard her offer prayer, perhaps leading the other women in their Sabbath day devotions.

Lydia is known to us from three verses narrated by Luke in Acts 16:14-15, 40. From that scant reference, we know that she owned a house in Philippi, over which she was householder; that she was a substantial businesswoman in the market for purple-dyed fabric products, and originally from Thyatira in Asia Minor—and that she was a worshipper of God. When "the Lord opened her heart" to receive Paul's Gospel and she was baptized, she responded eagerly, generously opening her house to the Pauline missionaries as their home base.

Thus, Lydia became the first person recorded in Scripture to support Paul with hospitality. Although it may have been unusual for first-century women to be householders on their own, and to carry on financial transactions, it is not without precedent. *New Documents Illustrating Early Christianity* offers several examples of papyrus evidence indicating women as homeowners independently conducting business.[29] Additionally, it is generally

---

[28] Bernadette J. Brooten, "Early Christian Women and their Cultural Context: Issues of Method in Historical Reconstruction," in *Feminist Perspectives on Biblical Scholarship*, Adele Yarbro Collins, ed. (Chico, CA: Scholars Press, 1985), p. 68.

[29] *New Documents Illustrating Early Christianity: A Review of the Greek Inscriptions and Papyri*, G.H.R. Horsley, S.R. Llewelyn, eds (North Ryde,

recognized among New Testament scholars that Macedonian women from the Hellenistic period onward were known for greater independence and more visibility and influence in public affairs.[30]

Cities were named after wives, female money-earners funded tomb-building, women were being permitted to join their husbands at table fellowship and in other activities, and there are examples in inscriptions of women's names where "a metronymic takes the place of the usual patronymic."[31] The fact that women may have taken on leadership roles in the Early Church in Philippi is demonstrated by the reference to the dispute between Paul's co-workers, Euodia and Syntyche in Phil. 4:2.

In any case, under Roman law, "women enjoyed far more freedom and privileges than traditionally has been supposed."[32] In some cases "free marriage" had dissolved the restraints of *manu mariti,* where a woman's rights passed "into the hands of her husband" from the hands of her father. In *sine manu,* women were on an equal par with their spouses in terms of rights of ownership. Furthermore, *ius trium liberorum,* the law of three children, exempted freeborn women with three children or freed women with four children from the necessity of employing a guardian or tutor to transact business.[33] Some women were therefore free to dispose of their own property as they saw fit, and the widow could stand in the place of her deceased husband for execution of household

---

N.S.W.: Ancient History Documentary Research Centre, Macquarie University, 1981-95), 2:28.

[30] Ferguson, *Backgrounds of Early Christianity,* p. 78.

[31] Witherington, *Women in the Earliest Churches,* p. 12. Both types of names convey lineage: a patronymic is based on the name of the bearer's father or an earlier male descendent; more unusual is a metronymic which is derived from the bearer's mother or another female ancestor.

[32] Caroline Whelan, "*Amica Pauli*: The Role of Phoebe in the Early Church," *Journal for the Study of the New Testament* 49 (1993), p. 73.

[33] Among the Oxyrynchus archeological documents recovered is a third-century request "applying to the prefect's office for the right of *ius liberorum,* 'so that I may henceforth be able to conduct my affairs without any impediment.'" P.Oxy XII.1467.

business activities. Thus, Lydia's position as the head of a household was not uncommon for widows.[34]

The character Lydia who greeted Paul at Philippi, then, had a home large enough to accommodate Paul and his group, as well as the finances to care for their needs. The various aspects of her life referenced in Scripture—purple-dealing, heading a household, showing hospitality, and traveling—each one contributes to a picture of some wealth. Lydia's offer of hospitality may well mean that she became host to one of the original core groups of the Primitive Church,[35] for "she was the nexus for the network of Jesus believers in and around Philippi,"[36] a vibrant and flourishing community that filled Paul with pride and joy (Phil.1:3-4).

In fact, archeological evidence has been found which supports the existence of people similar to Lydia, but not Lydia herself. An inscription has been uncovered in Thessalonica, for example, which cites a purple dealer named Menippus from Thyatira;[37] and not far from Lydia's home city of Thyatira, due north in the city of Aphrodisias, a stele was found with an inscription naming benefactors to the synagogue. Almost half were labeled *theosebeis* or God-fearers, and among them was also a dealer in purple cloth.

Luke's narration of the development of the Early Church in Acts, with its detail-rich storyline, offers a different type of resource than the more impressionistic evidence provided in the letters of Paul; "[Luke] is a painter rather than a photographer."[38] Of course, the contemporary reader is also separated from Luke's story by the imperfect lens of translation and editorial redaction over the centuries. Nevertheless, at its heart Acts reflects some grounding in reliable historical events. To its credit, the text demonstrates the accomplished treatment and theology of an

---

[34] Cohick, *Women in the World of the Earliest Christians*, p. 188.
[35] James D.G. Dunn, *Beginning from Jerusalem* (Grand Rapids, MI: William B. Eerdmans Publishing Co., 2009), p. 671.
[36] Richard S. Ascough, *Lydia: Paul's Cosmopolitan Hostess* (Collegeville, MN: Liturgical Press, 2008), p. 1.
[37] Ascough, *Lydia*, p. 18.
[38] Pervo, *Acts*, p. 9.

author who may have been significantly close to the story, and it should not be discounted merely because of the expansive style of its narrative literary genre. Furthermore, the Acts of the Apostles serves as an important bridge to the next generations of recorded memory at a time when the Primitive Church and its theology were still coming into being.

While it is possible that Luke's characterization of a person like Lydia, one who is not corroborated in Paul's letters, could have been creatively influenced by the author in some measure, even modeled on the memory of more than one conversion experience of a woman in the missionary field, Raymond Brown estimates that Luke has recorded the Lydia story from "the fabric of genuine local tradition...She is an exemplary case of the success of the early Christian household mission."[39] And after all, as he observes, "there is no reason to think that the tracing of everything carefully from the beginning promised by Luke 1:3 stopped with the Gospel."[40]

As Paul makes his way from Asia Minor across the Aegean Sea toward Philippi, "a leading city in the district of Macedonia"(Acts 16:12), Luke is able to portray his encounter with the purple textiles dealer, Lydia, and other characters there in compelling detail, but, a glance at the parsing of the verbs may indicate a tantalizing hint as to why. Abruptly, without explanation, the text shifts from third-person plural into first-person plural for eight verses (16:10-17), which creates a distinct "we" section, the first of four. The majority of Acts gives no indication of an author's point of view, and indeed "from the biblical tradition comes the technique of omniscient narration and its companion, anonymous authorship,"[41] melding humility with expertise for the sake of authority. Nevertheless, the Evangelist Luke crafts distinctly intimate-sounding narrative in these "we" sections, appearing to write himself into the missionary picture alongside the Apostle Paul.

---

[39] *The New Jerome Bible Commentary*, Raymond E. Brown *et al*, eds (Englewood Cliffs, NJ: Prentice Hall, 1990), p. 753.
[40] Brown, *Introduction to the New Testament*, p. 316.
[41] Pervo, *Acts*, p. 15.

Although it is unlikely that the missionary band came to town and swept up the young physician Luke in their evangelistic fervor, the text does convey the author incorporating himself into his description of their group and identifying himself with their ministry. While it has been suggested that Philippi, with its famous school of medicine, could have been the hometown of the physician/evangelist, Luke, who was "still based in Philippi at a later time when that epistle was written, somewhere between 60-62 C.E.;"[42] this view is inconclusive. It is just as likely that here, as in three other places in Acts (20:5-16; 21:1-18; 27:1-28:16), Luke has incorporated an eye-witness testimony known to him as a source or is simply including Paul in the narrator's point of view.[43] Yet, whatever the relationship is between the author of Acts and Paul's eye-witness companion, it adds to the reliability of the story of Lydia in Acts 16 that it is contained in one of the "we" sections.[44]

Named after the father of Alexander the Great, Philippi was located on the eastern border of the Roman province of Macedonia; only ten miles inland from the Aegean Sea, it was a busy port of call along the first-century trading route. As a Roman colony, Philippi was granted the honor of the "Italian law" (*ius italicum*), which meant that the town was to be treated as if it were located on Italian soil and given equal status with other Roman cities, governed by collegiate magistrates under Roman law and kept free from direct taxation. This is demonstrated in Scripture by the mention of the technical Roman job title, *stragtegoi*, in Acts 16:35-38.[45]

Philippi was the gateway into the rest of Macedonia and what is today northern Greece. One of the significant accomplishments of the Roman Empire, and of particular benefit to Philippi, was the building of the Via Egnatia, a major 500-mile road, which stretched across Macedonia from the Adriatic coast to the Aegean

---

[42] Witherington, *Acts of the Apostles*, p. 490.

[43] This issue is comprehensively examined in Richard Pervo's "Excursus: 'We' in Acts," in *Acts*, pp. 392-396.

[44] Brown, *Introduction to the New Testament*, p. 317.

[45] Ascough, *Lydia*, pp. 19-21.

Sea and ran through the center of town. Between the well-con-
structed road running through Philippi and the busy seafaring enterprise nearby, Lydia's purple-dealing business probably involved the import of goods from Asia Minor via the trade routes
by either land or across the sea.

When he arrived in Philippi, Paul set out to follow the usual
mode of operation for mission he had been using since his commissioning by the Holy Spirit (13:2). As he had done in Salamis
on Cyprus (13:5), and in Antioch of Pisidia (13:14), and also in
Iconium (14:1), Paul embarked on the Sabbath day to find a gathering of Jewish worshippers in order to proclaim the Gospel to
them first. He and his group proceeded outside the gate by a
river;[46] where they supposed there was a "place of prayer"
(proseuche), sometimes translated as a "Jewish assembly." Here,
"we sat down and spoke to the women there" (16:13). This is a
fascinating observation on many levels!

Were men there as well, faithfully occupied in liturgical affairs, while Paul meanwhile engaged in conversation with the
women present? Paul's group may have been unable to find any
local Jewish assembly yet in Philippi; if indeed there was one, it
may not have met formally in a designated synagogue building.
Given the possibilities of gathering for religious rites, certain
women from the synagogue group, including interested Gentiles,
could have met on the Sabbath without the men.[47] Perhaps Luke
would not share the author's surprise that the Jewish prayer gathering which was found by Paul and his co-workers consisted of
women and that Paul approached them and even sat down among
them like a rabbi to teach the Gospel message.[48]

---

[46] When Paul encountered Lydia, he may have gone outside the Krenides
Gate by the river where the Via Egnatia intersected Philippi on the western side. Ascough, *Lydia*, p. 23.

[47] Cohick, *Women in the World of the Earliest Christians*, p. 188.

[48] Since it is unusual because of the gender of the recipients, this episode
echoes the story of the twelve-year-old Jesus teaching in the Temple,
radically unusual because of the age of the "rabbi" (Lk. 2:41-52). Thus,
Luke appears to be authenticating the apostleship of Paul by imbuing
him with Christ-like characteristics.

This story may indicate a different kind of assumed Jewish ritual setting than can be expected in a contemporary situation today where liturgical and study activities take place in the synagogue, while ritual cleansings are done elsewhere. Additionally, this may have been the women's part of the group, or the special day or time when the women rather than the men met for prayer, at a location convenient for cleansing rituals as well. Nevertheless, it is fascinating that, for whatever reason, this group at this time seems to have consisted of women. Moreover, it is most interesting to note that Luke doesn't describe this as in any way unusual, though it seems astonishing to our ears.

Here, then, by the river we are introduced to Lydia, one of the remarkable characters witnessed in Luke's story. She has a name well-known from Horace's *Odes*;[49] yet since most Roman women were usually called by their family name, Lydia's name, with its likely geographic reference to the region of Lydia, might mean that she was of Greek descent or a freed slave.[50] It is probably significant that Luke calls her by name; although, the name Lydia has sometimes been interpreted as an ethnic nickname, implying "the Lydian."

Lydia is described as a "worshipper of God" (*sebomene ton Theon*), probably meaning someone familiar with and sympathetic to Jewish religious practice. She is also a "dealer in purple cloth" (*porphuropolis*) from Thyatira, a city on the mainland of Asia Minor. Purple dye in antiquity was extracted principally from mollusk shells. Purple fabric was considered so luxurious that it was often monopolized by the imperial family, to the extent that those engaged in the production and sale of it were sometimes referred to as "Caesar's household."[51] It so typified glamorous adornment that Luke, probably influenced by the

---

[49] *Odes* 1.8. Hans Conzelmann, *Acts of the Apostles: A Commentary on the Acts of the Apostles*; (Philadelphia: Fortress Press, 1987), p. 130.

[50] "A number of inscriptions suggesting that several people involved in the purple trade were ex-slaves might imply that she was herself a freed slave." Ascough, *Lydia*, p. 7. See also Pervo, *Acts*, p. 403.

[51] *New Documents Illustrating Early Christianity*, 2:28.

moralizing reaction against purple,[52] characterized the rich man, in the parable with Lazarus, as being clothed in it (Lk. 16:19).

"The Lord opened her heart to listen eagerly to what was said by Paul" (16:14). This fulsome description of one woman's divinely inspired response to Paul's teaching of the Gospel leads her as well as her entire household to be baptized; she becomes the first convert in Europe. But what does it mean for the Lord to have "opened her heart?" Here, "the Lord" probably indicates the Spirit of Jesus in action by the riverside. Luke might have considered Lydia among those who respond to the Word of God with "a good heart and bear fruit with patient endurance," (Lk. 8:15) as Jesus himself taught.

Lydia's spiritual openness also has echoes of the skilled women in Exodus whose hearts were moved by the Lord (Ex. 35:25-26) to a generous enterprise. By her conversion, she has, like them, "now come face to face with God's incredible graciousness and willingness to begin again."[53] Lydia's conversion is unique in actually taking place within the scope of the scriptural text (Acts 16:13-15). Like other conversions, this one was life-changing and the reader hears the outcome in Lydia's faithful action; and in contrast to other characters attested in Scripture, we glimpse Lydia at the very heart of the evangelizing moment.

The successful outcome of Lydia's evangelization along with her household is demonstrated by the fact that, by the time Paul and Silas depart from Philippi, they have won over enough people that Paul is reported to have encouraged the brethren (*tous adelphous*), in the plural form. This could indicate the development of a group of believers meeting in Lydia's home, which had become a house church. Her story is significant in illustrating how the house church came to be developed.

Earlier in Acts (10:48), the conversion of Cornelius's household is the first of the examples of an entire household being Baptized in Acts. Other examples include those cited at Acts 11:14

---

[52] *New Documents Illustrating Early Christianity,* 2:25.
[53] Walter Brueggemann, "The Book of Exodus: Introduction, Commentary, and Reflections," in *The New Interpreters Bible,* v.1 (Nashville, TN: Abingdon Press, 1994), p. 961.

and 18:8. In considering what the Baptism of Lydia and her household looked like, the Cornelius story may provide an effective exemplar for the pattern of early Baptism. According to this account, Cornelius "feared God" (10:2), heard Peter's message (10:33, 44), and believed (10:43); he received the Holy Spirit and spoke in tongues (10:46), and extolled God (10:46).[54]

The make-up of Lydia's household is not specified, but it probably consisted of other women employed by her for the purple-fabric business and her slaves, or freed servants—and even some of the local poor, for whom Lydia may have served as a patron.[55] Only women are indicated in Scripture, though; so, if there were other males in her family and household in general, they were probably not present at the river for prayer on the Sabbath day. In contrast to the next Baptism described in the story, which takes place "without delay" (16:33), in the case of Lydia's household the conjunctive phrase (hos de) in 16:15, which the NRSV translates as "when," indicates some passage of time. In the natural course of events, the group Baptism of Lydia's household may have taken place directly but not immediately, with an opportunity for the entire group to come along, including men and children, if any.

Baptism is attested in Acts as administered in the name of Jesus Christ. Lydia's Baptism likely included a confession of faith in him. As in other accounts in Acts, such as that of the Ethiopian eunuch (8:26-40), her Baptism follows a transformational hearing of the spoken Word of God (16:13-14). Baptism was viewed as "both a human act and an act in which God was at work."[56] The coming of the Holy Spirit is suggested by the fruit of Lydia's faithful commitment in generously opening her home to Paul and his band of missionaries, and it is notable that her invitation of hospitality is recorded as a remembered quotation: "If you have

---

[54] Everett Ferguson, *Baptism in the Early Church: History, Theology, and Liturgy in the First Five Centuries* (Grand Rapids, MI: William B. Eerdmans Pub. Co., 2009), p. 178.

[55] Ascough, *Lydia*, p. 32.

[56] Ferguson, *Baptism in the Early Church,* p. 184.

judged me to be faithful to the Lord, come and stay at my home" (16:15).

Luke shows God working through the new faith of Lydia by interacting with the faith of Paul, challenging him to accept hospitality from a new believer, who was in all likelihood sharply different from him: a non-Jewish woman, from a different culture, operating without the guardianship of a man. Here is a case where a woman's established role of providing hospitality to visiting guests "became a means by which they could support and sustain the Church."[57] Lydia's statement appears to reflect hesitancy of some sort of Paul's part, perhaps a normal aspect of polite conversation, but more likely it is an honorable acknowledgment of their differences.[58]

Showing sensitivity to the dangerous circumstances facing itinerant Jewish preachers in the Roman Empire, Lydia offers him hospitality, in the same way that the disciples from Emmaus welcomed the itinerant Jesus whom they did not recognize (Lk. 24:29). Lydia prevailed, or perhaps the Spirit working in her effectively prevailed. As often recorded in stories about Jesus, both host and guest show generosity in engaging with one another in this exchange, and from this acceptance of hospitality, the church in Philippi began to grow.

After the experience of encountering women at the Philippian "place of prayer" outside the city gates, and settling into the residential hospitality of Lydia's house, it is interesting to note that the text describes Paul and his band of missionaries still returning to the riverside "place of prayer" again in Acts 16:16. While it is plausible that this is a mere stylistic place-holder to mark the beginning of a new story in the same narration, it may indicate as well that Luke's "eyewitness" source knew that Paul repeatedly returned to preach the Gospel among the group of women praying by the river.

While Luke mentions an earlier house church back in Jerusalem, where many had gathered in prayer and fellowship "in the house of Mary, the mother of John" (Acts 12:12), the story of

---

[57] Witherington, *Women in the Earliest Churches*, p. 145.
[58] Ascough, *Lydia*, pp. 5, 13.

Lydia's conversion in Philippi signals another important shift from a Jewish place of prayer to a believer's home as the missionary base. This becomes increasingly a pattern in the emerging Church and in the continuing story of Acts as it unfolds. Thus, as Witherington observes, it is probably not accidental that "at the only two points in Acts (12:12, 16:40) where Luke clearly tells us of a Church meeting in a particular person's home, not just a place of lodging or hospitality, it is the home of a woman."[59]

Three centuries later in his commentary on Philemon, St. Jerome described hospitality to Paul as participating in Paul's apostleship. "When Paul would arrive at a new city to preach the crucified one...he needed before anything an appropriate place in the city where all could gather, a place without disturbances, large in order to receive many listeners, not near the places of spectacles with disturbing neighbors."[60] Jerome reflects a Church memory which made a significant connection between early Christian hospitality and effective missionary work. Not only is the peripatetic preaching disciple necessary for the progress of the Gospel, but also the ministry of the host in whose household the missionary is welcomed and given provisions.

After an ordeal of persecution, imprisonment, and miraculous manumission by the work of the Holy Spirit (Acts 16:19-26), note that Paul and Silas retire again to the comfort and mission fellowship of Lydia's house (16:40), even though they had actually been asked to leave town (16:39). Acts 16:40 acknowledges the hospitality of Lydia's home in the formation of the Philippian group, since it is there that Paul and Silas encourage the brethren before leaving the city, demonstrating that her house had become the meeting place for the early believers in Philippi.

In this, "Luke wishes us to understand that what began as a lodging for missionaries became the home of the embryonic church in Philippi."[61] Furthermore, the fact that Paul and Silas

---

[59] Witherington, *Women in the Earliest Churches*, p. 146.

[60] PL 26.616.22; for English, *St. Jerome's Commentaries on Galatians, Titus, and Philemon*, Thomas P. Scheck, trans. (Notre Dame, ID: The University of Notre Dame Press, 2010), p. 377.

[61] Witherington, *Women in the Earliest Churches*, p. 149.

retreated to the encouraging atmosphere of Lydia's house, when in fact they had been instructed to leave town may indicate the possible danger inherent for Lydia and her household, as indeed is the case for Paul's host, Jason, in Acts 17:5-9. It must have been courageous hospitality for her to harbor the recently incarcerated pair; this may have been a dangerous action on the part of Lydia. Although Luke doesn't describe them, it cannot be assumed that there were no further negative consequences for Lydia and her household—and she is, after all, never heard of again.

The fact, nevertheless, that we still have the women's stories in the scriptural text demonstrates that their remembered presence has remained strong. The persistence of the memory of Lydia's contribution has won out over the natural tendency, especially throughout the early centuries, to editorially diminish or to even delete entirely female presence in the processes of redaction. "Luke expresses by this arrangement that man and woman stand together and side by side before God. They are equal in honor and grace; they are endowed with the gifts and have the same responsibilities."[62]

As Paul and Silas move on to embark on mission work in Thessalonica, and after experiencing opposition again in Beroea, the Church is described as continuing to grow; and the attested presence of male and female followers throughout the story demonstrates that "the strength of Christianity's appeal to women was a function from the first."[63] Luke makes a point of stressing the number of women who became believers, and their socio-economic prominence. The emerging Church is shown, therefore, as dependent on its female benefactors, like Lydia, for their philanthropic ability to seed the growth of house churches, and also to witness to the women's leadership in the earliest faith communities.

Note in the verse adjacent to it that the women of high standing who came to belief were among those observed having the

---

[62] Quoting H. Flender, Witherington, *Women in the Earliest Churches*, p. 129.

[63] Elisabeth Schüssler Fiorenza, *In Memory of Her: A Feminist Theological Reconstruction of Christian Origins* (New York: Crossroad, 1992), p. 167.

intellectual capacity and spiritual desire to examine the Scriptures daily "to see whether these things were so" (17:11). The verses in Scripture do not specify whether Lydia served as a leader of the group of believers which gathered at her house, yet: "Lydia's status as Paul's benefactor would make a leadership role in the Church likely."[64] The witness of "not a few of the leading women" (17:4) contributes to an overall picture of converts being added to the growing community of believers from both Jews and Gentiles; and the character of Lydia stands out among them, as a purple-dealer and also as a God-fearer whose heart was opened by the Lord.

Regarding the root term from which *porphuropolis*, describing Lydia, derives, "It is uncertain whether we are to translate this word as 'trader in' or 'maker of purple,' perhaps 'purple dealer;'" but, epigraphical evidence indicates the importance of the purple trade in Tyre and in the provinces of Lydia and Phrygia, and in Macedonian cities such as Philippi. In fact, in Tyre, Christian purple dyers are attested in archeological inscriptions;[65] purple-dyeing in the Lydia region can be traced back as far as the Iliad.[66] The purple which Lydia was selling was not likely the imperial Tyrian murex extracted from shellfish, but a less luxurious dye from the roots of the madder plant (*rubia*), which was generically called "turkey red;"[67] it was an industry "well-known in association with Tyratira."[68] There was a vigorous market for desirable goods; togas, for example, garments which could only be worn by Roman citizens, often featured a purple-dyed border. Pliny the Elder described how purple fabric could be double-dyed to achieve a greater depth and consistency of purple, but that double-dying also raised the price.[69]

---

[64] Cohick, *Women in the World of the Earliest Christians*, p. 307.

[65] *New Documents Illustrating Early Christianity*, 2:26.

[66] Homer, *The Iliad*, 4.141-42.

[67] *New Documents Illustrating Early Christianity*, 3:53.

[68] Craig Steven De Vos, *Church and Community Conflicts: The Relationships of the Thessalonian, Corinthian, and Philippian Churches with their Wider Civic Communities* (Atlanta, GA: Scholars Press, 1999), p. 257.

[69] Pliny the Elder, *The Natural History* 9.125-34.

Lydia is also identified as a "worshipper of God" (*seboumene ton Theon*). Luke uses two different expressions in Greek to convey this category, "God-fearer" (*phoboumenos ton Theon*) in Acts 10:2, 22, 35; 13:26 and "God-worshiper" (*seboumenos ton Theon*) or simply "worshipper" in Acts 13:43, 50; 16:40; 17:4, 17; 18:7. The Septuagint speaks of God-fearers in Ps. 119:9-11 and Ps. 135:19-20, so Luke in Acts may have adapted this phrase to describe Gentile sympathizers with Jesus, since God-fearers stood on the boundary between Judaism and paganism—and often Christianity as well. They were associated with Judaism, but had not become proselytes; not yet having taken the radical step of circumcision in the case of men. God-fearers represent an important Christian category; and analyzing epigraphic evidence shows that over 75% of God-fearers may have been women.[70] Lydia is a prominent example of a God-fearer. She also presents an intriguing character, not only with regard to her role as a businesswoman in the market for purple fabric goods, but also as one of Paul's benefactors. Luke understands her to be making a significant contribution as "a patron of the seminal Jesus group in Philippi."[71]

In his own writing, Paul offers a glimpse, both in 2 Cor. 8:1-5 and Phil. 4:14-18, of his gratitude for the abundant hospitality he received from men and women in the young churches of Macedonia "in the early days of the Gospel." He assures his readers that their hospitality to the Gospel and to his little band of missioners is earning them bountiful grace from God. Thus, "the generous openness and support of Lydia, a gentile devotee of Jewish worship, is a model for the Christian household."[72]

The foundation for the ministry of the benefactor offering hospitality as a necessary component of missionary work is not only laid down in the Gospel, but Paul in his letters acknowledges that the generosity of the giver fulfills one of the divine attributes God lives out in the work of the Holy Spirit through God's people. The liberal giving of money in Rom. 12:8 is understood as a

---

[70] Cohick, *Women in the World of the Earliest Christians*, p. 187.
[71] Cohick, *Women in the World of the Earliest Christians*, p. 53.
[72] Brown, *An Introduction to the New Testament*, p. 310.

spiritual charism; 2 Cor. 9:6-15 makes the additional point that the gift may not be consciously experienced as your own until you actually practice it. "Sometimes, Paul says, we must act out of a conviction that God is magnanimous, even though we do not feel particularly gifted."[73]

Although the historical veracity of the character, Lydia, cannot be firmly established, the "argument from silence is not strong enough to erase a real person from history; we can be reasonably confident that Lydia was an actual person described by Luke, who molded her story to reinforce theological points recurrent in Luke/Acts."[74] The reliability of Lydia's story is also enhanced by being contained within the first "we" section, which confirms its "eyewitness pedigree."[75] Ultimately, the story of Lydia's faith journey and her connection to Paul's ministry are significant to the development of the Early Church, whether or not the historicity of Lydia can be reliably proved. Her colorful lifestyle and eager response to the Lord opening of her heart are remembered as a contribution to the origin of the Primitive Church in Philippi.

---

[73] John Koenig, *Charismata: God's Gifts for God's People* (Philadelphia, Westminster Press, 1978), p. 118.
[74] Cohick, *Women in the World of the Earliest Christians*, p. 190.
[75] *The New Jerome Bible Commentary*, p. 753.

CHAPTER I.2
THE VOICE OF ST. THEKLA: INWARDLY TUNED BY GOD[1]

I am a slave of the living God.[2]

Thekla's luminous first-person account of divinely inspired deliverance from martyrdom and her subsequent preaching ministry inspired by the Apostle Paul captured the imagination of innumerable Christians in the early centuries of the Jesus movement, a time when the organization of the Church lacked as yet full episcopal and creedal development, and was still markedly fluid and collaborative. Her story is known to us from the *Acts of Paul and Thecla*;[3] one of the apocryphal documents circulating alongside the authorized books of Scripture in the late second century,

---

[1] The title cites the Church Father, Bishop Methodius, in "Logos 8—Thekla" of his *Symposium* (8. Proem.3-5), where he describes Thekla as a "cithara, inwardly tuned and prepared to speak carefully and nobly" the Gospel of Jesus Christ.

[2] Acts of Paul and Thekla 4.2, Jeremy W. Barrier, trans.

[3] "Praxeis Paulou kai Thekles" in *Acta Apostolorum*, R.A. Lipsius, M. Bonnet, eds (Hildesheim: Georg Olms, 1958), pp. 235-272. For English translation, see "The Acts of Paul," in *New Testament Apochrypha*, revised ed., W. Schneemelcher, ed., R. McL. Wilson, trans. (Louisville, KY: Westminster/John Knox Press, 1992), pp. 2:213-270. See also Jeremy W. Barrier, *The Acts of Paul and Thecla: A Critical Introduction and Commentary* (Tübingen: Mohr Siebeck, 2009).

41

when the New Testament Canon was still in the process of being formally codified.

This, and the *Acts of Paul*, of which it became a part, is attested in Greek, Latin, and Syriac versions, among others. Thekla's account is considered to be extracanonical; however, it reflects remarkably accurately the experience of many second-century women who ventured away from the family hearth to follow the Gospel taught by Paul and found themselves, like Thekla, in "violent confrontation with society."[4] The *Acts of Paul and Thecla* is a tale of high adventure and divine miracles, and it brings into sharp focus the incarnational tension living between the ascetic and erotic components of the text.

Note that Thekla was held up as an example by the martyr Perpetua, and by Gregory of Nyssa's sister, Macrina, and by Patriarch John Chrysostom's soul-mate, Olympias. The model of Thekla was used as an endorsement in support of women's active ministry in the Early Church, including preaching and baptizing, as can be seen by Tertullian black-listing of it in *De Baptismo* 17.[5] Tertullian's criticism of the *Acts of Paul and Thecla* places the document, if not the actual characters, into an historical framework, with a *terminus ante quem* of 206 C.E., although a date of 160 has been suggested for its authorship.[6] Origen cites it twice approvingly;[7] Athanasius extolls Thekla in *De Virginitate* as the ideal of ascetic piety. Thus, even as Thekla's sacramental efficacy was

---

[4] Margaret Y. MacDonald, "Rereading Paul: Early Interpreters of Paul on Women and Gender," in Ross Shepard Kraemer, Mary Rose D'Angelo, eds, *Women and Christian Origins* (New York: Oxford Press, 1999), p. 249.

[5] In around 206 C.E., Tertullian cautioned: "But if certain acts of Paul, which are falsely so named, claim the example of Thecla for allowing women to teach and to baptize, let men know that in Asia the presbyter who compiled that document, thinking to add of his own to Paul's reputation, was found out, and though he professed he had done it for love of Paul, was deposed from his position." *Tertullian's Homily on Baptism*, Ernest Evans, trans. (London: SPCK, 1964), p. 36.

[6] Jan Bremmer, "The Apocryphal Acts: Authors, Place, Time and Readership," in *The Apocryphal Acts of Thomas* (Leuven: Peeters, 2001), p. 153.

[7] Origen, *De Principis* I.2.3; *Comm. in John* 20.12.

being invalidated by Tertullian, she could claim the mantle of righteous popularity throughout Asia Minor.

The historicity of Thekla, unfortunately, cannot be determined with any reliability at this point. While earlier scholarship saw some hope of historical accuracy,[8] and questions have been explored about the *Acts* as evidence of an active Early Christian group of ascetic widows,[9] more recently it is thought that "there may have been someone Thekla represents who was an historical figure, but the actual details of her life are beyond our grasp."[10]

The success of her popularity, however, paradoxically bypasses the challenges presented in any quest for the historical Thekla, "much as the literary Thekla repeatedly escapes martyrdom and yet is remembered and revered as a martyr."[11] Rather than intending to portray the historical Paul and Thekla, the original purpose of the *Acts of Paul and Thecla* may have been to assist the faithful in remembering the theology and personal experience of the Pauline Churches of the first century.

The cult of Thekla enjoyed robust development and expansion, especially throughout the fourth and fifth centuries.[12] A shrine to her devotion built up at Seleucia of Isauria,[13] for

---

[8] See William M. Ramsey, "The Acta of Paul and Thekla," in *The Church in the Roman Empire Before 70 A.D.* (London: G.P.Putnam, 1893), pp. 390-410.

[9] See Stevan L. Davies, *The Revolt of the Widows: The Social World of the Apocryphal Acts* (Carbonville, IL: Southern Illinois University Press, 1980), pp. 95-109; Dennis Ronald MacDonald, *The Legend and the Apostle: The Battle for Paul in Story and Canon* (Philadelphia: Westminster Press, 1983), pp. 17-35; Virginia Burrus, *Chastity as Autonomy: Women in the Stories of the Apocryphal Acts* (Queenston, ON: Mellon, 1987), pp. 88-90.

[10] Barrier, *Acts of Paul and Thecla*, p. 11, where he characterizes the assessment of Willy Rordorf.

[11] Gail Corrington Streete, *Redeemed Bodies: Women Martyrs in Early Christianity* (Louisville, KY: Westminster John Knox Press, 2009), p. 139.

[12] For a comprehensive survey of the development of the cult of St. Thekla, see Stephen J. Davis, *The Cult of Saint Thecla: A Tradition of Women's Piety in Late Antiquity* (Oxford: Oxford University Press, 2001).

[13] Seleucia of Isauria is modern-day Silifke, in Turkey. See Troels Myrup Kristensen, "The Landscape, Space, and Presence in the Cult of Thekla at

example, on the southeastern coast of Asia Minor, at the place where Thekla is said to have died. Athanasius visited;[14] Gregory of Nazianzus, who regarded Thekla as an apostle-martyr,[15] went into retreat there for at least three years when his parents died.[16] Egeria records visiting the holy site in May of 384 and encountering a beautiful church with numerous monastics living in the hills above it. She reports:

> In Insauria, only three staging-posts on from Tarsus, is the Martyrium of Holy Thekla... When I got there, I called on the Bishop, a very godly man who had been a monk. Holy Thekla's is on a small hill about a mile and a half from the city... Round the holy church there is a tremendous number of cells for men and women... and in the middle a great wall round the martyrium itself, which is very beautiful. In God's name I arrived at the martyrium, and we had a prayer there, and read the whole Acts of Holy Thekla, and I gave heartfelt thanks to God."[17]

The chapel received imperial favor from the Emperor Zeno in the fifth century, adding the basilica and cutting a cross-shaped Baptistery into the rock floor of the crypt.

Also, in the fifth century, another document, *The Life and Miracles of Thekla*, testified to the numerous miracles attributed to Thekla experienced after her death, as well as the lively theological debates of the period.[18] In the sixth century, Emperor

---

Meriamlik," *Journal of Early Christian Studies* 24:2 (Summer 2016), pp. 229-263.

[14] Greg. Naz. Or. 21.22 *In Laudem Athanasii*.

[15] Greg. Naz. Or. 4.69 *Against Julian*.

[16] Greg. Naz. *De Vita Sua*, vv. 547-549. That Gregory calls it the "Parthenona"—that is, the House of Virgins—indicates that it was a well-developed monastery, at least by the 370s, probably operating as a healing center. See John A. McGuckin, *Saint Gregory of Nazianzus: An Intellectual Biography* (Crestwood, NY: St. Vladimir's Seminary Press, 2001), pp. 99, 230.

[17] *Egeria's Travels*, John Wilkinson, trans. (Warminster: Aris & Phillips, 2002), 23:1-6, excerpted, pp. 141-42.

[18] "Thaumata tes Hagias kai Proto-martyros Theklas," in Gilbert Dragon, in collaboration with Maria Dupré La Tour, *Vie et miracles de Sainte*

Justinian erected a shrine in Thekla's honor in Constantinople. Although the Roman Catholic Church suppressed her cult in 1969, the Orthodox Church venerates St. Thekla on September 24.[19]

Among the miracles associated with Thekla, we witness the action of the Spirit of God working through her, demonstrating divine approval of her choice of celibacy and her Baptism, from a time when virginity was an essential virtue of Christian sanctity— what Peter Brown calls "the apostle's call to continence."[20] Indeed, for many at that time, she stood prominently among "the cloud of witnesses" surrounding the faithful cited in Hebrews 12:1. The *Acts of Paul and Thecla* provided well-needed encouragement to believers in the second-century Church, assuring them that God delivers his followers, especially in the face of Christian persecution and martyrdom at the hands of Roman authority.

In a story often uniquely crafted in its observance of her point of view, especially during her martyrdom trials, we are introduced to Thekla in her hometown of Iconium at the very instant of her conversion to Christian belief. Her call to faith is a sunlit moment in the narrative, filled with "overabundant joy" (3.7). And as we encounter the characters, a new literary genre is being crafted, "a new type of fictional prose narrative, which can

---

Thecle: Texte Grec, Tradution et Commentaire (Bruxelles: Societé des Bollandistes, 1978). For selected English translation, see: Scott F. Johnson, *The Life and Miracles of Thekla: A Literary Study* (Washington, D.C.: Center for Hellenic Studies, 2006). See also "The Miracles of Saint Thekla," in *Miracle Tales from Byzantium*, Alice-Mary Talbot, Scott Fitzgerald Johnson, trans. (Cambridge, MA: Harvard University Press, 2012), pp. 1-202.

[19] In fact, McGuckin, who characterizes Thekla as a "megelo-martyr," observes that, "In the Eastern Church the female martyrs are remembered at every Eucharistic liturgy...the memory that innumerable women were among the company of the early martyrs endures. The *proskomedia* ritual," enumerating the principle martyrs, includes Thekla in the list. John Anthony McGuckin, *The Path of Christianity: The First Thousand Years* (Downers Grove, IL: IVP Academic, 2017), p. 902, footnote 32.

[20] Peter Brown, *The Body and Society: Men, Women, and Sexual Renunciation in Early Christianity* (New York: Columbia University Press, 1988), p. 156.

in a certain sense quite legitimately be labeled the 'Early Christian novel.'"[21]

Thekla is swept up in newfound faith by hearing the "Word of Christ" (*tou Christou Logou*) from her upstairs window as the Apostle Paul is preaching the Gospel across the way in the house next door. This kind of access will be familiar to listeners in urban settings who witness their neighbors' lives in sudden snapshots of overheard dialogue through apartment walls and studio windows.

St. Paul, whose missionary visit to Iconium is mentioned in Acts 13:51, is teaching about the Resurrection by crafting a magisterial gloss on the Beatitudes of Jesus heard in the Gospel of Matthew (5:3-12), and he is redefining "Blessed are the pure in heart" (Mt. 5:8) as those who keep the flesh chaste:

> "Blessed are the pure in heart," Paul teaches, "for they shall see God. Blessed are those who have kept the flesh chaste, for they will be a temple of God...Blessed are they who are set apart from the world, for they will be well pleasing to God...Blessed are they who receive the wisdom of Jesus Christ, for they shall be called sons of the Most High...Blessed are the bodies of the virgins, for they shall be well pleasing to God, because the word of the father shall be to them a work of salvation in the day of his son, and they shall have rest forever" (3.5-6).

Remember that Paul operated in an eschatological tension that anticipated the imminent demise of the present age, and therefore, demanded behavior congruent with the expectation of impending judgement, including sexual abstinence. Nevertheless, this message did not match the concerns of Roman parents for their vulnerable teenage daughters.

While Thekla longs to "be made worthy to stand in the presence of Paul and hear the word of Christ" (3.7), her burgeoning faith alarms her mother, as it might any parent dealing with the impulsive behavior of an impressionable teenager exploring new subversive ideas. She finds her daughter's infatuation with Paul's teaching to be "a new desire and a fearful passion" (*epithumia*

---

[21] Niklas Holzberg, *The Ancient Novel: An Introduction* (London: Rutledge, 1995), p. 23.

kaine kai pathei deino) (3.9). Thekla's betrothed is heartsick as well and has Paul brought before Governor Castellius and imprisoned.

In a midnight scene reminiscent of Mary Magdalene dispensing with her jewels as she turns to Jesus, Thecla offers her bracelets and silver mirror to the gate-keepers holding Paul and enters his prison to sit at his feet; and while kissing his chains, her faith in Christ grows yet more. In the classic ancient novel, these two characters would be lovers brought together; but here, both are Jesus-lovers, engaged in the holy work of Christ (*tois hosios autou ergois tou Christou*) (3.18).

Thekla's late-night expedition, even faith-inspired, is seen as scandalous by her mother, who is enraged, fearing the loss of a valuable family fiancé. She demands that Thekla be burned at the stake, in the hope that it will effectively deter any other young, marriageable daughters from contemplating Christian conversion, rather than the conjugal duties of the bridal bed. Thekla's mother cries out, "Burn the one who is no bride in the midst of the theatre, in order that all the women who have been taught by this one might be afraid" (3.20). Paul is interrogated and flogged, and Thekla condemned to the stake by the governor.

As an agitated crowd departs for the Roman stadium and Thekla's martyrdom is imminent, she has a vision of the presence of the Lord seated near her, and she stands transfixed in the chaos around her. This divine appearance is traditionally regarded as equivalent to the Lord appearing to Stephen before he was stoned, as described in Acts 7:55-56, causing St. Stephen and St. Thekla to be characterized as Brother and Sister Proto-Martyrs by the Orthodox Church.

Soon, Thekla finds herself stripped and thrust into the municipal arena before an excited crowd. The Roman stadium is hierarchically arranged with spectators above looking down upon the victim, in such a way as to publicly exhibit their power; quite effectively creating an "exercise in terror."[22] Governor Castellius weeps at the sight of Thekla, and is said to have "marveled at the

---

[22] Alice Futrell, *Blood in the Arena: The Spectacle of Roman Power* (Austin, TX: University of Texas Press, 1997), p. 47.

power in her" (*ethaumasin tenaute dunamin*) (3.22). Heroically, she makes the sign of the Cross, climbs the pyre, and it is lit from beneath.

With the flames rising, "even though a great fire was shining, it did not touch her" (3.22). Because God rained down a great storm of life-damaging hail, Thekla, like Polycarp before her, was saved.[23] As the first part of her story draws to a conclusion, Thekla sees "the destruction of her former identity and the emergence of a new one as the unassailable and powerful virgin slave girl of God."[24]

Having been sent out of the city, Paul, meanwhile, is ministering to friends in an open tomb; and when he and Thekla are united, an overjoyed dialogue of prayer breaks forth. He is already praying, when she finds him, that God may protect her from being "overtaken in the fire." Seeing Paul, she prays to Jesus Christ in thanksgiving for salvation and for finding him again; seeing Thekla, Paul then prays to "God, knower of hearts" (*Thee cardiognosta*) in thanksgiving for the divine deliverance of Thekla (3.24). Joyful thanksgiving and Eucharistic celebration ensue.

By not going home after her ordeal by fire, and leaving her betrothed in order to follow Christ with the Apostle Paul, Thecla is described committing herself to a celibate vocation serving in the life of the Gospel. Although she eventually was sent into a leadership role in Early Christian ministry, there were costly consequences for her discipleship. Thus, the *Acts of Paul and Thecla* can be seen as a document providing "remarkable insight into the social tensions experienced by women who joined early Christian groups."[25]

Paul and Thekla are soon on their way to Antioch; but almost immediately, martyrdom is threatened once again. Thekla is

---

[23] See the *Martyrdom of Polycarp* 13:1-15:2.

[24] Maureen A. Tilley, "The Ascetic Body and (Un)Making of the World of the Martyr," *Journal of the American Academy of Religion* 59:3 (1991), p. 467.

[25] Margaret Y. MacDonald, "Rereading Paul: Early Interpreters of Paul on Women and Gender," in Ross Shepard Kraemer, Mary Rose D'Angelo, eds, *Women and Christian Origins* (New York: Oxford Press, 1999), p. 249.

discovered by the city's grandiose Syrian council leader, Alexander, who sizes her up and is immediately smitten. After first trying to buy her from Paul, he then attempts to sexually accost her out in the open city quarter. Thekla gamely struggles against him, grabbing his draped robe in the process, and knocking off his crown of authority, and she ends up proudly unmolested. Though she defends herself as "the servant of God" (*tou Theou doulen*) (4.1), having wounded the pride of a prominent male city official, retaliation comes quickly.

In an uncomfortable *frisson* of desire and dishonor, Alexander has Thekla hauled before the governor of Antioch and sentenced *damnati ad bestias*, even providing his own menagerie of wild beasts. Thekla cries out to the governor for salvation from rape; and, in the face of certain violation, begs to be kept inviolate. She is offered refuge from her impending martyrdom by a wealthy royal widow who is grieving the recent loss of her daughter; and we are introduced to Queen Tryphaena, perhaps from Pontus and related to the Emperor Claudius. Tryphaena's story is examined in the next chapter, where she steps forward to offer a night's refuge to Thekla, until she fights the wild beasts.

While there, Tryphaena requests that Thekla pray for her daughter, and the grateful mother experiences the spiritual efficacy of her prayer (4.4). In this, Thekla can be seen exercising the charism of forgiving sins and healing which was popularly thought to be invested in her as an imprisoned confessor of the Church. Furthermore, in the early centuries of Christianity, "the line between the confessor and the martyr who dies was thin indeed, and the terminology is sometimes used interchangeably."[26]

Imagine the chaos and racket of a large stadium with the crowd's excitement growing to almost apocalyptic proportions, when a nude maiden was about to be paraded into the Roman theatre. "Nearly every major theme of the Roman power structure was deployed in the spectacles: social stratification; political theater; crime and punishment; representations of civilization and

---

[26] Susan E. Hylen, *A Modest Apostle: Thecla and the History of Women in the Early Church* (New York: Oxford University Press, 2015), p. 100.

the empire; repression of women; and exultation of bellicose masculinity."[27]

Thekla is taken from the protective embrace of Tryphaena and prepared for display in the arena. Stripped again and assigned prisoner's undergarments, Thekla is cast into the stadium. The martyr's scene is rich with sensations for all the senses: the tremendous "rumbling of the beasts" (*patagos ton therion*) (4.7), and the people's hysteria, pierced by the frenzied cries and high-trilling *ululation* of the women, and here surrounded by an aromatic abundance of fragrant ointments; the sight of bulls goaded with hot irons, and God intervening with a cloud of flames to save Thekla.

A lioness is cast upon Thekla, but the animal responds by coming to lie at her feet. The lioness does battle with a bear set upon her and is killed. Then, a conflagration of Alexander's wild beasts is sent in to destroy Thekla; and, in the face of them, Thekla stands calmly, with her hands raised *en orans*, praying to God. All those gathered see a cloud of fire surrounding her, protecting her from the fierce attack and covering her nakedness.

As she continues to pray, a vat of water is revealed to her. Even though it is filled with man-eating sharks (*phokai*), Thekla realizes that this is the water of her Baptism. She immerses herself into the water God has provided, saying, "In the name of Jesus Christ, I baptize myself (*baptidzomai*) for the last day" (4.9), using language similar to that found in Matt. 28:19, Acts 2:38, and Acts 10:48.

Whether or not the reader or intervening centuries of Church Fathers affirm her unusual Baptism, the Apostle Paul endorses it and eventually commissions Thekla, sending her out as a teacher of the Word of God. More importantly, the Lord "sends several divine signs to suggest that this has been sanctioned by God."[28] As such, she is providentially selected, and her eventual commissioning is no different than the vocation of Paul and the other Apostles to preach.

---

[27] Erik Gunderson, "The Ideology of the Arena," *Classical Antiquity* 15:1 (Apr. 1996), p. 149.
[28] Barrier, *Acts of Paul and Thekla*, p. 164.

In the stadium, women outraged by the violation to Thekla have gathered and are dropping down upon the wild beasts a shower of "herbs and spices, nard, cassius, amomum," creating a haze of fragrant ointments, and the fierce animals are dazed into lethargy. So, Alexander suggests to the governor, in one last sadistic attempt to destroy the young Christian virgin who spurned his advances, that Thekla be bound by the feet to two of his bulls; so that, as they are enraged by torture, they will dash away and rip her apart.

This gruesome image of Thekla bound is dramatically captured in a well-known fifth-century sculpture, probably from Oxyrynchus.[29] It portrays in high relief the moment when the presence of the Lord is about to transform an intense scene of violation and potential death, with a promise of the saving presence of God in times of strife for all believers. The Proto-Martyr Thekla stands before the viewer praying, yet stripped and bound, and exposed to public view in the arena in Antioch. The shapely nude figure in the carving is surrounded by rampant threatening lions, but divinely protected by angels. She is covered in only a prisoner's loin-cloth, with the aura of a halo surrounding her face and nobly braided hair.

Additionally, what contemporary viewers may miss, but fifth-century viewers of the relief sculpture knew well, was that the woman depicted was about to be drawn and quartered. Harness-style straps stretch across her breasts binding her hands behind her back, and the young Christian is also tied by her feet to "two fearful bulls" (4.10). Reflecting his own sexual frustration, Thekla's attacker has bragged that he will torture the beasts with red-hot irons pressed to their private parts, enraging them to run in opposite directions and tear apart Thecla's body.

At the very moment of violent pandemonium, however, God intervenes and saves the newly baptized convert to faith in Christ with a cloud of fire. Indeed, the bulls "leapt up, but the flame

---

[29] "Thecla with Wild Beasts and Angels," fifth-century limestone roundel (9.5 x 64.8 cm.), Collection of the Nelson-Atkins Museum of Art, Kansas City, MS. See David R. Cartlidge, J. Keith Elliott, *Art and the Christian Apocrypha* (London: Rutledge, 2001), pp. 134-171.

inflaming itself burned through the good ropes, and it was as if she had not been bound" (4.10).

Thus, as Thekla's martyrdom, her second trial, climaxes, the conflict in the story is seen, finally, to be less between Alexander and Thekla; but rather, between Alexander and God, who wins. Thekla remains untouched. It must have been quite a spectacle in the arena; and in fact, Queen Tryphaena faints at the sight of it. So, the governor orders the action stopped immediately, for fear of offending Caesar, her kinsman.

Appalling as all that sounds, acts of exploitative sadism were actually standard practice in the Roman arena, and were often the manner of death for prisoners and Christian martyrs. "Roman audiences reveled in the spectacle of bloodshed, even as their moralists feared its corrupting effects."[30] Further, as Brock and Harvey note, accounts of female martyrs "are stunning in the regularity with which they depict either mutilation or sexual violence against women."[31]

Yet, even with such violence—why do we watch? It may seem unimaginable that anyone would take prurient interest in such displays of violence. Yet, even St. Augustine himself reminds us in his *Confessions* of a companion who was taken unwillingly by friends to the arena in Rome, but ended up enthralled by his own irrational passion and compelled to open his eyes to the screams and gaze fully at the violence unfolding before him.[32]

In the stadium with Thekla, the council leader Alexander sees his imperial favor evaporate before his eyes, and falls at the

---

[30] Michael Gaddis, *There is No Crime for Those Who Have Christ: Religious Violence in the Christian Roman Empire* (Berkeley, CA: University of California Press, 2005), p. 19.

[31] S. Brock, S.A. Harvey, *Holy Women of the Syrian Orient* (Berkeley, CA: University of California Press, 1987), p. 24.

[32] "For, directly he saw that blood, he imbibed a sort of savageness; nor did he turn away, but fixed his eye, drinking in madness, and was delighted with the guilty contest, and drunken with the bloody pastime...He looked, shouted, was excited, carried away with the madness...And from all this did Thou, with a most powerful and most merciful hand, pluck him, and taught him not to repose confidence in himself, but in You— but not till long after." Augustine, *Confessions*, 6:7-8.

feet of the governor. "Have mercy on me and the city," he cries, "and release the beast-fighter (*thariomakos*),[33] lest the city be destroyed with her!" But the governor speaks instead to Thekla, who is standing among the wild animals, naked and unscathed; for the Lord has delivered her. Thekla names Jesus Christ to the governor as the Son of God and her savior, her answer rising to a homiletic proclamation. The governor is enthralled.

"Who are you?" he asks. "And what is it about you, that none of the beasts touched you?" In answer, Thekla declares, "I am a slave of the living God...For to the one being storm-tossed, he is a place of refuge, a deliverer to the one being oppressed, a shelter to the one who is in despair" (4.12). With her refusal to marry and her commitment to remain virgin in the name of Jesus Christ, Thecla proudly apparels herself in the new title, "the slave of God" (*he doule tou Theou*); and from this transformation, she eventually becomes a traveling preacher.

Notice how the silent teenage bride who was shyly enamored with Paul's Gospel has developed throughout the arc of the story, through the threshold of violent martyrdom and Baptism, into a persuasive defender of the new faith in Jesus Christ. Furthermore, "it is clear that the author of the *Acts of Paul and Thelca* is bringing to a climax the theological agenda associated with women and authority in the Early Church."[34]

As Thekla stands uncovered before the governor, but clothed for salvation by the deliverance of God and Baptism, "this reorientation of Thekla's 'body' and 'person' serves to contrast the nakedness and eroticization of Thekla, while at the same time Thekla stands before the governor as pure, chaste, and a virgin."[35] The governor calls for clothes for Thekla; but, she wisely remonstrates with him. "'The one who has clothed my nakedness while

---

[33] The usage of this dramatic Greek compound term, "the feminine *thariomakos*, is unprecedented." Annewies van den Hoek, John J. Herrmann, Jr., "Thecla the Beast Fighter: A Female Emblem of Deliverance in Early Christian Popular Art," *The Studia Philonica Annual: Studies in Hellenistic Judaism* 13 (2001), p. 225.

[34] Barrier, *Acts of Paul and Thecla,* p. 172.

[35] *Ibid.*, p. 175.

with the wild beasts; this one will clothe me with salvation on the day of judgement.' And then, receiving the garments, she put them on."[36] The governor now diplomatically responds, "Thekla, the slave of God, the God-fearer (*ten Theosebe*), I release to you" (4.13).

Paul has been gone for quite a while in the story and Thekla has managed to Baptize herself, overcome wild beasts by divine intervention, and live to preach about it. When reunited, Paul "marvels much" to hear her story, and the faith of others who hear it is strengthened as well. Thekla announces that she is going home to Iconium to witness to the salvation of God. Having been baptized, and with the approval of God miraculously demonstrated, Paul responds, "Go and teach the Word of God" (*didaske tou logou tou Theou*) (4.16), commissioning her to go out and preach, as he is doing.

Martyrdom, then, while violent, has become the test of true discipleship in Christ, and it can be seen now that those facing martyrdom are granted heightened authority to teach, and even to forgive sins.[37] On the face of it, God's reported intervention among Early Christian victims of violence may seem cold comfort to readers surviving violence themselves. Yet, it is the fact of the Lord's living presence and potential transformation which makes this story relevant and vital for survivors; and especially, for all those drawn into tense moments of modern-day decision-making which may lead to violence. Thekla's story is a compelling reminder of the divine at work in our lives.

Here in New York City, worshiping at a parish church dedicated to one of the earliest Church Fathers, St. Ignatius of Antioch,

---

[36] For a thorough examination of recent translations of Thekla's response to the Governor, see Robert Doran, "Thecla and the Governor: Who Clothes Whom?" in Susan Ashbrook Harvey *et al*, eds, *A Most Reliable Witness: Essays in Honor of Ross Shephard Kraemer* (Providence, RI: Brown University Press, 2015), pp. 17-25.

[37] Frederick C. Klawiter, "The Role of Martyrdom and Persecution in Developing the Priestly Authority of Women in Early Christianity: A Case Study of Montanism," *Church History* 49:3 (Sept. 1980), p. 254.

morning sun glitters through the large stained window[38] dedicated to the patron saint of the church, a Christian who was
thrown to the beasts in the arena, like St. Thekla. In it, the late
first-century Bishop Ignatius prays *en orans* in the midst of rampant lions in the Colosseum under the watchful eye of Roman authorities enthroned above him. Polycarp and several other saints
watch nearby.

Although no women are depicted, it is good to remember the
pervasive tendency to diminish or erase the witness of women
from text and image and Early Christian history in general. "One
must always ask, not only what is being said, but also what is
being assumed, or ignored, marginalized or repressed."[39] As sun-
shine flooding in blots out the celebrated martyr from Antioch for
a moment, it is easy to see Thekla standing there *en orans* in his
place, praying among the lions, with her hands raised to God.

At the conclusion of the *Acts of Paul and Thecla*, she finds herself back home in Iconium, in the house where she first heard Paul
preach the Gospel of Jesus Christ, and she offers this prayer (4.17):

> O, Our God even of this house
>> where the light was revealed to me,
> Christ, son of God,
>> O, My helper in prison,
>> My helper before governors,
>> My helper in the fire,
>> My helper before the wild beasts,
> He is God, and the glory is yours forever.

---

[38] The English stained glass was executed by John Hardman & Co, Birmingham.

[39] Sheila E. McGinn, "The Acts of Thecla," in *Searching the Scriptures: A
Feminist Commentary,* Elizabeth Schüssler Fiorenza, ed. (New York: Crossroad Publishing Company, 1994), p. 801.

CHAPTER I.3
QUEEN TRYPHAENA: THE LORD'S REFUGE IN HOSPITALITY

While being a queen, she has humbled herself with me,
because of the desire and fear she has for you, Lord.[1]

The Christian virtue of hospitality as a marker of saintliness acknowledged in Early Christian women carries scriptural warrant (see "Lydia: Speaking Up to the Apostles") and is modelled in the *Acts of Paul and Thekla* in an exemplary fashion by Queen Tryphaena, a kinswomen of Emperor Claudius. The story of the Early Christian martyr, St. Thekla,[2] in which she appears, presents

---

[1] Scott F. Johnson, *The Life and Miracles of Thekla: A Literary Study* (Washington, DC: Center for Hellenic Studies, 2006), p. 52.

[2] On St. Thekla: Stephen J. Davis, *The Cult of St. Thecla: A Tradition of Women's Piety in Late Antiquity* (Oxford: Oxford University Press, 2001); Susan E. Hylen, *A Modest Apostle: Thecla and the History of Women in the Early Church* (New York: Oxford University Press, 2015); Edgar Johnson Goodspeed, "The Book of Thekla," *American Journal of Semitic Languages and Literatures* 17 (1901), pp. 65-95; B. Diane Lipsett, *Desiring Conversion: Hermas, Thecla, Aseneth* (Oxford: Oxford University Press, 2011); Dennis Ronald MacDonald, *The Legend and the Apostle: The Battle for Paul in Story and Canon* (Philadelphia: Westminster Press, 1983); Sheila E. McGinn, "The Acts of Thecla," in *Searching the Scriptures: A Feminist Commentary*, Elizabeth Schüssler Fiorenza, ed. (New York: Crossroad Publishing Company, 1994), pp. 2:800-828; William M. Ramsay, "The Acta of Paul and Thekla," in *The Church in the Roman Empire Before A.D. 170* (New York: G.P. Putnam, 1893), pp. 390-410.

the kind of disoriented intersection of faith and passion especially evident in times of radical cultural change, making the value of Tryphaena's generous hospitality and conversion to Christ all the more relevant for today's readers.

The vast popularity of Thekla in the early centuries of Christianity demonstrates that she fulfilled a need in the emerging faith for a female hero exercising agency in the spiritual world around her. Pilgrims to her shrine at Seleucia,[3] such as Gregory Nazianzus in the 370s C.E. and Egeria in 384, found a healing center for hospitality and prayer already actively functioning in memory of Thekla's martyrdom[4] and of her rescue by Queen Tryphaena. Note that the name Tryphaena is mentioned by Paul in Romans 15:12. Material evidence exists for an historical Queen Tryphaena from Pontus in the form of two sets of minted coins identifying her image. Although, as a first cousin of Emperor Claudius, the character of Tryphaena adds a reliable historical element to the story; nevertheless, the intention of the author may not have been to represent the actual queen from Pontus.

Still, with the heartfelt support and funding of Tryphaena as her philanthropic patron in Thekla's story, and inspired by her life with Paul, and furthermore surviving by the grace of God at the hands of persecutors and tormentors, Thekla carries on an effective ministry on her own. Then, "having brought to light many by the Word of God (*pollous photisasa to Logo tou Theou*), she lay down with a good sleep" (4.18).

---

[3] Seleucia of Isauria is modern-day Silifke in Turkey. See Troels Myrup Kristensen, "The Landscape, Space, and Presence in the Cult of Thekla at Meriamlik," *Journal of Early Christian Studies*, 24: 2 (Summer 2016), pp. 229-263.

[4] See Gregory Nazianzus, *De Vita Sua*, vv. 547-549, where Gregory characterizes it as the "Parthenoma," meaning the House of Virgins, evidence that it was a well-established monastery when he was in retreat there. See John A. McGuckin, *Saint Gregory of Nazianzus: An Intellectual Biography* (Crestwood, NY: St. Vladimir's Seminary Press, 2001), pp. 99, 230. See also *Egeria's Travels* 23 John Wilkenson, trans. (Warminster: Aris & Phillips Ltd., 2003), pp. 141-42.

All this high drama is told in the second-century Apocryphal document, the *Acts of Paul and Thekla*,[5] with the mighty arm
of God ever-present, saving Thekla from martyrdom in the flames;
and again, with the help of Queen Tryphaena when she was condemned *ad bestias*, from violation in the Roman arena in Antioch
by "terrible beasts" (4.10). This is Thekla's second martyrdom
trial: Whereas at home in Iconium, she functioned as a dutiful,
then rebellious, daughter within the societal hierarchy of an élite
Roman family, now in the second section of the narrative, Thekla
abandons her fiancé and follows Paul on his missionary journey,[6]
and is therefore viewed as a stranger sojourning in Antioch, an

---

[5] "Praxeis Paulou kai Thekles" in *Acta Apostolorum*, R.A. Lipsius, M. Bonnet, eds (Hildesheim: Georg Olms, 1958), pp. 235-272. For English translation, see "The Acts of Paul," in *New Testament Apocrypha*, revised ed.,
W. Schneemelcher, ed., R. McL. Wilson, trans. (Louisville, KY: Westmin-
ster/John Knox Press, 1992), pp. 2:213-270. See also Barrier, *The Acts of
Paul and Thecla: A Critical Introduction and Commentary*.

[6] Although the *Acts of Paul and Thekla* is not to be seriously considered
as an historical work, it is nevertheless helpful to establish where the
author intends for the narrative to fit into the historical life of Paul, who
did in fact embark on missionary journeys which encompassed both Iconium and Pisidian Antioch; this consideration, in fact, contributes to its
integrity as a document. Paul's preaching visit described in the *Acts of
Paul and Thekla* could be part of his first, second, or third missionary
journeys described in Acts 23-14, or Acts 15-18, or Acts 18, respectively.
Reconstructing a chronology for Paul's travels which coordinates with
the evidence of the Acts of the Apostles and his own correspondence is
challengingly complicated; and thus, Paul's ministry in Iconium described in the *Acts* could signify any of his three missionary journeys.
Nevertheless, since Paul mentions the suffering he endured; and additionally, the cultural environment described is not Jewish, in terms of
dietary or liturgical practice, and is probably pagan, the *Acts of Paul and
Thekla* could refer to Paul's third missionary journey toward the end of
his life, even though Paul is not mentioned appearing in Iconium in Acts
18. See "Graph of Dates and Time-Spans," in Robert Jewett, *A Chronology
of Paul's Life* (Philadelphia: Fortress Press, 1979), p. 161. See also Theresa Angert-Quilter, *A Commentary on the Shorter Text of the Acts of Thecla
and its New Testament Parallels* (North Sydney: Australian Catholic University, 2014), pp. 31-39.

unwelcome outsider who spurns the advances of a Syrian regional council leader. Her peripatetic circumstances make her vulnerable, and highlight the generosity of Tryphaena, the royal widow who offers hospitality to Thekla.

Throughout the *Acts of Paul and Thekla*, we read of God's deliverance manifesting itself in spectacular light-shows of fire and hail in the story; but, the Lord can also be seen working through Queen Tryphaena, who provides the righteous deed of asylum to the condemned stranger, becomes a second mother to the Christian virgin—and thereby saves her honour and her life."[7] As with Thekla herself, it is unlikely that either woman's story in the *Acts* is historical "as a real personage in real history;" but, rather, that the benevolent Queen Tryphaena is established as a salvific character, "as a figure in the tale of Thekla."[8]

In a close reading of Thekla's life and trials in the previous chapter, we heard from the *Acts of Paul and Thekla* the humiliatingly gruesome details of her martyrdom; and afterward, explored why we tend to lean in with interest to glean the violent details of suffering. But most do—it is part of the human condition, in need of God's mercy and deliverance, of the Lord's refuge in hospitality.

This reality is partly why Thekla's story resonated with such clarity to Church Fathers[9] and early Jesus-followers, as devotion to her memory grew exponentially in the generations after her death. And it is also why Queen Tryphaena's pious response in reaching out to the condemned virgin prisoner resonates with the generosity preached by Christ himself in Mt. 25:34-40.

With martyrdom again imminent in Antioch, a vision of prayer in a dream indicates God's approval of Thekla during her

---

[7] William M. Ramsey, "A Lost Chapter in Early Christian History," *Bible Expositor & Illuminator*, vol. VI (London: Hodden & Stoughton, 1902), p. 283.

[8] Ramsey, "Lost Chapter," p. 284.

[9] Among examples from the Fathers of the Church, Thekla is praised: in the *Symposium* by Methodius; by Gregory of Nyssa, as the secret soul-name of his sister, Macrina, in the *Vita Macrinae*; by Gregory Nazianzus who regards her as an apostle-martyr in his *Oration Against Julian*; by John Chrysostom in his Homily on Acts 25; in the *Panegyric to Thecla* by Pseudo-Chrysostom; and, by Ambrose in the *De Virginibus*.

trial. The widowed Queen Tryphaena steps forward, offering her the comfort of her home, in her hour of need; for at this juncture, Thekla is viewed as a "deserted stranger" in Antioch (*ten zenen ten eremon*) (4.3). She is condemned to be thrown to wild beasts; and, as the sentence is declared, she cries out to the governor for fear of rape, begging to be kept inviolate, and Tryphaena responds, taking Thekla "into her protection" (*eis teresin*) and welcoming her "in consolation" (*eis parmuthian*) (4.2). She is moved to do this because her daughter, who had recently died, speaks to her in a dream, inspiring her to compassionate and philanthropic action. She implores her to take in Thekla to stand in her place as a daughter and beseeches her intercession to help translate her, even in death, "into a place of the righteous" (*eis ton dikaion topon*) (4.3).

The *Acts of Paul and Thekla,* as well as other apocryphal documents, depict a pivotal threshold time in the early generations after the Resurrection of Christ, when the Spirit of the Lord was distinctly experienced operating in the world. The followers of Jesus are reported unmistakably receptive to the action of the Holy Spirit. This is the spiritual environment richly evident in the Acts of the Apostles, and the Apocryphal Acts as well, with visions of God and divine messages remembered in dreams and the witness of God's intervention active within the stories in acts of deliverance from suffering.

Here, a dream of Tryphaena demonstrates God's approval of Thekla as an intercessor able to assist in translating the one on whose behalf she prays into a better place. The thoughts and actions of Queen Tryphaena, even her prayers and dreams, are captured with such sensitivity in the *Acts of Paul and Thekla* that female authorship for the document has been considered by some commentators.[10]

---

[10] See Stevan L. Davies, *The Revolt of the Widows: The Social World of the Apocryphal Acts* (Carbonville, IL: Southern Illinois University Press, 1980), pp. 95-109; Dennis Ronald MacDonald, *The Legend and the Apostle: The Battle for Paul in Story and Canon* (Philadelphia: Westminster Press, 1983), pp. 17-35; Virginia Burrus, *Chastity as Autonomy: Women in*

Notice how the carefully constructed observation of compassion in the description of Tryphaena creates a striking contrast with Thekla's own mother earlier in the story, who is portrayed so threatened by Thekla's newfound faith and virgin celibacy commitment that she cries out (*anekragen*) (3.20) for her daughter's violent execution. Queen Tryphaena's protecting outcry (*anekrazen*) (4.5), on the other hand, puts Thekla's bellicose attacker, Alexander, to flight, at least for the night.

The widowed queen offers support for Thekla's faith and grants her protection from the added violation which would have surely exacerbated her sentence.[11] Note that the exploitative dimensions of Thekla being thrown to the wild beasts are resonant of the indignities suffered by St. Ignatius, which he describes in his Letter to the Romans (5:2), and by St. Clement in his First Letter (6.2), both Fathers of the Church, her fellow martyrs.[12]

Tryphaena welcomes Thekla into her home, for an evening of refuge and consolation between her degrading exposure in the Roman parade, previewing the violence of the upcoming games, and the spectacle itself the next morning, when she fights the wild beasts. In doing so, she provides an environment of cooperation

---

the Stories of the Apocryphal Acts (Queenston, ON: Mellon, 1987), pp. 88-90.

[11] "It would have been nothing for Thekla to have been violently and repeatedly raped and beaten. She could have been abused in disgusting and distasteful ways, tortured and shamed, made a spectacle both by being the victim of sexual violence, and the victim of sadistic torment and exhibition. In her day, jailors and spectators would have unscrupulously both laughed and wept at her plight, but it would have all been entertainment for them." Theresa Angert-Quilter, *A Commentary on the Shorter Text of the Acts of Thecla and its New Testament Parallels* (North Sydney: Australian Catholic University, 2014), p. 334.

[12] St. Ignatius of Antioch, Letter to the Romans 5:2: "May I have joy of the beasts that have been prepared for me; and I pray that I may find them prompt; nay I will entice them that they may devour me promptly." The First Letter of St. Clement 6:2, speaks of: "women being persecuted, after they had suffered cruel and unholy insults...safely reached the goal in the race of faith, and received a noble reward, feeble though they were in body."

for the gifts of the Spirit. The two women embark on a mutually beneficial relationship; and as they do, they experience the fluid roles of host and guest, which so often feature in scenes of hospitality when Jesus is visiting families. Note, for example, the Wedding at Cana (John 2:1-11), Mary and Martha (Luke 10:38-42), the Anointing at Bethany (John 12:1-8), these are times when Jesus can be seen functioning as both guest and host. In fact, "in a number of New Testament stories, people who initially come as guests end up exercising roles that are normally associated with hosts, and vice versa."[13]

Here, while Tryphaena's invitation brings Thekla into the protection of her home, the royal widow finds herself in need of compassionate action from her adopted daughter as well. In the nourishing exchange of hospitality offered and received, Tryphaena discerns in Thekla the vocation of one who can pray to God effectively. So, as she shares the comfort of her home, Tryphaena requests prayer on behalf of her daughter. Her plea for prayer reflects the belief that Thecla, as an expectant martyr, was being granted the power to forgive sins during her imprisonment and her trials as a Christian martyr.

Thekla responds immediately, and the grateful mother experiences the successful efficacy of her prayer, confident that her daughter has been spiritually rescued and will rest in peace. "It is well-known that in Early Christianity, martyrs awaiting death could exercise and manifest extraordinary power. They even had 'the power of the keys;' that is, the power to forgive the sins of those who had denied the faith and were therefore thought to have lost salvation."[14]

"O God of the Heavens," Thekla prays, "the son of the Most High; give to Tryphaena according to her need, in order that her daughter might live forever" (4.4).

---

[13] John Koenig, *Soul Banquets: How Meals Became Mission in the Local Congregation* (Harrisburg, PA: Morehouse Publishing, 2007), p. 50.

[14] Frederick C. Klawiter, "The Role of Martyrdom and Persecution in Developing the Priestly Authority of Women in Early Christianity: A Case Study of Montanism," *Church History* 49:3 (Sept. 1980), p. 254.

For Tryphaena, who is on the threshold of faith, the result is life-changing. "Reward Tryphaena," Thekla prays, "the one who has sympathized with your slave, and who has kept me pure" (4.6). She witnesses that, by this invocation, Thekla, the stranger and arena victim, begins to function as a prayer leader. Tryphaena's offer of refuge, and also her request for prayer, set in motion a dynamic collaboration for the action of the Holy Spirit, the space where God works; and, the story marks the beginning of Jesus followers gathering around Thekla.

Tryphaena's home, like the houses of Lydia and Prisca, witnessed in the Acts of the Apostles, becomes a haven for Thekla's evangelization and preaching—in Tryphaena's house and later as she travels teaching. Thus, the seed of an Early Christian house church is planted in Tryphaena's home, and grows to fulfillment throughout the story. And it can be expected of Queen Tryphaena, as with Chloe (1 Cor. 1:11) and Nympha (Col. 4:15), that "these Christians of means must have exercised some leadership in the house churches that they hosted."[15]

"I am the slave of the living God," Thekla proclaims before the governor, "for to the one being storm-tossed, he is a place of refuge, the deliverer to the one being oppressed, a shelter to the one in despair" (4.12).

After Thekla's miraculous deliverance from the violent beasts in the stadium, Tryphaena is able to declare; "'Now I believe that the dead are raised. Now I believe that my child lives. Come inside, my child, into my house, and I will transfer all of my property to you.' Therefore, Thecla entered with her and refreshed herself in the house for eight days, teaching her the Word, so that she believed in God, and also many of her servants, and great was the joy in her house" (4.14). Tryphaena is convinced that her daughter, Falconilla, now lives eternally, because Thekla prayed on her behalf.

The outcome of Tryphaena's hospitality is a synergistic spiral of mission in the name of Jesus Christ, where spiritual welcome

---

[15] John Koenig, *New Testament Hospitality: Partnership with Strangers as Promise and Mission* (Eugene, OR: Wipf and Stock Publishers, 2001), p. 65.

and material welcome merge; and new burgeoning familial connections grow, supporting those brought to the faith throughout her household. Tryphaena's home demonstrates the seeds of a house church, and her philanthropic generosity supports the traveling virgin missionary preaching the Gospel of Jesus Christ taught to her by the Apostle Paul.

"Taken as a feature of Christian life," reports Amy Oden in her *Sourcebook*, "hospitality is not so much a singular act of welcome as it is a way, an orientation that attends to otherness, listening and learning, valuing and honoring. The hospitable one looks for God's redemptive presence in the other, confident it is there."[16]

Tryphaena becomes Thekla's patron and a significant patron for the poor as well on the behalf of Paul's ministry (4.16). It is noteworthy that Queen Tryphaena's progress in faith, leading her to offer intercessory prayer and to be remembered for her impressive philanthropy, is in keeping with one of the earliest Christian institutions, the Order of Widows, witnessed in Scripture in Acts 6:1 and 9:39.[17] From this, it can be inferred that the *Acts of Paul and Thekla* "assumed an audience would find such a woman plausible because it knew of such women."[18]

Even though Queen Tryphaena's story with Thekla cannot be established as historical, the *Acts of Paul and Thecla* provide description which the second-century hearers found familiar of women who were inspired to open their homes as a saintly refuge to the spread of the Gospel of Jesus Christ. And in the case of Thekla, the text portrays well how women, who were drawn to follow Christ by leading Paul's celibate lifestyle, became part of the growing tension and hostility between early groups of Jesus-followers and the surrounding Roman society. Yet, as the story

---

[16] Amy G. Oden, *And You Welcomed Me: A Sourcebook on Hospitality in Early Christianity* (Nashville, TN: Abingdon Press, 2001), p. 14.

[17] Also noteworthy is Tertullian's mention of widows in *De Praescriptione Haereticorum* 3.5, where he regards it as a formal "order," listing it among other church offices.

[18] Ross Shepherd Kraemer, *Unreliable Witnesses: Religion, Gender, and History in the Greco-Roman Mediterranean* (Oxford: Oxford University Press, 2011), p. 122.

closes, Thekla begins functioning as a teacher—the shy, silent maiden sitting at Paul's feet speaks with authority as she has been nourished by hospitality.

Explaining her Baptism to the Apostle, when she is united with him again, she declares: "I took the bath, Paul: for the one who worked with you in the Gospel has even worked with me in the washing" (4.15).

In the fifth-century *Life and Miracles of Thekla*,[19] a fuller version of Thekla's prayer on behalf of Tryphaena's daughter is given, which well-expresses her gratitude for the charism of hospitality:

> Fulfill this reward for her, Lord Christ, on my behalf.
> For behold, as you see,
>> she herself has become a guardian of my virginity.
> After Paul, she has assisted me and has delivered me
>> from the frenzy of Alexander.
> She has comforted me in her bosom
>> after the fright of the wild beasts.
> While being a queen, she humbled herself with me,
>> because of the desire and fear
>> she has for you, Lord.

---

[19] "Thaumata tes Hagias kai Proto-martyros Theklas," in Gilbert Dragon, *Vie et miracles de Sainte Thecle: Texte Grec, Tradution et Commentaire* (Bruxelles: Societé des Bollandistes, 1978). For selected English translation, see: Scott F. Johnson, *The Life and Miracles of Thekla: A Literary Study* (Washington, D.C.: Center for Hellenic Studies, 2006). See also "The Miracles of Saint Thekla," in *Miracle Tales from Byzantium*, Alice-Mary Talbot, trans., Scott Fitzgerald Johnson, trans. (Cambridge, MA: Harvard University Press, 2012), pp. 1-202.

CHAPTER I.4
PERPETUA'S STORY IN HER OWN WORDS: HOPE FACING MARTYRDOM

We have heard as they were read aloud those words,
so shining and luminescent, we have taken in by ear,
we have considered in our minds,
and honoured in our belief.[1]

Inside the holding cells for condemned prisoners where Perpetua prayed beneath the Carthage amphitheater and received her visions from God, the ancient stones now look skyward among its well-preserved ruins.[2] Christian pilgrims visiting the site can stand where martyrs were incarcerated and gaze heaven-ward—not so when Perpetua prayed there, and wrote about the terrifying heat and the darkness, before being executed in a most barbarous manner for her faith in Christ. Even today, the martyrdom experience witnessed by this early third-century catechumen stands out for its clarity of voice, audacity, and the evidence of the Holy Spirit at work among the faithful, charging them with eschatological hope.

Perpetua's martyrdom can be seen as emblematic of the Early Christian experience in North Africa, in a community who

---

[1] Augustine, *Sermo* 280.1.1, "On the Anniversary of the Deaths of Perpetua and Felicity."

[2] The Carthage Amphitheater UNESCO World Heritage site still exists and is a popular pilgrimage site.

understood themselves as the "Spirit-filled elect whose hope was focused on God's future vindication of people who had been faithful to him in the midst of a society which denied him."[3] "The Passion of Perpetua and Felicity"[4] is the earliest surviving example of autobiography in Latin, and furthermore, written by a woman. It has been praised as "an incandescent jewel of writing,"[5] and is named as "the primal document in the development of the conventions which were to shape female sacred biography for a millennium."[6]

Like the account of the first martyr in the New Testament, Stephen, "The Passion of Perpetua and Felicity" is significant for the history of the Church, because it is a document which was recorded very soon after the events took place and one which includes the recollections of eye-witnesses.[7] It is vividly rich in detail, encompassing first-person quoted text within a framing narrative of hagiographic biography crafted to provide context and exhortation, especially for those seeking admission to the body of the faithful in Christ. Like New Testament resources circulating at the same time, the text offers the reader unmistakable

---

[3] Richard A. Norris, "From the Gnostic Crisis to Constantine," in Williston Walker *et al*, *A History of the Christian Church*; Fourth Edition (New York: Charles Scribner's Sons, 1985), p. 80.

[4] *Passion de Perpétue et de Félicité suivi des Actes*, J. Amat, ed. "Sources Chrétiennes," no. 417 (Paris: Les Éditions du Cerf, 1996). The English translation edition used for this study is Thomas J. Heffernan, *The Passion of Perpetua and Felicity* (Oxford: Oxford University Press, 2012), which includes a new critical edition of the Latin text based on the Monte Cassino 204 manuscript. The Latin text is here favored over the Greek as likely earlier and containing the fullest witness of Perpetua's visions. Hereafter, the text shall be cited as *Passio* with chapters indicated in Roman letters and verses in numerals; for example, *Passio* X.1, or simply chapter and verse—X.1.

[5] Brent D. Shaw, "The Passion of Perpetua," *Past & Present* 139:1 (May 1993), p. 16.

[6] Thomas J. Heffernan, *Sacred Biography: Saints and Their Biographies in the Middle Ages* (Oxford: Oxford University Press, 1988), p. 186.

[7] See Louis Bouyer, *The Spirituality of the New Testament and the Fathers* (New York: The Seabury Press, 1963), p. 191.

descriptions of Early Christians experiencing the clarifying and empowering action of the Holy Spirit.

The number of women named among the early martyrs is a striking testimony to the memory of their courage in defense of the Christian faith, even at the expense of defying societal norms. Especially from the Orthodox perspective, "in the liturgical commemoration, the memory that innumerable women were among the company of the early martyrs endures to this day."[8] Beyond this, the record of Perpetua and other early Christian martyrs stands as a hallmark of a new concept of religious suffering as resistance and as spiritual reward,[9] with its victims acknowledged as saints. Indeed, this was a pivotal time in the use of the term "martyr;" since in the earliest generations after the life of Jesus, it was used of the Apostles as witnesses to Christ, but gradually came to signify someone testifying to commitment in faith at the cost of her life.

Like others who had followed Christ's example literally, Perpetua quickly became the focus of veneration. Her remembered words were treasured, especially her prophetic dreams, and they were thought to be inspired by the Holy Spirit, as promised by Jesus himself for those who came after him: "When they bring you to trial and hand you over, do not worry beforehand about what you are to say; but say whatever is given you at that time, for it is not you who speak, but the Holy Spirit" (Mk. 13:11). In the generations following her martyrdom, Perpetua was acknowledged as an authoritative figure in Early Christian history and elaborately memorialized on the anniversary of the death. As her Passion-story was rehearsed and remembered, she was lifted up as a role model for courageous Christian behavior.

---

[8] John Anthony McGuckin, *The Path of Christianity: The First Thousand Years* (Downer Grove, IL: IVP Academic, 2017), p. 902.

[9] Perpetua presents the reader with a woman transcending society's restrictions, one who is "buttressed by a growing sense of her empowerment through suffering." Judith Perkins, *The Suffering Self: Pain and Narrative Representation in the Early Christian Era* (London: Rutledge, 1995), p. 105.

Perpetua's story is relevant for a new audience as well, since it reveals the depth of transformation possible in the experience of commitment to Christian identity, and witnesses with confidence that the Holy Spirit continues to be present in the lives of her Church. By reflecting on the martyrdom experience of Perpetua, we can discern a nuanced tension which exists between aspects of our own identification as victim, as oppressor, and as faithful commemorator of the saint-martyr; since also operating in this narrative is the presence of the spectator. The text is addressed to some who were eyewitnesses of the events and to us as continuing witnesses across time. This chapter examines Perpetua's startling confession of faith and martyrdom.

While lively debate has questioned the authenticity of the "Passion of Perpetua and Felicity,"[10] there is now scholarly consensus that the surviving text represents Perpetua's own voice and was probably composed between 203 and 213 C.E. Like most early Christian texts, it is difficult to date the composition of the *Passio Sanctarum Perpetuae et Felicitatis* with any certainty. A *terminus post quem* can be established, however, from the martyrdom events themselves, which likely took place on the March 7 birthday of Caesar Geta (VII.9), possibly as part of the pageantry associated with his coming-of-age celebration, when he was fourteen years old in 203 C.E., and assumed his *toga virilis*. A *terminus ante quem* can be marked by Tertullian's reference to the *Passio* in *De anime* (55.4), written around 210-213.[11]

Regarding its authenticity, one commentator has concluded that in Perpetua's prison diary, "we have an authentic first-hand narrative of the last days of a gallant martyr."[12] The dreams especially, "are truly extraordinary in the quality of their reportage," another has observed; "whatever the traditional and stereotypical

---

[10] The title, *Passio Sanctarum Perpetuae et Felicitatis,* is not original to the document; but was introduced by a Vatican librarian, Lukas Holstenius, in the seventeenth century. "Brief Introduction," in Jan N. Bremmer, Marco Formisano, eds, *Perpetua's Passions*, p. 2.
[11] See Heffernan, *Passion*, pp. 317-318.
[12] E.R. Dodds, *Pagan and Christian in the Age of Anxiety* (Cambridge: Cambridge University Press, 1965), p. 52.

images contained in them, there is no reasonable question of their authenticity."[13] An anonymous redactor later compiled and perhaps edited the document to some extent; and in fact, the editor may have been the very eyewitness speaking in the final climactic section of the narrative. Perpetua even salutes her redactor as she goes to her death in faith, "What happened at the spectacle itself, let who will, write (*si quis voluerit, scribat*)" (*Passio* X.11-12).

In a single sentence of the introduction (II.1-3), her family name is identified for the reader, and her personal name, Perpetua; her social class and educational level are acknowledged (*honesta nata, liberatiter instituta*), and her honorable marital status (*matronaliter nupta*). Finally, the members of her nuclear family are named, including her parents, her three brothers, one now deceased, and the infant son at her breast, all from the illustrious Roman Vibii family.[14] Among her retinue in the arrest before their martyrdom are two household slaves, Revocatus and Felicity, who is included in the title of the document; and two other catechumens, Saturninus and Secondulus. Also present is the man responsible for successfully converting all of them to Christianity, Saturnus. Although not initially arrested, his ministry participation in the scene provokes arrest by the authorities and subsequent martyrdom along with them.

The specific reason the group is arrested in Carthage is not provided in the text, but it was likely in response to an imperial

---

[13] Shaw, "Perpetua," p. 26. Furthermore, in the Preface to his 1972 translation of the *Passio*, Musurillo claims the text as "an apocalypse in its own right, reminiscent of the Book of Revelation and "The Shepherd of Hermas." Herbert Musurillo, *The Acts of the Christian Martyrs* (Oxford: Clarendon, 1972), p. xxv.

[14] Note that Perpetua mentions her son throughout the *Passio*, but never her husband. While her unnamed spouse could have been related to her by an arranged marriage *sine manu*, which would explain the continuing authority of her father operating in her life *in potestate patris*, Heffernan contests this notion; ably demonstrating that legal precedent existed at the time for custody to be granted to the mother in cases of irresponsible accusation against the husband. See Thomas J. Heffernan, "*Ius Conubii* or *Concubina*: The Marital and Social Class of Perpetua in the *Passio Sanctarum Perpetuae et Felicilatis*," *Analecta Bollandiana* 136 (2018), p. 34.

Roman decree meant to identify and eradicate members of the troubling dissident Christian sect. For by the end of the second century, faith in Christ had "penetrated deeply into the fabric of North African life;"[15] and with the Severin dynasty occupying the throne in Rome, local outbreaks of persecution against Christians were springing up throughout the Empire, including in Latin North Africa, as Eusebius describes: "When Severus, in his turn, was instigating persecution of the churches, the champions of true religion achieved glorious martyrdoms in every land. By their heroic endurance of every kind of torture and every form of death, they were wreathed with the crowns laid up by God."[16] Although not yet a state-wide sanctioned mandate, district legislation was put in place to root out religious trouble-makers, especially recent converts to Christianity from the upper classes.

Apart from its historical details, several aspects of the story, including the group of catechumens arrested all being impressionable teenagers (*adolescentes*) on the vulnerable cusp of adulthood, jolt this ancient scene into the present-day complexities of parental life, making it challenging to know where to identity first. Perpetua's own memoir within the document opens in the middle of a painful debate with her father who is visiting the prison to persuade her to recant. Their dialogic encounter establishes the increasing domestic tension building between them, as she and an increasing number of Christian converts navigate the insurmountable conflict between the authority of Rome and the power of faith. Even mention of the word "Christian" sends him into a violent rage.

Yet, in examining Perpetua's situation, it can be seen that a familiarity with the traditional mystery religions, with magic and astrology, and the Roman spiritual world within the Vibii household with its complex pantheon of moody gods, may have prepared the way for Perpetua's receptiveness to new faith available on the margin of society. However, if the mocking tone of her father's arguments and the guards' strategy to break her down are

---

[15] Thomas M. Finn, *Early Christian Baptism and the Catechumenate: Italy, North Africa, and Egypt* (Collegeville, MN: Liturgical Press, 1992), p. 112.
[16] Eusebius, *Eccles Hist*, Book 6.1.1-2.

meant to disarm and discourage Perpetua from her commitment to faith in Christ, they fail; for she is swept up among many who were facing persecution. She was not the first, nor would she be the last, to find her life in peril because she confessed her identity as a Christian with confidence. For like Bishop Ignatius, martyred a century earlier, her desire is to "move beyond simply being *called* a Christian to really *being* a Christian."[17]

Following the fraught episode with her father, lyrical images in a compressed chronology reveal the anxious days spent enduring the hardship of the municipal prison, as well as fragmented glimpses of her Baptism. While the details of Perpetua's Baptismal liturgy cannot be described with any certainty, "quite a number of the motives in the visions and in the narration of the editor allude to her Baptism:" including the sweet food she enjoys in the first vision, the unreachable water basin (*piscina*) in her visions about Dinocrates, and martyrdom characterized as a second Baptism in XXI.1.[18] Throughout her story, the shocking physicality of the guards (*concussurae militarum*) (III.6) is contrasted with the pleasure of nursing her baby, and yet again, the anguish of relinquishing him to her visiting family for safekeeping. Perpetua is able to comment honestly "on her fear at being isolated in an unfamiliar, dark prison; but, at the same time she senses a completeness and a joy in herself that she never felt before."[19] Even faced with the pressures of maternal demands and filial loyalty, she identifies her true self as a Christian to her father. She can no more be called something other than a Christian, she declares, than a water jug can be called anything else (III.2).

Thus, Perpetua's story is "full of subtleties in her simultaneous adoption of the roles of noblewoman, mother, publicly vocal Christian, and eventually, martyr."[20] But note now, how her

---

[17] Elizabeth A Castelli, *Martyrdom and Memory: Early Christian Culture-Making* (New York: Columbia University Press, 2004), p. 86.

[18] Katharina Walder, "Visions, Prophecy, and Authority in the *Passio Perpetuae*," in Bremmer, ed., *Perpetua's Passions*, p. 215.

[19] Elizabeth Alvilda Petroff, *Medieval Women's Visionary Literature* (New York: Oxford University Press, 1986), p. 35.

[20] Margaret Cotter-Lynch, *Saint Perpetua across the Middle Ages: Mother, Gladiator, Saint* (New York: Palgrave Macmillan, 2016), p. 2.

priorities are changing. The certainty of her Christian identity
leads Perpetua to reject her father's increasingly desperate attempts to dissuade her from criminal action in the eyes of the
Roman authorities, and her spiritual commitment is affirmed and
upheld by divine intervention in her visions. Her narrative inter-
weaves terrifying details of her imprisonment with moments of
joyful serenity achieved as the Spirit of the Lord distracts her from
the terror of the moment and comforts her with beatific visions
in which she experiences herself supported and cared for by beautiful angelic creatures.

Perpetua's first vision begins abruptly: "I see a bronze ladder
(*Video scalam aeream*)" (IV.3). It is rising to heaven before her,
treacherously accessorized with implements of cruel terror, leaving her with bloody images of torn flesh sticking to the iron weap-
ons from those who try to climb, but are careless in their focus
heaven-ward. Also at the ready to vanquish her is a crouching
serpent curled at the foot of the ladder. "In the name of Jesus
Christ," she treads upon its head as she mounts the first step
(IV.6). The proclamation of the Holy Name functions as a powerful shield against the evil gathered around her.

An allegorical garden paradise awaits her above and the vision of a new god-like father figure appears to her, clothed as the
Good Shepherd, offering welcome and sweet-tasting sustenance,
which lingers on the tongue after her vision subsides. Awakening,
she realizes that, as a God-beloved confessor, she will not be able
to escape suffering a martyr's death in the arena (IV.10). Yet,
filled with hope, "Perpetua the martyr emerges with a kind of
shimmering clarity separated from the 'hope of this age' and
poised inexorably on the verge of a different existence."[21]

Indeed, after interrogation by the local governor, the group
is condemned to be thrown to the beasts (*ad bestias*) (VI.6) on the
birthday of the Emperor's younger son, Caesar Geta. The gladiatorial games in Carthage and throughout the Empire were "moments of important social statement of loyalty to the augustus as
divine *Kyrios*-Lord;"[22] but from the first, Perpetua confesses that

---

[21] Castelli, *Martyrdom and Memory*, p. 178.
[22] McGuckin, *Christianity*, p. 902.

Christ is Lord. Christians who refused to burn incense in honor of the Emperor provided ideal sacrifices for the gladiatorial games.[23] Much of Perpetua's prison account describes her responding to her family's pleas that she recant and acknowledge the Roman Emperor as Lord. By merely renouncing her conversion, Perpetua could then return to the aristocratic comfort of her family life as mother and daughter.

Obstinate in faith, however, as a fresh convert to Christianity, she refuses and is remembered down through the ages for her defiant confession of faith and for her martyrdom in the arena. While the expectation of an appallingly grisly death at the hands of wild beasts in the municipal arena sounds unconscionable today, the Roman state, like most premodern judicial systems, "relied on gruesome exemplary punishment as a substitute for effective law enforcement." The bloody spectacle of public executions, often staged alongside celebratory games, "served both to deter and to entertain."[24]

Following her vision, pathos and tension mount as Perpetua's fellow prisoners realize that death is the price they will all pay for salvation. Reflecting on similar terrifying circumstances in our own time, former Archbishop of Canterbury, Rowan Williams, has observed: "When things are leveled to the ground, when our security is taken away, when terror reigns, when violence triumphs, our ability to sit with that intensely painful reality without either false consolation or despair is a moment that somehow opens us up, opens the world up."[25]

In this case, the imprisoned group becomes open to the belief that Perpetua has received a special spiritual gift for healing. This

---

[23] "The special value of rarity attached to females, when coupled with the dangerous and yet alluring spectacle of witnessing the public violation of norms of sexuality and the mutilation of otherwise protected and honourable female bodies, gave a special edge, a sharper culmination to the display." Shaw, "Passion," p. 18.

[24] Michael Gaddis, *There is No Crime for Those Who Have Christ: Religious Violence in the Christian Roman Empire* (Berkeley: University of California Press, 2015), p. 19.

[25] Rowan Williams, "Perspectives on the Stations of the Cross," Public Art Project, New York City, Lent 2018.

conviction, that confessor-martyrs awaiting death exercise "the power of the keys,"[26] is supported by Tertullian's treatise *Ad Martyras*, which illustrates the view of Christians in Carthage that imprisoned confessors of the faith possessed efficacy for healing in their intercessory prayer. "Some, not able to find peace in the Church, have become used to seeking it from the imprisoned martyrs (*a martyribus in carcere exorare*). And so you ought to have it dwelling with you, and to cherish it, and to guard it (*et fovere et custodire debetis*), that you may be able perhaps to bestow it upon others."[27] Perpetua's spiritual charism eventually evangelizes several people around her, including the adjutant of the guards, who all become believers in Christ (XVI.4).

In her next two visions Perpetua is given confirmation of the realization that she has the power to intervene in prayer for her brother, who is still in a place of suffering from his cancer death. Her fervent prayer is mobilized day and night, "groaning (*ingemescere*) to the Lord," that his suffering be relieved, even as she is herself suffering confined in the prison's stocks (*in nervo*) (VIII.1).[28] In her vision, she senses a great gulf (*diastema*) between them,[29] and she sees her brother dirty, hot, thirsty and pale, and unable to reach healing relief at a huge pool (*piscina*). Pleading

---

[26] Frederick C. Klawiter, "The Role of Martyrdom and Persecution in Developing the Priestly Authority of Women in Early Christianity: A Case Study of Montanism," *Church History* 49:3 (Sept 1980), p. 258.

[27] Tertullian, *Ad Martyras* 1.6.

[28] Heffernan's use of "stocks" in translating *nervo* is supported with a similar usage by Cyprian and probably signifies a prison device fastened to the floor restraining the feet as well as the upper body, since Latin expressions exist for feet or neck bindings alone, *compes* and *furca*, respectively. Noted are "the skeletons of four prisoners found still bound in the stocks in the excavation of Pompeii's *Ludus Gladiatorius*." Heffernan has suggested as well that thirst and open sores caused by chafing of the stocks may have precipitated Perpetua's vision; or as in the author's experience, blinding *scotomatic* migraines with associated flashing *scintilla*. Heffernan, *Passion*, p. 229.

[29] Perpetua uses here a Latin transliteration, *diastema*, of the Greek word meaning great gulf; probably indicating her educated knowledge of Greek.

that "this gift might be given to me (*ut mihi donaretur*)" (VII.10), the answer to her prayer is realized in her next vision, and she rejoices to see that, as a result of divine mercy, Dinocrates is refreshed, released from suffering, and enjoying the miraculous refreshment of a never-ending golden cup (*fiala aurea*) (VIII.3).[30]

Perpetua's intercessory plea for Dinocrates, like the prayer of the first-century martyr, Thekla,[31] is one of the earliest known instances of someone praying for the benefit of the dead. By the grace of her spiritual charism, Perpetua has helped to restore Dinocrates to a new life, "albeit one among the happy dead."[32]

The final hours of Perpetua's life are described from two perspectives: one is an account from the narrator reporting on the gladiatorial games from the point-of-view of an eye-witness to the events. Intriguingly woven into this narrative, however, are several subtle pivot-points which invite a fluid interpretation of Perpetua's last dream as her own visionary experience of her martyrdom ordeal viewed as a cosmic struggle, even though the dream is described beforehand in the text.

The familiar opening words "I saw (*Video*)" (X.1) introduce the appearance of Perpetua's new spiritual father, the Deacon Pomponius, as he welcomes her to the amphitheater, encouraging her with fatherly Christ-like teaching: "Do not be afraid (*Noli expavescere*). I am here with you (*Hic sum tecum*), and I will struggle with you" (X.4). This is luminously juxtaposed against her father's last devastating visit, before her dream; for now, Perpetua experiences the shifting and re-prioritizing of her primary relationships in response to the compelling press of Christian conversion and in the face of impending death.

---

[30] The Latin term *fiala* is another transliteration from the Greek word meaning cup or bowl, perhaps signifying familiarity with Rev. 15:7. See Heffernan, *Passion*, p. 234.

[31] See the previous two chapters.

[32] Heffernan, *Passion*, p. 238.

Handsome young men approach Perpetua and prepare her to fight;[33] "and I was stripped naked (*et expoliata sum*), and I became a man (*et facta sum masculus*)" (X.7). Some see this candid declaration as a "gender transformation," like Heffernan;[34] yet others, such as McGuckin, see, rather than a transformational metaphor, an analogy incorporating traditional masculine tropes. She is prepared "for contest now as a fighter in the arena, just as in the men's gymnasium; she is a man among men, by virtue of the courage she feels;"[35] so, she may have been understood by contemporary ears to become virile and fearless, rather than transsexual.[36]

Perpetua can be seen as well modelling the image of Christ, who was stripped before his salvific ordeal (Mt. 27:28). Therefore, the mounting tension about the expectation of impending violence and shame is resolved as she envisions her transformation into a powerful fighter in the arena. As she prays, she experiences divine intervention in her dream and the unfolding of new restorative relationships. An environment of increasing terror from religious persecution, one which is steeped with keen awareness of the coming of the end-time, led early Christians like Perpetua "to envision the appearance of a new world, a world symbolized by the unity of male and female in Christ, a world in which Christ appeared to them in the form of a woman as well as in the form of a man."[37]

While Perpetua's observations are reported from the vantage point of a visionary daze in her last dream (*Passio* X), a literal

---

[33] In the early centuries of Christianity, the mention of beautiful beardless characters would have been recognized by Perpetua's readers as indicating angelic beings.

[34] Heffernan, *Passion*, p. 249.

[35] McGuckin, *Christianity*, p. 903.

[36] Cotter-Lynch adds that "reading this vision as one in which Perpetua 'becomes male' misreads the inherent ambiguity of the Latin. English does not attach gender to adjectives and participles, as Latin does. Thus, the phrase signaling Perpetua's putative transformation—'facta sum masculus'—loses its gendered difficulty." Cotter-Lynch, *Saint Perpetua*, p. 29.

[37] Frederick C. Klawiter, "The Role of Martyrdom and Persecution," in *Women in Early Christianity*, Ferguson *et al*, eds (New York: Garland, 1993), p. 115.

account of the tragic events is provided by the redactor in the closing section (*Passio* XVI-XXI). There, too, Perpetua and her slave are stripped and displayed in the arena clothed in diaphanous nets to sensational affect, like the martyrs Thekla and Blandina endured before them. Their predicament does not go unnoticed by Tertullian, who warns that "a young woman must necessarily be endangered by the public exhibition of herself, while she is penetrated by the gaze of untrustworthy and multitudinous eyes, is fondled by pointed fingers, and is too well loved by far."[38]

Perpetua's dream ordeal involves kick-boxing a foul Egyptian gladiator, while the crowds look on in astonished wonder, rather than moral ridicule, and a white-clad trainer, another divine idealized father figure, towering over the entire amphitheater in her vision moderates the scene (X.5-13). He awards her a branch of golden apples for treading upon her foe and greets her with peace and a kiss.

"Daughter, peace be with you (*Filia, pax tecum*)" (X.13). And, as Perpetua walks in triumph toward the Gate of Life (*ad Portam Sanavivarium*) and awakens from her dream, she is given the realization that she will be wrestling against the devil (*sed contra diabolum*) and not the beasts (X.12). Thus, while readers may "linger over the physical details of her nakedness, much as the eyes of the spectators may have done, at once repelled and drawn to the sight,"[39] Perpetua and other martyrs like her, and the persecuted Christian community as well, "understood their ordeal in terms of struggle, active spiritual combat against the forces of evil."[40]

On a literal level, however, the "cruelty of the crowd (*populi duritia devicta*)" and its lust for the traditional Roman rituals of violence demanded that the young female martyrs be whipped through a gauntlet of gladiators in the amphitheater (XVIII.9), before being set upon by a ferocious wild cow (*ferocissimam*

---

[38] Tertullian, *De virginibus velanidis*, 14, quoted in Shaw, "Passion of Perpetua," p. 4.
[39] Castelli, *Martyrdom and Memory*, p. 92.
[40] Gaddis, *No Crime*, p. 24.

vaccuuam) (XX.1).[41] The Passion of Perpetua and Felicity plays out in heart-rending details of violence and noble modesty, but mention again of the Gate of Life reminds the reader that Perpetua's last quoted words, "her final depiction of herself, immediately before she wakens, is of a solitary victorious figure walking from the floor of the arena in triumph" toward the gate.[42]

The martyrdom account even mentions that when she awakened (*expergita*) from her dream, "she was so deep in the spirit (*adeo in spiritu*) and in ecstasy (*et in extasi*)" (XX.8), that the reader is drawn to shift back and forth, pivoting between her witnessed violation and her confessed visions. Note that the Early Church "appears to have believed that the revelations received in ecstasies were particularly beneficial in times of travail and persecution."[43] Perpetua's refusal to see that she is being gored to death reinforces her visionary state and "the miraculous nature of God's protecting grace."[44] In fact, to the last moments of her life, Perpetua is represented as rejecting any concept of herself as a victim, "refusing to be a spectacle for the crowd's gaze."[45]

In her farewell exhortation to those being martyred with her, Perpetua cries out, "Stand fast in faith (*In fide stale*) and love one another (*et invicem omnes diligite*) and do not lose heart (*ne scandalize mini*)" (X.10). This message was far more likely familiar to the ancient Christians who heard it in the amphitheater than to today's hearers as an intentional *catena* of 1 Cor.16:13, 1 John 4:7 and 2 Cor. 4:16, stringing together a rhetorical necklace of powerful words of encouragement from Scripture. In the last fleeting moments of Perpetua's life, when the trembling sword hand of the gladiator wavered, she herself guided it to her throat. Perhaps

---

[41] "Being matched by a wild cow is a sign that their maternity is being mocked and ridiculed. Both Perpetua and Felicity have voluntarily given up their children, a behavior which Roman women would have found incomprehensible and savage." Heffernan, *Passion*, p. 344.

[42] *Ibid.*, p. 271.

[43] *Ibid.*, p. 350.

[44] *Ibid.*, p. 350.

[45] Perkins, *Suffering Self*, p. 112.

so great a woman (*fortassa tanta femina*) "could not have been killed if she herself had not willed it (*nisi ipsa voluisset*)" (XXI.10).

Thus, "where the spectators in the past saw suffering flesh, those who now participate in the commemorative liturgy in the present see moral triumph."[46] The cult of St. Perpetua developed rapidly in the third and fourth century in North Africa, so that her unique spiritual vision was reenacted annually and played out liturgically in a living tradition in which the audience, male and female, could witness replayed the heroic experiences of the saint. In fact, it was a mark of her spiritual authority that Augustine himself had to warn sternly that her words, her views, "were not canonical Scripture."[47]

So, what are we to make of Perpetua's martyrdom? Her story certainly demonstrates that the action of divine presence can be seen resolving tension by creating a synergy of transformation within personal roles and relationships. Perpetua's radical honesty in faith provides an invitation to engage with and better understand other events experienced by Early Christians, and it also equips us to question the meaning of martyrdom, and religious violence as a whole. In fact, even in the midst of courageous response to the reality of persecution, it is useful to recognize that, as spectators, we continue to this day to witness "Christian identity forged in the heat of martyrdom" in every new encounter with the *Passio* and with situations of religious tension in our lives.[48] For certainly every rereading of Perpetua's story "tells us more about us as readers, as retellers, than it ever can about a woman who lived, and died, nearly two millennia ago."[49]

---

[46] Castelli, *Martyrdom and Memory*, p. 125.

[47] "*Nec scriptura ipsa canonica est.*" Augustine, *De natura er origine animae*, 1.10.12.

[48] Lynn H. Cohick and Amy Brown Hughes, *Christian Women in the Patristic World: Their Influence, Authority, and Legacy in the Second through Fifth Centuries* (Grand Rapids, MI: Baker Academic, 2017), p. 64.

[49] "These dreams invite Perpetua's readers, whether ancient or modern, to posit a world in which the future is present, genders collapse, the body is spiritual, and the damned are saved." Cotter-Lynch, *Perpetua,* pp. 34, 156.

Additionally, this reflection invites us to engage in sacred listening to the stories of those persecuted in faith, and to the dreams they reveal; that we, too, might experience the wisdom of the Spirit revealed in them. Continuing exploration of the confession of Perpetua affords the reader an enlightening, if uncomfortably sobering, realization as well that faithful non-retaliation in the face of oppressive violence is particularly challenging in any age, including today's environment.

Furthermore, there is a significant spiritual thread which connects the lives of early martyrs with the developing wisdom of the saints in the next generations, and into the desert experience, as we shall see in the chapters ahead. For as the history of Christian martyrology unfolds, the capacity of Christian women to be transformed into heroes "translates eventually into a new type of spiritual virtuosity, when asceticism supplants martyrdom as the privileged form of Christian suffering."[50] Finally, as these stories were read, marked, learned, and inwardly digested by women and the men around them, we can be encouraged that "these are legends that have influenced women's consciousness of themselves, of the possibilities open to them, and of the female role in salvation history."[51]

---

[50] Castelli, *Martyrdom and Memory*, p. 126.
[51] Petroff, *Visionary*, p. 60.

II.
THE LONG BYZANTINE HYMN OF PRAISE

Chapter II.1
St. Helena: Becoming
a Christian Roman Empress

For her God-loving deeds...Constantine honored her
with imperial rank, she was acclaimed in all nations
and by the military ranks as Augusta Imperatrix,
and her portrait was stamped on gold coinage.[1]

Rising in a unique trajectory from stark obscurity to national prominence and finally wielding the treasury beside her son Emperor Constantine the Great (ca. 272-337 C.E.), St. Helena presents a significant character in the history of Early Christianity. She also poses a fascinating challenge in navigating the historical evidence of her life alongside her legendary reputation. Helena is venerated as an Orthodox saint together with her son, Constantine, on May 21. She also appears in the Orthodox liturgical texts for the Elevation of the Holy Cross on September 14. Virtuous Roman empresses reigned before her, virtuous Roman empresses came after; but, Dowager Empress Helena Augusta (ca. 249- ca. 329 C.E.) stands at the threshold of a new Christian ethos for the Roman Empire. Both history and legend contribute to this transformation.

As he gained political and military power, Constantine I raised up his mother into prominent visibility and authority; and, after her death, honored her by burying her in his own newly

---

[1] Eusebius, *Vita Constantinii*, PG 20.III.47. For English, Averil Cameron, Stuart G. Hall, trans., *Eusebius: Life of Constantine* (Oxford: Clarendon Press, 1999); hereafter VC III.47.

crafted porphyry sarcophagus. He also set up a statue of her in the central ceremonial square; which in fact became named after her, the Augustaian, in his new capitol city, Constantinople.[2]

Treasured memories and legends of Helena spiraling into circulation in the generations after her death became a significant touchstone for the role and even the ideal image of a Roman empress; to such an extent that her life and achievements influenced the archetype of the female ruler for the next several centuries. For the purposes of our study, however, this chapter explores sources for encountering the Empress from some of the earliest historians, since these texts are most likely to be still conserving possible threads of personal memory of the historical Helena.

In the sea change from pagan to Christian imperial Roman administration, it is no surprise that the first Christian emperor and empress would be held up in idealized legendary narrative; but, devotion to Helena, especially, enjoyed tremendous popularity. In some ways Helena joins the traditional progress of narratives with her sister Roman empresses; but in other ways, she steps forward into the history of Christianity, and her story is told reflecting her laudable achievements through the prism of the new religion. While Helena Augusta continued to embrace time-honored Roman virtues; nevertheless, as the first Christian empress, she can also be seen embodying the ideals of Jesus Christ proclaimed in the Gospels. By the time she completed her journey to the holy sites around Jerusalem, Eusebius praised her for her generosity and piety, as he might any previous pagan empress; but also for her Christian virtues, among them humility and relieving the suffering of those condemned to the mines for debt.

Furthermore, although she is now considered a model Christian empress because she is thought to have discovered the True

---

[2] Demonstrating how quickly Christianity was penetrating imperial Roman culture: a few score years later, for Empress Eudocia in the same location, "the inauguration of a silver statue in her honour on the Augustaian, accompanied by traditional music which disturbed the Liturgy nearby," garnered memorable condemnation from Patriarch John Chrysostom. Judith Herrin, "Late Antique Origins of the 'Imperial Feminine:' Western and Eastern Empresses Compared," *Byzantinoslavica* 74 (2016), p. 8.

Cross,[3] it may be that her faithful life and memory were prized as exemplary long before popular thought focused on the wood of the actual Cross at all. In fact, it is remarkable that, in a span of Early Christian centuries often notorious for diminishing or erasing the contributions of women, this particular memory of female agency—in the Finding of the True Cross—would become so firmly attached to one woman, Helena Augusta, and come to be regarded as historical reality for untold generations of Church History.

This phenomenon indicates the fluid and persistent ability of the faithful to cooperate in the construct of memory by tending to connect narrative details with beloved characters. In one location after another, as the generations unfolded, threads of tradition about Helena knitted themselves together to include local nobility and biblical figures into a mighty scenario acclaiming Helena's "discovery" of the Cross.

Associating Helena with the narrative of the *Inventio Sanctae Crucis* added an additional star in the crown of her popular memory. And what is more, this connection neatly resolved the concern about veracity for the innumerable True Cross relics which had come into abundant circulation by the end of the fourth century, when Cyril of Jerusalem boasted that: "Already, the world is filled with fragments of the wood of the Cross."[4]

The matchless appeal of the cult of the Holy Cross strengthened devotion to both Empress Helena and her son, Constantine the Great. For our purposes, though, what is fascinating in examining Helena's life is less the question of who discovered the True Cross, and more the depth of admiration for her demonstrated in her powerful connection with its discovery. For in Helena, we can see an imperial female paradigm shift in the making, and in the progress of Byzantine ruling women which followed, Helena Augusta became regarded as a prototype of the exemplary Christian

---

[3] "For centuries, this story enjoyed the greatest vogue, blossoming into a full-blown legend of the Cross which traced its genealogy all the way back to the Garden of Eden." H.A. Drake, "Eusebius on the True Cross," *Journal of Ecclesiastical History* 36:1 (Jan. 1985), p. 1.
[4] Cyril of Jerusalem, *Catechesis* IV.10, PG 33.470.

empress[5]—yet, she navigated a world still largely pagan. But even a portrait of St. Helena derived from mostly non-legendary material reveals an early fourth-century Roman empress driven by Christian faith and commitment to her noble son.

Imperial coinage provides a fascinating window into the changing world of Roman governance and royal favor—and offers an enduring glimpse of St. Helena in history. "When empresses appear on coins, they are always meaningful, and they often appear at points of fracture or transition."[6] In an age before cinema and news journalism, imperial coinage served a vital function; not only economically, but also as official state communication. Roman coinage can be a useful aid in understanding the social and ethical environment of any generation of the ruling Roman families, and can verify historical details about Helena in a relatively durable medium. While the minting process produced only crude facial features, familiar and recognizable elements of faces were nevertheless carefully incorporated into the crafted product, such as the long sharp, slightly hooked Constantinian nose on both Helena and her son.

Indeed, for the majority of the empire at the time, one of the most significant means of communication about the likeness and rising status of Helena were the state issues of coinage.[7] In fact, "her own numismatic depiction at times reached as much as twenty percent of the issue."[8] The Latin text on the front faces of Roman coins, "the coin obverses, were official documents—the legends, no less than the portraits, wore the stamp of officialdom;"[9] and they

---

[5] See Jan Willem Drijvers, "Helena Augusta: Exemplary Christian Empress," *Studia Patristica* XXIV (1993), p. 501.
[6] Leslie Brubaker, Helen Tobler, "The Gender of Money: Byzantine Empresses on Coins (324-802)," *Gender & Money* 12:3 (Nov. 2000), p. 590.
[7] Liz James, *Empresses and Power in Early Byzantium* (London: Leicester University Press, 2001), p. 101.
[8] Anne McClanan, *Representations of Early Byzantine Empresses: Image and Empire* (New York: Palgrave Macmillan, 2002), p.17.
[9] Patrick M. Bruun, *The Roman Imperial Coinage, VII, Constantine and Licinius A.D. 313-337*, C.H.V. Sutherland, R.A.G. Carson, gen. eds (London: Spink and Son Ltd., 1966); hereafter, RIC VII.27.

were "streamed to the ends of the world, imperishable, minted in discs of gold and bronze."[10]

After the last Battle of Chrysopolis, which brought civil war to a close in the Roman Empire in September of 324 C.E., and summarily terminated the experiment of the Tetrarchy style of government, Constantine gained supremacy over the whole Roman world. "On 8 November 324 he celebrated his victory by conferring the rank of *Augusta*[11] upon his mother Helena and his wife Fausta and by officially confirming the Caesarship of young Constantius," his son;[12] and he began at that time to be called Constantine the Great.[13]

In one coin, a *follis* struck in 326, the empress is appareled in the mantle of Roman court dress, in a bust facing right, with her head prominently positioned so that no words rise above it, which honors her in the "broken legend" style.[14] Indicating Helena's senior imperial rank, she wears a distinctly "ladder-shaped diadem decorated with a single pearl (dot) in each division."[15]

---

[10] Brubaker, "Gender of Money," p. 574.

[11] Her title, *augusta*, was originally bestowed upon Empress Livia after the death of her husband, the first emperor, Augustus, in 14 C.E. and remained in use until the thirteenth century. Brubaker, "Gender of Money," p. 575.

[12] RIC VII.69.

[13] "The *titulus primi ordinis*, 'Maximus,' conferred upon Constantine by the Roman Senate after the capture/liberation of Rome, becomes a regular feature." And in his minted imperial coinage, "the obverses of Constantine gradually develop from *Constantine aug* to *Constantinus max aug*." RIC VII.28, 73.

[14] This empty space above the head in imperial Roman coins mirrored one of the concepts of kingship: nothing man-made was to stand between the imperial head and heaven with its gods. While Helena was alive, Constantine bestowed the "broken legend" upon both her and Fausta; but after her death, he issued it only for himself. RIC VII.28. Note that a later Christianizing development included the hand of God (*manus Dei*) within the broken legend reaching down from heaven to crown the empress. "It is a device confined to the East and to empresses' coins." James, *Empresses and Power*, p. 105.

[15] RIC VII.672.

Christian empresses in the Byzantine era after Helena developed even more elaborate diadems pressed across the forehead, embellished with strands of pearl *pendilia* draped from the ears.

Helena's hair is drawn back and fashioned into a prominent braid, assisted by ropes of pearls visible on the coin. It sweeps up the back of the head to form a distinctive "crest-like feature" on top of the head in a hairstyle named after Magnia Urbica, wife of Emperor Carus (282-283). An interesting question arises around the precedence of the two elevated empresses—who comes first: Helena or the Emperor's wife?—but the evidence of Roman "coin portraits showing Helena with a diadem and Fausta as bare-headed imply a distinction of rank despite identical titles."[16] Thus, "Helena is thought to have been higher in rank than her daughter-in-law."[17]

So, what did it mean for Helena Augusta to be the first Christian Roman empress and first among women (*princeps femina*) in a new era? With Christianity on the rise, the ideal virtues and social ethos of imperial ruling women were in transition. First of all, since Jesus Christ was becoming acknowledged as Lord God throughout the empire, it was paramount in this transformation of priorities that the Empress Helena not be seen raised to the status of a goddess, as had been several of her royal forebears. Annia Galeria Faustina, for example, wife of Emperor Antonius Pius, was deified by senatorial decree in the year 140. The situation was changing, however; and even in 312, it was seen as a significant gesture that Constantine I, when processing into Rome in triumph "declined to ascend the Capitol to perform the customary sacrifices and to give thanks to Jupiter for his victory."[18]

Therefore, while the position of Roman empress continued to exemplify ideal womanhood, the expectations of the idealized paradigm with which Helena was associated were shifting. On the reverse side of Roman coins, for example, the personification of a

---

[16] RIC VII.45.

[17] Jan Willem Drijvers, *Helena Augusta: The Mother of Constantine the Great and the Legend of Her Finding of the True Cross* (Leiden: E.J. Brill, 1992), p. 42.

[18] Timothy D. Barnes, *Constantine and Eusebius* (Cambridge, MA: Harvard University Press, 1981), p. 44.

Roman virtue was often displayed. Thus, Faustina could be seen symbolizing imperial harmony (*Concordia*), or standing in for the goddess Juno, wife of Jupiter, or for Venus, "the divine ancestress of Rome."[19]

Like Faustina, Helena as the first Christian empress was also "used by the imperial administration as a vehicle for propaganda;"[20] therefore, the reverse side of many of her coins shows her exemplifying "Security for the Nation (*Secvritas Reipvblice*)" and "Peace of the Nation (*Pax Pvblica*)." During this time as well, Helena was described in Latin inscriptions as "righteous (*piisima*)" and "venerable (*venerabilis*)" and "benevolent (*clementissima*)."[21]

In examining the early Greek Church historians, the transition becomes more pronounced. The praise Eusebius lavishes on Helena Augusta "the God-beloved mother (*Theophiles mater*)" in the *Vita Constantini*[22] describes her in ways unrecognizable from any previous Roman Empress. She is not only remembered for her generosity (*philanthropia*), but also for her humility (*tapeinophrosyne*) and her pious zeal (*eusebeia*)[23]—thus, the virtuous ideal was being distinctly transformed by imitating the teaching of Christ.

Because it was likely written less than ten years after Helena died, Eusebius' *Life of Constantine* remains an important, if opinionated, primary source for information about Helena. Describing her journey and the family's building projects commemorating the sacred events of the life of Jesus, he reports: "This lady, when she made it her business to pay what piety owed to the all-sovereign God (*kaisarsi Theophilestatois*)...in prayers and thank-offerings for her son...came, though old, with the eagerness of youth...to inspect with imperial concern the eastern provinces...according adoration to the footsteps of the Savior."[24]

---

[19] Bettina Bergmann, Wendy M. Watson, *The Moon and the Stars: Afterlife of a Roman Empress* (South Hadley, MA: Mount Holyoke College Art Museum, 1999), p. 15.

[20] Bergmann, *Moon and Stars*, p. 13.

[21] Bergmann, *Moon and Stars*, pp. 50-52.

[22] VC I.42.

[23] Drijvers, "Helena Augusta: Exemplary Christian Empress," p. 501.

[24] VC III.42.

Eusebius continues: Often seen "in modest attire," Helena "showered countless gifts…with a magnificent hand (*megaloprepei dienemen*)…to the unclothed and the unsupported poor…abundantly supplying to cover the body. Others she set free from prison and from mines. She released victims of fraud, and others she recalled from exile."[25] The "supreme piety (*eusebeias huperbolen*)" of the first Christian Empress[26] is lifted up as an exemplar; for she is noticeably emulating the familiar teaching of Jesus from Matthew 25, exhorting the faithful to compassionate deeds, such as feeding the poor, clothing the naked and visiting prisoners. By the time of the Socrates *Ecclesiastical History*, Helena is even seen humbly serving supper to virgins of the Church;[27] thus, "presenting herself as a servant of the servants of God."[28]

Ambrose's "Funeral Oration for Theodosius,"[29] which incorporates the story of Helena, is one of the earliest historical sources to connect her with the re-discovery of the True Cross,[30] although the lost *Church History* of Gelasius[31] was written earlier and may

---

[25] VC III.44.

[26] VC III.47.

[27] "So devout was she that she would pray in the company of virgins of the churches, inviting them to a repast and serving them herself." Socrates, *Hist. Eccl.* I.17, PG 67.121; for English, NPNF II.22.

[28] Drijvers, *Helena Augusta*, p. 102.

[29] Ambrose, *De Obitu Theodosii Oratio*, PL 16:1447-1468; for English, Mary D. Mannix, trans. (Washington DC: Catholic University of America Press, 1925).

[30] Naming the True Cross "the remedy of immortality, the mystery of salvation (*remedium immortalitas, sacramentum salutis*)…Mary visited to liberate Eve; Helena was visited that emperors might be redeemed." Ambrose, *De Ob. Theod.* 46.

[31] The *Church History* of Metropolitan Gelasius of Caesarea, although lost, is generally accepted as a primary resource "included in the *Church Histories* of Rufinus, Socrates, Sozomen, Theodoret, as well as in the letter of Paulinus of Nola and the Chronicle of Sulpicius Severus." Drijvers, "Helena Augusta, the Cross and the Myth: Some New Reflections," *Millennium 8, Yearbook on the Culture and History of the First Millennium* (2011) p. 151. See also, the careful reconstruction of Gelasius' *Inventio Crucis* in Stephen Borgehammar, *How the Holy Cross was Found: From*

be his source. Actually, the Ambrose version of the story "gives the impression that the Bishop thought that Helena had a more important role in Christianization of the Empire than her son, Constantine."[32]

In fact, Ambrose's treatment of the empress "as the discoverer of the True Cross—whether original or not—laid the foundation for a new appreciation of Helena's role by the members of the imperial court as the ideal Christian empress and promoter of Orthodox Christianity."[33] Helena's renown grew in the West as well, but most prominently in the East, where "she was celebrated as an equal partner with her son," and regarded as an Orthodox saint "equal to the Apostles."[34]

Additionally, in looking back, "it is not improbable that Cyril of Jerusalem was responsible for the origin and composition of the Legend of the Cross, and that he even suggested to Metropolitan Gelasius of Caesarea that he include the story in his *Church History*"[35]—since, after all, Gelasius was his nephew.

Like many of our most celebrated Early Christians, not much is known about Helena's early life—she steps into the sunlight of historical memory only in her old age. The scant references to her youthful years pieced together from ancient sources still leave her veiled in mystery.[36] In attempting to decipher even a birthplace

---

Event to Medieval Legend (Stockholm: Almqvist & Wiksell International, 1991).

[32] Drijvers, *Helena Augusta*, p. 112.

[33] Andriani Georgiani, "Helena: The Subversive Persona of an Ideal Empress in Early Byzantium," *Journal of Early Christian Studies* 21:4 (2013), p. 604.

[34] Edward D. Hunt, *Holy Land Pilgrimage in the Later Roman Empire AD 312-460* (Oxford: Clarendon Press, 1982), p. 29.

[35] Jan Willem Drijvers, "Promoting Jerusalem: Cyril and the True Cross," in *Portraits of Spiritual Authority: Religious Power in Early Christianity, Byzantium, and the Christian Orient*, Jan Willem Drijvers, ed. (Leiden: Brill, 1999), p. 91.

[36] Even the date of Helena's birth is only extrapolated by Eusebius' report of her death at about eighty years of age. (VC III.46) Her date of repose is established in this study by the excellent gloss of Patrick Bruun

for Helena, one can only guess. Several quite disparate locations, however, have claimed her with robust legendary traditions.

The most likely places her as an inn-keeper or a tavern girl (*stabularia*)[37] in Bythynia, possibly in Drepanum, which Constantine renamed Helenopolis, now modern-day Herkes in Turkey. Constantine's father, Constantius Chlorus, was an upper-level Roman officer, with a peripatetic military lifestyle; and because of that, any of the proposed childhood sites and circumstances are plausible for the location of Helena's youth[38] and the initial encounter between Helena and Constantius Chlorus.

Where ever they first met, the triumphant Roman warrior was quite the romantic prize for a young girl to encounter, perhaps unknowingly initiating an historically significant match—and sometime after, there was a son in Helena's arms. An endearing legend of the birth story from the seventh century later incorporated into the *Church History* of Kallistos Xantosphulos even goes so far as to paint a hagiographic association of Constantine being indirectly "born in the purple"—that is, in the imperial purple cloak given to Helena by Constantius Chlorus after their first night together.[39] Legend notwithstanding, Constantius and

---

calculating when Helena Augusta died to 329; and therefore, she may have been born around 249 C. See RIC VII.72-73, footnote 6.

[37] Ambrose, *De Obit. Theo.* 42.

[38] "Trier, Colchester, and Edessa are named in the medieval legendary material as her place of origin." All these proposed cultural details are of interest in exploring possible connections to Helena's background; but, are difficult to substantiate. Drijvers, "Helena Augusta: New Reflections," p. 130.

[39] In this early seventh-century legend, later reported in the *Church History* of Kallistos Xantophulos, Constantius stops for the night at a tavern in Drepanum on his way to the East and is offered the innkeeper's daughter, Helena. In the morning, he rewards her with his imperial purple cloak and instructs her father to take great care of her and the infant she will bear, because he had an overwhelming vision in the night about the child's future, as if the sun was rising in the West. When later delegates of Constantius, who had by then been proclaimed as Augustus, visit Drepanum and recognize Helena because of the purple cloak, they bring

Helena appear to have had a stable and enduring relationship of almost twenty years from ca. 270-289.

Although "spouse" (*coniunx*) has been used to describe their relationship,[40] because of his higher social status, it is probable that Helena served as some sort of concubine to the upwardly mobile commander, a practice common among Roman military élite.[41] And in fact, Constantius Chlorus separated from her in order to make a politically expedient marriage with the daughter of his commanding officer, Augustus Maximian, as he was strategizing a promotion to the status of a Caesar.

Helena, however, managed in later life to become a compelling presence in the Imperial court of her son, especially after the scandal surrounding the death or murder of Constantine's second wife, Fausta, and his son, Crispus. While little is reliably known about the domestic trouble in the imperial household during the time of Constantine's marriage to Fausta, her death and the death of his son, Crispus, have been interpreted in differing ways, placing blame on relations between one or another member of the family. In one scenario, Helena is seen as an "anxious mother" peace-making and redeeming the scandalous reputation of Constantine's household by making her journey to the holy sites in the East in remarkably old age.[42] In the *damnatio memoriae* that followed Fausta's death and erased her from official public memory, "her role was assumed by Helena."[43] When Constantine was acclaimed in York as his father's successor in 306,[44] it is

---

her to court with the child. Kallistos Xantophulos, *Church History*, PG 145.1241.

[40] Sextus Aurielius Victor, *Liber de Caesaribus* 39.25; CIL X.517.

[41] "Indeed, Constantine himself fathered Crispus by his concubine, Minervina." See B. Leadbetter, "The Illegitimacy of Constantine," in Samuel N.C. Lieu, ed., *Constantine: History, Historiography and Legend* (London: Rutledge, 1998), p. 79.

[42] Hunt, *Holy Land*, p. 33.

[43] Leslie Brubaker, "Memories of Helena: Patterns in Imperial Female Matronage in the Fourth and Fifth Centuries," in *Women, Men, and Eunuchs: Gender in Byzantium*, Liz James, ed. (London: Rutledge, 1997), p. 59.

[44] A well-developed English Helena tradition, even including a royal connection as the daughter of an old King Coel, enjoys enthusiastic

generally accepted that Helena joined his court,[45] and was present with him in Trier,[46] in Rome,[47] and later in Constantinople.[48] Therefore, even having been put aside by his father, Helena later "resumed her rank with consummate dignity as the companion of her son."[49]

A puzzle remains: between the imperial mother and son, who evangelized whom? But the history of Helena coming to Christian faith cannot be reliably established, nor her plausible influence on the upbringing of her imperial son. While we do not know whether Helena converted her son, Theodoret maintains that Helena raised the young Constantine as a Christian.[50]

Although the Christianizing process of the empire took place gradually, Constantine's financial and political support of his mother's travel and building projects became a visible part of his own philanthropic program of Christian patronage quite soon after he convened the Council of Nicaea in 325. Eusebius writes

---

popularity, and it gained visibility by its inclusion of Evelyn Waugh's clever novelization of Helena's life. See Antonina Harbus, *Helena of Britain in Medieval Legend* (Suffolk: D.S. Brewer, 2002).

[45] From the time that she joined Constantine's court, "Helena bore the official title of *nobilissima femina*, indicating that she was a member of the imperial house, as we know from a small quantity of bronze coins which have her image and the lettering *Helena NF*." Drijvers, "Helena Augusta: New Reflections," p. 136.

[46] Trier retains a lively Helena tradition, complete with a *Vita Helenae* which claims she was born there.

[47] In Rome there is even clearer evidence of Helena in residence; and in fact, she is likely to have stood in for the imperial presence at Rome, since Constantine was seldom there. A large estate just southeast of the city became an official possession of hers—a legal *possessio Helenae*—and eventually Constantine had a mausoleum built on its grounds, and Helena was later buried there.

[48] Even though she never resided there, it is likely that Helena spent time in the new developing capitol city as part of her extended sojourn to the eastern provinces.

[49] Joseph Vogt, "Pagans and Christians in the Family of Constantine the Great," in *The Conflict between Paganism and Christianity in the Fourth Century*, Arnaldo Momigliano, ed. (Oxford: Clarendon Press, 1963), p. 43.

[50] Theodoret, *Hist Eccl*. I.18.1.

that Constantine "even remitted to her authority over the imperial treasuries (*basilikon thesauron*), to use them all at will and to manage at her discretion, in whatever way she might wish and however she might judge best in each case, her son having accorded her distinction and eminence in these matters."[51]

Helena can be seen most clearly at a threshold of cultural and religious change as she travels to the sacred Christian sites in the eastern provinces of the Empire, probably embarking on her voyage in the Autumn of 326 or in the early Spring of 327.[52] In this undertaking, time has shown that she single-handedly transformed the spiritual and ethical components of the imperial progress as it had been established by previous Roman reigns, including the dramatic state journeys of Emperor Hadrian.[53]

In the process, Christian pilgrimage, as we know it today, was born. Thus, it was not so much that Helena visited the holy sites as a pious pilgrim—for that was a later reality for travel to Palestine—but rather, that she embarked on a state visit, "in the magnitude of imperial authority (*magalprepia basilikes edzousias*)."[54] Furthermore, her royal progress as Empress Dowager on behalf of her son, the Emperor Constantine, drew attention to the sites of Our Lord's Passion in Palestine, contributing to a transformation in identity, for they were coming to be regarded now as the Christian Holy Land.

The idea of Christian pilgrimage as a devotional act was only in its earliest stages of development; and, while Helena was by no means the first pilgrim to the Holy Land, the Dowager Empress's sojourn, intended in all likeliness to inspect the progress of her son's building projects honoring the Christian holy sites, galvanized the burgeoning practice of pilgrimage over time. Now, with her son increasingly sanctioning the new religion, Helena's royal

---

[51] Eusebius, VC III.47.

[52] Drijvers, *Helena Augusta*, p. 13.

[53] See Kenneth G. Holum, "Hadrian and St. Helena: Imperial Travel and the Origins of Christian Holy Land Pilgrimage," in Robert Ousterhout, ed., *The Blessings of Pilgrimage* (Urbana, IL: University of Illinois Press, 1990), p. 73.

[54] VC III.44.

progress was regarded as a significant new element of Christian piety.[55]

Thus, as the story of her journey was told and retold, it became "reconstructed as a *peregrinatio religioso*."[56] After her, there came a multitude of visitors, many of them aristocratic women, following her lead. Subsequent Christian Roman empresses after Helena now "re-inscribed themselves onto the landscape of imperial power, virtue and religion, using travel to the Holy Land as their medium."[57]

All this contributed to a transformation of even the term "pilgrim," which originally meant a kind of stranger or foreigner; but, it came to be understood in a new sense of piety and intentionally sacred exploration. In fact, it could even be said that Christian pilgrimage was "essentially a new phenomenon that first flourished during the age of Constantine."[58] And it is clear that, during the re-assessment of Constantine's life, soon after his death, when he became regarded as a Christian saint, his mother's reputation, and even the narrative of her life, expanded exponentially.

It may be difficult to pinpoint the ground-breaking moment in Jerusalem when digging apart the Venus temple commenced and exposed the cave of the Holy Sepulchre during the imperial building project patronized by the Emperor Constantine and the visiting Empress Dowager. Yet it is likely that during the excavation, fragments of cross-wood were unearthed in the process of uncovering the nearby hill identified as Calvary, a place where crucifixion executions were regularly carried out. In addition, "the balance of probability is that the site of Golgotha, like certain other biblical sites, remained known to the Palestinian Christians during the first three centuries."[59]

---

[55] Holum, "Hadrian and Helena," p. 70.

[56] Georgiou, "Helena: The Subversive Persona of an Ideal Christian Empress," *Journal of Early Christian Studies* 21:4 (Winter 2013), p. 604.

[57] Noel Lensky, "Empresses in the Holy Land: The Creation of a Christian Utopia in Late Antique Palestine," in *Travel, Communication, and Geography in Late Antiquity: Sacred and Profane* (Aldershot: Ashgate, 2004), p. 119.

[58] Holum, "Hadrian and Helena," p. 70.

[59] Colin Morris, *The Sepulchre of Christ and the Medieval West* (Oxford: Oxford University Press, 2005), p. 13.

Yet, interest in the actual Cross of Christ had not even begun to arise in Helena's lifetime; and, it must be noted that at the time of her journey, the Cross was still regarded as a substantially negative symbol of Christ's humiliating manner of death. "Initially an object identified with disgrace, it later became a highly revered token of salvation."[60] Indeed, Early Christian thought focused on the victory, not the suffering, of Jesus Christ. During the years 350-385, however, Cyril of Jerusalem was able to deploy the Cross in his teaching, playing down the negative aspect of the Crucifixion,[61] and this marks a significant transition in ideology.

The connection of Helena Augusta with the Discovery of the True Cross is one of the most significant and best-known stories of faith in Late Antiquity. "Shortly after its origin, most probably in Jerusalem in the second half of the fourth century, the story rapidly became widespread and available in various versions in Greek, Latin, and Syriac."[62] While Eusebius does not specifically acknowledge Helena's association with the Finding of the True Cross, his historical texts may have, nevertheless, effectively contributed to her expanded representation as the first Christian empress; an idealized imperial status rich with pious attributes—in some ways similar to the idealized pagan empress, but with the addition of Christian virtues. By the ninth century, the Legend of Helena and Constantine was much more fully developed, and for hagiographers, "all their creativity was funneled toward the Cross as a vehicle of military success."[63]

Ultimately, though, concern about locating the Cross of Christ may have more to do with the issue of agency—who is responsible? under whose auspices was the Calvary site excavated?—rather than who did the literal digging and discovery. The fact is that churches were built in Jerusalem and its

---

[60] Drijvers, *Helena Augusta*, p. 81.

[61] For Cyril, the Cross had become the glory of the Church, a source of illumination and redemption, the end of sin, the source of life, a crown of honor instead of dishonor, the basis of salvation, and the symbol that brings the faithful together. Cyril of Jerusalem, *Catechesis* 13, 15.22.

[62] Drijvers, "Helena Augusta: New Reflections," p. 126.

[63] Alexander Kazhdan, "'*Constantin Imaginaire*:' Byzantine Legends of the Ninth Century about Constantine the Great," *Byzantion* 57 (1987), p. 229.

surrounding region, many under the auspices of the Byzantine throne. In excavating the site, the Tomb was discovered, and likely at the nearby Golgotha Crucifixion site, cross fragments were dug up in the rubble.

The fabric of the Legend was strengthened by a growing desire several years later to identify the specific Cross on which Jesus died, because of the increased significance and symbolism which came to surround it. Furthermore, the proliferation of treasured True Cross reliquaries necessitated the increased authentication of shards of legendary tradition to justify them. The contradictory evidence of the earliest Church historians demonstrates that focused interest in the actual wood of the Cross—and whose agency was being exercised when cross pieces were found—took a few years, even a few generations, to catch up with the original memories of the events. When it did, however, it triggered the fascination of the world. Yet, acclamations in the various early versions of the *Inventio Sanctae Crucis* may still reflect back upon a kernel of truth about Helena herself and the compelling strength of her virtuous actions and building projects. The story certainly endeared her to the people, and won her favor in her own generation and increasing esteem in the generations after.

Later comparisons demonstrate that, by emulating her and by embodying her compassionate action and generous building projects throughout the new Christianized empire, Helena Augusta was kept in such glowing memory that it justified making idealized comparisons with her, placing later empresses in relational juxtaposition with her. Thus, the moniker "New Helena" came to describe several subsequent royal women who were regarded as just and charitable; several of their lives are explored in the last section of the book.

Not only have many pious and merciful female rulers been described as a "New Helena," but the *topos* "New Constantine and New Helena" was bestowed on imperial couples as well. In some cases, significant conciliar achievements were marked by the comparison: thus, the Acts of the 451 Council of Chalcedon proclaimed Empress Pulcheria and her new husband, Marcian, as the "New Constantine and New Helena," and the same description was deployed by Pope Hadrian I to describe Constantine VI and his mother Irene at the time of the Second Council of Nicaea in 787, which restored the Orthodox veneration of icons.[64] And indeed, Helena and Constantine, as mother and son, stand together signifying an idealized couple in icons commemorating their Orthodox feast together in May 21.

On balance, what emerges from examining the fabric of memories evoked by Helena Augusta is a clearer focus on the changing role of the Roman empress at the dawn of global Christianity. The nuanced variety of versions of Helena's connection with the True Cross flowering over the centuries demonstrates the continued enthusiasm for her memory in the mind of the faithful.[65] "By words and deeds," says Eusebius, "she has produced luxurious growth from the Savior's commandments (*ton soterion paraggelmaton*)."[66]

Although legendary, the *Inventio Sanctae Crucis* was a useful explanation for its time and enjoyed hearty and persistent popularity for the next several centuries. Furthermore, the development and evolution of her legend provide a vivid example of how memory is constructed in a changing religious environment. Yet, there is, amid the elaborately embellished tapestry of varying legends about Helena, a unique strength which was remembered as hers alone, some persistent thread of admirable character which captured the hearts of the people around her. And in the same way, there is a golden thread of reality which is shot through the fabric of her legend and still describes the actual Helena today.

---

[64] Drijvers, "Helena: Exemplary Empress," pp. 88-89.

[65] In our own generation, "we discovered that legend, however ornamented by gorgeous inventions, had a value in its own right, no less precious for understanding the past than the most firmly ascertained facts." Kazhdan, "*Constantin Imaginaire;*" p. 196.

[66] VC III.43.

CHAPTER II.2
DIVINE FIRE: THE MYSTIC ST. SYNCLETICA SPEAKS

There is struggling and great toil at first
for all those advancing toward God; but afterward,
inexpressible joy. Indeed, just as those seeking
to light a fire at first are engulfed in smoke and
teary-eyed, thus they obtain what they desire.
As it is said, Our God is a consuming fire.
So, we ought to kindle the divine fire in ourselves
with tears and toil.[1]

Even among Early Christian spiritual elders who discerned the image of God as divine fire,[2] St. Syncletica and her sayings[3] make

---

[1] The translation of the Divine Fire saying of Syncletica is here synthesized from the Greek words duplicated in *Vita Syncletica* (PG 28, Saying No. 60) and the *Apophthegmata Patrum* (PG 65, Syncletica Saying No. 1).
[2] Others include: Makarios the Great, Abba Isaiah, Abba Poemen, Evagrius, and Diodochus, Bishop of Photike.
[3] For the sayings of St. Syncletica: PG 65.421-428. These are traditionally supplemented by J.-C. Guy, "Recherches sur la Tradition Grecque des *Apophthegmata Patrum*," *Recherches de Science Religieuse* 48 (1955), pp. 252-259. For an English translation, see *The Sayings of the Desert Fathers: The Alphabetical Collection*, Benedicta Ward, trans. (Trappist, KY: Cistercian Publications, 1975), pp. 230-235; *Give Me a Word: The Alphabetical Sayings of the Desert Fathers*, John Wortley, trans. (Yonkers, NY: St. Vladimir's Seminary Press, 2014), pp. 302-308. See also, Pseudo-Athanasius, *Vita Syncleticae*, PG 28. 1487-1558. For an English translation, see "Pseudo-Athanasius: The Life and Activity of the Holy and Blessed

a remarkable contribution to the history of the Church. In fact, with twenty-seven sayings in *The Saying of the Fathers* (*Apophthegmata Patrum*), including the additional nine supplemented by J.-C. Guy from another manuscript—even with nearly all of them originating from among the eighty-one sayings in *The Life of Syncletica* (*Vita Syncletica*) in PG 28—and over twenty sayings also present in the *Verba Seniorum*, not to mention the thirty-four sayings included in Abba Isaiah's Russian *Matericon* collection, it is evident that the significance of the sayings of Syncletica has been under-valued in the standard literature about the Desert tradition.

Nevertheless, we are fortunate that robust evidence exists for Syncletica's textual memory, with multiple surviving texts for the fourth-century desert elder, two of them within the *Patrologia Graeca*. And a good thing it is, because her personal identity remains a mystery.

Standing beside St. Antony, who is hailed as the "father of monks," Syncletica can be "rightly named as the 'mother of female ascetics.'"[4] Indeed, she is called *Amma* Syncletica in Patristic literature. Since scholars have suggested that her *Vita*, originally attributed to Athanasius the Great (296-373 C.E.), was likely written even before Gregory of Nyssa's "Life of Macrina" (ca. 380-383), it can be identified as the first surviving Christian woman's biography. Further, as the first recorded leader of an organized women's ascetical community, she is known to be the first female founder in the early development of monasticism. Just as the *Vita Syncletica* characterizes St. Paul the Apostle as the "leader of the bride" (*nymphagogos*) for both she and the early Christian martyr,

---

Teacher Syncletica," Elizabeth A. Castelli, trans. in *Ascetic Behavior in Greco-Roman Antiquity: A Sourcebook*, Vincent L. Wimbush, ed. (Minneapolis, MN: Fortress Press, 1990), pp. 265-311; *The Life & Regimen of the Blessed & Holy Syncletica by Pseudo-Athanasius; Part One: English Translation*, Elizabeth Bryson Bongie, trans. (Toronto: Peregrina Publishing Co., 2003).

[4] John Anthony McGuckin, *The Westminster Handbook of Patristic Theology* (Louisville, KY: Westminster John Knox Press, 2004), p. 321. Also note that Nikephoros Kallistos in his *Ecclesiasticae Historicae* praises St. Syncletica as the Mother of Ancient Monasticism alongside St. Antony as the Father. PG 145.VIII.40.155-158.

Thecla, leading them to Christ,[5] Syncletica functioned as a bride-leader for her monastic followers. The Orthodox Church venerates St. Syncletica on January 5.

Although the Greek word, Syncletica, has come to be used as a given feminine name, in earlier times it meant literally "called together, summoned," or even "the heavenly assembly." It also signified association with Byzantine nobility, probably identifying the saint's father.[6] Thus, the term Syncletica is a social rank descriptor, and not likely the ascetical elder's personal name. The strongest historical foundation for the saint is therefore her textual evidence; the fact of its survival is remarkable, considering it quotes the theological teaching of a woman.

In much the same way as the remembered sayings of Jesus—raw, abrupt and piercing in essential wisdom—many of the sayings of Syncletica undoubtedly trace back to an individual disciple's memory of a hallmark experience receiving a very personal answer from a spiritual guide, a word (apophthegm) now writ large on the heart of the one receiving it, and then handed down to generations of spiritual seekers. Finally, a saying or logos was written down and later nuanced in redaction, or editorially enlarged as part of a teaching discourse. This theory about the manner of development for the apophthegmata, the sayings of the early ascetical teachers, from the earliest primitive answer offered to an individual disciple, through to the more polished rhetoric of a teaching discourse, follows the concept introduced by J.-C. Guy.[7]

The two collections of Syncletica's sayings present in the volumes of the Patrologia Graeca raise interesting questions about how and when they came to be collected—and which came first. In the theological literature of the early centuries of Christianity, notable for scant treble voices, any opportunity to observe one

---

[5] Vita Syncletica 8, hereafter abbreviated as VS 8. Likewise, sayings from the Apophthegmata Patrum will be given as AP with number. A Patristic Greek Lexicon, G.W.H. Lampe, ed. (Oxford: Clarendon Press, 1961), p. 927.

[6] SV 4, Liddell & Scott, A Greek-English Lexicon, 1665b.

[7] Jean-Claude Guy, "Remarques sur le texte des Apophthegmata Patrum," Recherches de Science Religieuse 48 (1955), pp. 252-259.

collection of sayings illuminating another is a rare privilege. Even though the larger collection amassed in the *Vita Syncletica* probably informed the sayings present in the *Apophthegmata Patrum*, nevertheless, close study of her teaching texts from both collections in conversation with each other can shed light on the early monastic teacher herself, as well as the shifting development of the genre of *Apophthegmata* as a form of Early Christian writing.

The *Vita Syncletica*, probably of fifth-century provenance, offers a biographical portrait of Syncletica coming from prominent parentage in Alexandria, and beginning at an early age to devote herself to a theological life of virginity, "training her soul for the love of God," (*philotheia men to proton ten psyche eskeito*);[8] and after the rest of her family died, faithfully caring for her blind sister throughout her life. After years of ascetical hermit experience[9] at the family crypt in the desert hills outside Alexandria, during which she attracted followers, she is remembered answering the spiritual concerns of her disciples—requests traditionally expressed as "Give me a word, that I may live!"[10]

Another biographical tradition exists for Syncletica in a sixth-century manuscript.[11] Here, in a dramatic family story, a

---

[8] See VS 6. After all, as Augustine pointed out, every female is born a virgin in body, but it requires dedication to make a virgin soul. *De Sancta Virginitate* 10, CSEL 41:243.

[9] Curious about what ascetical practice actually meant in the fourth century?—good question. Syncletica's ascetical practices described by her hagiographer include: distributing her wealth to the poor (VS 12) and other good works, seeking stillness and humility, contemplation of the Old and New Testaments (VS 21), praying unceasingly (*adialeiptos proseukesthai*) (VS 19) with tears and penitential austerities (VS 17), as well as the "salvific remedy" (*soteriou pharmakou*) of fasting (VS 10).

[10] The traditional request to a spiritual elder is based upon Psalm 119:116, which continues to be associated with the monastic clothing service of a novice, to the present day.

[11] Bernard Flusin and Joseph Paramelle, "De Syncletica in Deserto Jordanis," *Analecta Bollandiana* 100 (1982), pp. 291-317; for an English translation, see Tim Vivian, "Syncletica of Palestine: A Sixth-Century Female Anchorite," *Vox Benedictina: A Journal of Translations from Monastic Sources* 10/1 (1993), pp. 9-37.

Constantinopolitan nobleman's daughter resists her impending betrothal by insisting on fulfilling a vow to visit the Holy Land while still a virgin, and flees into an ascetical life, until found by another monk in the desert twenty-eight years later. Although this Palestinian hermit tale likely describes a different ascetical teacher, in the economy of spiritual memory, these stories do share some of the same details and spiritual wisdom, especially about the *askesis* of seeking humility.[12] It is possible that both of these biographies have at times claimed the warrant of the Sayings. In any case, as with many Early Church figures, there is no known archeological evidence to support either hagiographic tradition.

While Syncletica's teaching explores the mystical arena of inner spiritual progress, her sayings also aim to convey down-to-earth advice. She taught her followers to strive for contemplation and spiritual enlightenment (*theorias kai gnosios*) by means of ascesis and practical study (*asketikes kai praktikes*).[13] Her style of spiritual teaching is based on frequent deep exploration of Scripture and probing observation. Her sayings offer personal examination for those seeking union with God's love and beauty.

Syncletica's ascetical instructions reveal remarkably intimate disclosure of the challenging experience of personal temptation with vividly illustrated Niptic advice aimed at guarding the purity of the heart against the threat of sinful thoughts (*logismoi*) by unceasing prayer (*proseukes apaustou*).[14] On balance, her sayings may have survived over the centuries because of their effectiveness in helping her disciples gain mastery over daily

---

[12] "The humility of Christ is a treasure difficult to acquire, yet necessary to be saved. It is the one virtue the Devil cannot mimic. So, even as it strips down, it clothes in salvation." (VS 56), Schaffer, trans., *Life & Regimen: Part Two: Study of the Life*, p. 70.

[13] See VS 43.

[14] Some of her cautionary advice borders on the grisly: Even for women living as solitaries, the Tempter conjures up handsome faces and old relationships, directed to the destruction of the soul. Amma Syncletica's strategy for confronting the temptation of an alluring image was to mentally gouge out its eyes and to imagine it as a stinking corpse, in order to frighten off the Devil. (VS 26, VS 29)

temptation,[15] increase competence in prayer,[16] and approach the ineffable joy of Christ's presence.[17]

With the élite education available to an Alexandrian aristocrat, Syncletica likely knew of her more celebrated forebears in the ascetical life, ones whom she and her hagiographer emulate. Her Vita, however, does not reveal if, like St. Antony, she sought the tutelage of a spiritual mentor experienced in prayer and ascetical practices; but, the Vita does indicate a priest in whose presence Syncletica sacramentally cut off her hair and entered the ascetical life.[18] Her writing demonstrates, though, the deep and specific influence that Evagrius of Pontios (345-399) made upon her theological teaching, especially with regard to the categorization of sinful thoughts (*logismois*) and the acquisition of virtue.

Evagrius arrived in Egypt around 383, gradually becoming the leader of the desert community thirty miles up the Nile from Alexandria in Nitria for the rest of his life.[19] Syncletica may acknowledge her formation in mystical theology according to the teaching of Evagrius by citing him in VS 88, "I know a servant of God living according to virtue," a saying which paraphrases Evagrius' Praktikos 50, attesting to his brilliance and his close analysis of the hierarchy of evil presented by the enemy, sin.[20]

VS 89 as well recommends novice formation according to Evagrian teaching. Here, the use of intentional observation of distracting, evil thoughts (*logismoi*) from the Enemy is an ascetical

---

[15] Here is an example of a saying of Syncletica to guard against temptation: "Stay wake! (*Pregoreite!*) for the Enemy continues to lurk in the crannies of your mind, inciting a battle of the Spirit." (VS 26)

[16] An example of a saying to guard the purity of prayer: "If you say, or even hear, foul-smelling slut words (*ten dusode ton logon ekatharsian*), you will stain your prayer." (VS 66)

[17] A saying concerning the spiritual strategy for approaching Christ's presence: "How great the *askesis* and skill needed to contemplate Him who merits indescribable glory! (*tes anekpsrastou dokses*)" (VS 86)

[18] See VS 11.

[19] Evagrius Ponticus, *The Praktikos: Chapters on Prayer*, John Eudes Bamberger, trans. (Kalamazoo, MI: Cistercian Publications, 1981), pp. xxv-xxix.

[20] Evagrius, *The Praktikos: Chapters on Prayer*, Praktikos 50, pp. 29-30.

practice deployed in order to overthrow them, and as a strategy
for attaining pure knowledge of the grace of God; lest by one mis-
take the "bloodsucking Devil" destroy all spiritual progress. The
very fact of Evagrian influence upon the *Vita Syncletica*, however,
thereby discounts it as written by Athanasius the Great, who re-
posed in 373. In fact, it may push the *terminus ad quem* for Syncletica herself over into the fifth century. Furthermore, since the
teaching of Evagrius was condemned at the Fifth Ecumenical
Council of 553, this might in fact account for the considerable
"silence about the *amma*" in the desert literature.[21]

Although it is likely, in comparing the two collections in the
Patralogia Graeaca, that the Syncletics sayings in the *Apophthegmata Patrum* were nearly entirely copied and redacted from the
larger collection of sayings present in the *Vita Syncletica*, it is also
possible that both collections were editorially chosen and redacted from another source, now lost, one which contained earlier versions of the sayings. Hints of the editing discernable in
several of the sayings which present differences between the two
collections support this suggestion.

Thus, several of the pairs of matching sayings, when compared and contrasted, are worded quite differently from one another; nevertheless, the one saying of Syncletica in the *Apophthegmata Patrum* with no basis in the *Vita Syncletica* is AP 11. It comes
instead from the "Adhortation ad Monachos" of Hyperechios;[22]
and the saying includes this pearl, "Choose the meekness of Moses
and you will find the stony places in your heart transformed into
springs of water."

Let us look at Syncletica's most popular saying, noted in English above,[23] where she uses the concept of "divine fire" to illumi-
nate the progress of seeking union with God. The version of this
teaching in the *Vita Syncletica*, VS 60, closes a loosely arranged
section of about a dozen *apophthegmata* in the *Vita* text examining
the spiritual discipline of humility and obedience in dealing with

---

[21] Schaffer, *Life & Regimen: Part Two: Study of the Life*, p. 10.

[22] Hyperechios, "Adhortation ad Monachos" 73-74. PG 79.1480.

[23] The text of Syncletica's Divine Fire saying is given on the first page of
the chapter, as its sub-title.

pride. The saying begins with female disciples demanding further teaching and the Amma responding. It closes with cautionary advice about faithfulness and perseverance, adding a Gospel citation as further gloss on the quote from Hebrews, in which the Old Testament definition of God as "a consuming fire" in Deuteronomy is set in an eschatological context.[24]

In the *Apophthegmata Patrum*, on the other hand, the Divine Fire saying opens the selection of Syncletica's sayings and includes her name, introducing the alphabetical section. Both versions of the saying in the Greek contain an almost duplicated forty-two-word inner saying illuminating the arduous process of approaching God by the powerful analogy of kindling divine fire (*to Theion edzapsai pur*) with tears and toil, but reaching finally the goal of ineffable joy (*kara aneklaletos*); text which may represent an attempt to identify a nugget of the earliest authentic sayings material.

In fact, by placing an edited-down version of VS 60 in first place among Syncletica's sayings in the *Apophthegmata* collection, the redactor has chosen it for special consideration. It can be seen functioning as a mantra for the rest of her sayings,[25] invoking the concept of "divine fire" to characterize Syncletica's mystical teachings as a whole.[26]

This edited-down appearance of the *Apophthegmata* version compared to the *Vita Syncletica* version of the Divine Fire saying may be the result of one redacted from the other, or of a further source for both. Other examples of sayings in the *Apophthegmata Patrum* which appear to edit down and synthesize a particularly

---

[24] Gerhard Kittel, *Theological Dictionary of the New Testament*, (Grand Rapids, MI: Eerdmans, 1964-1976), vol. 6, p. 945.

[25] Schaffer suggests that, by deploying VS 60 as a mantra, the collection as a whole is meant to function as "kindling to make the hearts of her listeners burn again with the fervour of the Gospel." *Life & Regimen: Part Two: Study of the Life*, p. 29.

[26] Other references to "divine fire" featured in the sayings of Syncletica include: Godly love (*Theios eros*) which is enkindled in us (*edzopurei hemon*) (VS 1); fire as spiritual testing in ascetical practice (VS 98/AP 7, VS 106); spiritual virtues described as fire (VS 54) and as lamps lit (VS 92); even a bit of good is characterized as a spark of divine fire (VS 37).

memorable didactic pearl from a longer narrative saying in the *Vita Syncletica* include her pithy observation about athletic competition, inappropriate laughter among monastics, and the use of sailing and ship-building as an analogy for spiritual progress.[27] Additionally, the fact of different fragments of text drawn together by theme in each collection is also consistent with the idea that both redactors may have borrowed from an earlier, less organized source.

It is interesting to note that the *Vita Syncletica* also makes occasional use of feminine plural participial verb constructions in the Greek, which are generally not chosen for the *Apophthegmata Patrum* with its principally male audience. In fact, as opposed to the *Vita* as a whole, which focuses predominantly on life within an organized female monastic community and its concerns, some of the sayings chosen for the *Apophthegmata* collection appear to purposefully characterize an earlier stage in the progress of Syncletica's ascetical spiritual life, when she was a more solitary desert elder and first beginning to attract individual disciples, before a monastic community developed around her.

In a sense, therefore, the selection of Syncletica's sayings for the *Apophthegmata Patrum*, may have intentionally attempted to exclude the voice of her hagiographer, whose description of Syncletica's early life and final illness in the *Vita* describe her life as a monastic founder. Although likely derived from a later stage in the transmission of her texts, the editorial choice of Syncletica's teachings for the *Sayings of the Fathers* appear to reflect an earlier stage in her spiritual teaching life, one closer to the original oral phenomenon of spiritual elder and disciple interacting.

In the centuries following her life and monastic career, as her reputation as a desert mother grew, Syncletica's *Vita* was

---

[27] "Just as athletes make progress, so they must contend with stronger opponents." Here, AP 14 is edited down from the twenty-five-line SV 26. Shaming immodest monastics, Syncletica observes, "Their gaze is unseemly and they laugh improperly." This is AP 2 redacted from the lengthier VS 24. Among several sayings about the lore of the sea: "Just as a ship is impossible to assemble without nails, a soul is impossible to save without a humble spirit." AP 26 is synthesized from the much longer SV 56.

translated into Latin, and references to her sayings appeared in scholia upon *The Ladder of Divine Ascent* by John of Climakas.[28] In addition, the *Vita* and its *apophthegmata* are quoted in a twelfth-century Russian anthology of Abba Isaiah's *Matericon*[29] and in the early thirteenth-century English manuscript, *The Ancrene Riwle*.[30]

Although several of the sayings, or *apophthegmata*, coalesce effectively into teaching discourses on a single theme,[31] the voice and content of most of the teachings in the *Vita* nevertheless clearly show that it was probably never intended to be received or read straight through as a whole, but rather to function as a compendium of remembered teachings from a beloved teacher. Thus, the compiler is offering the faithful a *vademecum*, a helpful palm-size handbook of Amma Syncletica's spiritual wisdom.

While Syncletica's sayings appear to have been crafted in response to persistent requests from members of her monastic community,[32] behind each one stands an ascetical disciple who strove to attain pure stillness of heart before the presence of the Lord. In many cases, the spiritual struggle described appears to be a personal confession of Syncletica's own progress toward a deeper love of Christ and the divine fire of God. Seen in this way, the sayings become textual evidence of the much-beloved desert elder wrestling with her own vivid images of temptation in the desert

---

[28] Schaffer, *Life & Regimen: Part Two: Study of the Life*, p. 31.

[29] *Matericon: Instructions of Abba Isaiah to the Honorable Nun Theodora* (Safford, AZ: St. Paisius Serbian Orthodox Monastery, 2001), for an English translation.

[30] From the Author's Introduction to the Rule: "Were not Paul, the first hermit, Antony and Arsenius, Macharius and the others, religious of the Order of St. James? And SS. Sarah and Syncletica and many other similar people, both men and women, with their coarse sleeping mats, and their harsh hair shirts, were not they of a good order?" *The Ancrene Riwle*; from the corpus MS: Ancrene Wisse, M.B. Salu, ed. (London: Burns & Oates, 1955), p. 5.

[31] These include her cautionary Niptic teaching (VS 40-48), as well as her teaching on Chastity (VS 22-29), on Humility versus Pride (VS 49-60), and two sections addressing Poverty (VS 30-39, VS 71-79).

[32] Indeed, her followers found her spiritual teachings to be "chalices of wisdom" (*sophias krateron*). (SV 30).

and purifying her soul by striving to attain humility, poverty, and
constant prayer. This is in keeping with Thomas Merton, who
characterized the spiritual path of the fourth-century desert solitary, like Syncletica, as one striving to surrender completely to
"the inner, hidden reality of a self that is transcendent, mysteri-
ous, half-known, and lost in Christ."[33]

The unique and remarkable woman revealed in these texts
offers original and discerning wisdom illuminating her "great ascesis,"[34] and her striving toward God. In this, her teaching has
been described as a rare pearl (*margerite*) veiled in iridescent lay-
ers of mystical meaning.[35] Syncletica stands as an exemplar of the
fourth-century Egyptian ascetical movement—an *amma* among
the desert *abbas*—women who were, as Wallis Budge observed,
"as well able to live the stern life of the solitary as any man."[36]
Her ascetic and mystical journey to the heights,[37] revealed in her
collected sayings, stands on the cusp of the historical transformation from solitary hermit to monastic community.

---

[33] Thomas Merton, *The Wisdom of the Desert: Sayings from the Desert Fathers of the Fourth Century* (Bardstown, KY: The Abbey of Gethsemane,
Inc, 1960), p. 7.

[34] Syncletica declares that the Great Askesis is: "to remain faithful, even
in great illness, ever chanting hymns of gratitude to the Almighty." (SV
99/AP 8)

[35] See VS 1.

[36] E.A. Wallis Budge, trans., *Paradise of the Fathers* (London: Chatto &
Windus, 1970), I, p. lxv.

[37] See VS 13.

CHAPTER II.3
ST. MACRINA: TEACHING GREGORY OF NYSSA ON THE PROGRESS OF THE SOUL

There is no other way to go up to God but by
constantly looking upwards (hupsothenai)
and having an unceasing desire
for sublime (hupselon) things...[1]

As we continue to examine the theological contributions of Early Christian women, it is fascinating to note that Gregory of Nyssa, one of the great masters of Cappadocian theology, addresses most probingly questions of the nature of the human soul in two documents focusing on his elder sister, Macrina, who he claims "raised herself by philosophy to the highest summit of human virtue (*tes anthropines aretes*)."[2] In her biography, which he provided in *The Life of Macrina*,[3] and especially in *On the Soul and Resurrection*,[4] it

---

[1] Gregory of Nyssa, Hom. 5 (GNOVII/2, 124.3, English trans., Norris).

[2] VSM 1.5, GNO 371.20-21.

[3] *Vita Sanctae Macrinae*, Virginia Woods Calahan, ed., in *Ascetica*, VIII,1, *Gregorii Nysseni Opera*, Werner Jaeger, gen. ed. (Leiden: Brill, 1958-1996); English translation is that of Anna M. Silvas, *Macrina the Younger, Philosopher of God* (Turnhout, Belgium: Brepols Publishers, 2008); hereafter cited as VSM with chapter and verse, and if appropriate, GNO with column and verse.

[4] *S. Gregorii Episcopi Nysseni de Anima et Resurrectione cum Sorore Sua Macrina Dialogus*, J. G. Krabinger, ed. (Leipzig: Gustav Wittig, 1837); English translation is that of Anna M. Silvas, *Macrina the Younger, Philosopher of*

was a poignant and lasting gesture of love for her that Gregory crafted a dialogue in Macrina's memory which has allowed readers down through the ages to study the manner in which she theologically taught him and others in the family.

Hailed by Jaroslav Pelikan as "the fourth Cappadocian," Macrina is remembered as both an early practitioner of Christian monasticism on her family's Cappadocian estates, and also as Gregory's "sister and teacher (*he adelphe kai didaskalos*)."[5] Furthermore: "not only was she a Christian role model by her profound and ascetic spirituality, but at the death of their parents she became the educator of the entire family, and that in both Christianity and Classical culture."[6]

The progress of Gregory's life suggests that grief and introspection brought him to a fresh acknowledgement of his sister as a sentinel spiritual influence in his life, at a time when he felt compelled to reappraise his own spirituality.[7] Indeed, he found himself unfortunately navigating the death of his celebrated brother, Basil the Great; and soon after, he was called to the deathbed of Macrina.

After his brother's untimely death, Gregory felt driven to complete much of his theological work; for when Basil first became Bishop of Caesarea, he had commissioned his younger brother to write *On Virginity* about the ascetical life. So, it is likely

---

God (Turnhout, Belgium: Brepols Publishers, 2008); hereafter cited as An Res with chapter and speech number, and if appropriate, Kr. with Krabinger page number.

[5] An Res, Intro 1, Kr. 2.

[6] Jaroslav Pelikan, *Christianity and Classical Culture: The Metamorphosis of Natural Theology in the Christian Encounter with Hellenism* (New Haven, CT: Yale University Press, 1995), p. 8.

[7] In fact, Rowan Williams considers Gregory of Nyssa's examination of Theological Anthropology to be "one of the more substantially original clusters of ideas in patristic theology." See Williams, "Macrina's Deathbed Revisited: Gregory of Nyssa on Mind and Passion," in *Christian Faith and Greek Philosophy in Late Antiquity: Essays in Tribute to George Christopher Stead* (Leiden: E.J. Brill, 1993), p. 227.

that Gregory had previously visited to seek his sister's advice from her practical experience with it.[8]

On the Soul and Resurrection demonstrates that Gregory was led at this time to see in Macrina an image of embodied virtue and to reflect deeply upon her teaching. He crafted a deathbed discourse explaining his interpretation of her theology, even as the speculation of his own theological thought was maturing toward mystical theology.

Among Gregory's most original concepts was his awareness of the restless striving forward toward perfection evident in virtuous souls, what he calls *epektasis*. This term is supported by scriptural warrant in Phil. 3:13-14, where the participle *epekteinomenos*, meaning "stretching out," expresses "his whole picture of the way of perfection as an unending ascent from lower to higher things," as Richard Norris explains it. "Since God is the Good, and since there is no limit to God's goodness, one's desire for the Good will therefore stretch out beyond all possible limits."[9]

On balance, Macrina's life-long spiritual transformation, as Gregory describes it, can be seen as an example par excellence of this endless stretching forward—*epektasis*—toward higher spiritual ground. By her gradual yet ceaseless steps forward in virtue, she came to embody for her grieving brother the angelic life, so that he envisioned his sister's story as a veritable "enactment of his theology."[10]

When Macrina was still of tender age, the man chosen by her father for her betrothal died, and her resolve to remain chaste is remembered as her entry-point into a life of asceticism for the sake of Christ; even to the point of considering herself a widow. This was, after all, "the one state of an unattached woman accorded dignity in pagan Graeco-Roman culture."[11] The establishment of this

---

[8] Silvas, *Macrina the Younger,* p. 87.

[9] Gregory of Nyssa, *Homilies on the Song of Songs*, Richard A. Norris, trans. (Atlanta: Society of Biblical Literature, 2012), p. xxxiv.

[10] Raymond Van Dam, *Families and Friends in Late Roman Cappadocia* (Philadelphia: University of Pennsylvania, 2003), p. 111.

[11] Anna M. Silvas, *Gregory of Nyssa: The Letters* (Leiden: Brill, 2007), p. 5. See VSM 6.

commitment transformed her personal life, and then gradually transformed the life of her entire nuclear family into one of the earliest examples of residential monasticism, one which eventually encompassed both men and women throughout the region from all social classes.[12]

Family crisis initiated further monastic development when the death of her father propelled Macrina to function as spiritual mother to her own mother and siblings, and finally for the entire household. In fact, with Macrina's life-long pursuit of saintly asceticism, every relationship within her family contributed to her progress: she convinced her father to allow her to remain virgin; step by step, she led her mother compassionately through her widow-grief toward the spiritual life.

Even with her gifted brother, Basil, Macrina "took him in hand, and drew him with such speed towards the goal of philosophy (*pros ton tes philosophias skopon*) that he withdrew from the worldly show...through perfect renunciation."[13] Finally, after the tragic fatal accident of her brother, Naucratius, she emerged as the maternal authority and spiritual leader for the entire household as it turned to live in spiritual asceticism.

"Macrina was for us a teacher of how to live, a mother in place of our mother...she was for us a strong tower and a

---

[12] VSM 6.8-10. "Macrina, from the 'virgin daughter' she once was, is transformed progressively into a 'virgin widow,' then a 'virgin mother,' and finally into what Gregory calls a 'manly virgin.'" So that finally for her youngest brother, Peter, "she was all for the child: father, teacher, pedagogue, mother, counsellor of all which is good (*pater, didaskalos, paidgogos, mater, agathou pantos sumboulos*)." Susanna Elm, *'Virgins of God:' The Making of Asceticism in Late Antiquity* (Oxford: Clarendon Press, 1996), p. 91.

[13] VSM 8.3, GNO 377.15. Note that "philosophy (*philosophia*)" as it is cited in Gregory's writing was at a threshold of fluid change in meaning: since during the second and third centuries, it signified the explanation of the Christian way of life and theological belief to a predominantly Greaco-Roman world; but in the fourth and fifth centuries came to mean the Christian ascetical life, including the early development of monasticism. Gregory uses the term over a dozen times in the VSM to describe Macrina's theological work and lifestyle of virtue.

shield..."[14] Here, among his earlier writings and likely composed within a year of Macrina's death, this "brief but intense cameo of Gregory's sister in his Letter 19:6-10, proved to be a foreshadowing and a promise of both the *Life of Macrina* and *On the Soul and Resurrection*,"[15] since it is the earliest documentation surviving of Macrina's existence, her way of life, and her significance for the theological development of her many celebrated Cappadocian siblings. In the *Life of Macrina*, Gregory "merges his sister's life with a vibrant theology of martyrdom, virtue, intercession, miracles, and beneficence."[16]

Gregory describes the extensive use of Scripture featured in the prayer life Macrina modeled for the family, including the entire Psalter, day and night, "since she recited each part of the Psalmody at its own proper time (*kairos idiois ekaston merostes Psalmodias*); when she went to bed or rose from it for prayers, she kept up the Psalmody wherever she went."[17] Ascetic life at Annisa was "not occupied with the pursuits of this life, but solely with meditation on divine things (*ton Theion melete*), unceasing prayer (*to tes proseuches adialeipton*), and uninterrupted hymnody (*kai he apaustos hymnodia*)."[18]

As the years went by, and those around her suffered from each death in the family, Macrina "continued firm, like an unconquerable athlete (*athletes akatagonistos*)."[19] After a long life of monastic leadership within her family and far beyond as her monastic community developed, Gregory's "providential participation in her dying hours"[20] made a lasting imprint on his heart—and on Cappadocian theological literature as well.

As Gregory received the alarming news that she lay dying when he was yet a ten-days' journey from his family's country

---

[14] Gregory of Nyssa, Letter 19:6-10, Silvas, trans., *Macrina the Younger*, p. 87.

[15] Silvas, *Macrina the Younger*, p. 83.

[16] Vasiliki M. Limberis, *Architects of Piety: The Cappadocian Fathers and the Cult of the Martyrs* (Oxford: Oxford University Press, 2001), p. 150.

[17] VSM 4.3-4, GNO 373.23.

[18] VSM 13.5, GNO 382.15-16.

[19] VSM 16.5, GNO 386.20.

[20] Silvas, *Macrina the Younger*, p. 83.

estate at Annisa, he reported the wrenching frustration of racing to be at her bedside: "It was the same as a traveler at noon whose body is exhausted from the sun. He runs to a spring, but alas, before he has touched the water, before he has cooled his tongue, all at once the stream dries up before his eyes and he finds the water turned to dust. So it was with me: I saw her whom I so longed to see, who was for me in place of a mother and a teacher and every good, but before I could satisfy my longing, on the third day I buried her and returned on my way."[21] As he reflected on his beloved sister at the threshold of her death, Gregory regarded her as nothing less than a luminous example of God's *theosis* of humanity, made possible by the divine Creator's experiencing human life in Jesus Christ in order to save His creation.

The middle sibling of the family, Basil the Great, Macrina's eldest younger brother, Gregory's older brother, left no such memorial of his sister, nor did he ever acknowledge Macrina's influence on his faith and his devotion to monastic asceticism. While this creates a startling silence in Early Christian literature, reasons for it can be discerned. First of all, several of Basil's texts undoubtedly refer to Macrina implicitly, especially those that describe the ideal monastic community and those that praise female virginity and women in the ascetic life. As an example: "The female too joins the campaign at Christ's side, being enrolled in the campaign thanks to her virility of soul, rejected in no way for weakness of body. Many women have excelled not one whit less than men. Indeed, some have proved themselves even more outstanding. Among their number are those who fill the choir of virgins."[22]

Furthermore, after years of significant influence by an earlier Christian ascetic leader and frequent family visitor, Eustathius of Sebasteia, Basil found his growing Homoiousian theological stance so heretical to his own Nicene Orthodoxy, and to the bishops under his leadership, that he turned away from him and completely deleted any mention of him from his family story. Because Macrina continued to maintain an association with Eustathius, she may have paid the price of future invisibility in Basil's

---

[21] Gregory, Letter 19.10, Silva, *Macrina the Younger,* pp. 88-89.
[22] Basil the Great, *Praevia Institutio Ascetica*, PG 31.621, Silvas, trans.

writing. Yet, "Macrina's trajectory as a virgin ascetic, a teacher, and a spiritual mother pre-empted, inspired and illustrated the maturation of Basil's own cenobitic teaching. She was the mother and preceptress of that monasticism that has come down under Basil's name."[23]

Gregory of Nyssa's writing, by which we have come to know Macrina, was influenced by the Classical tradition in which he was educated, and used its traditional Platonic trajectory as the foundation for his original theological thought. Casting her as a "Christian Phaedo," Gregory describes Macrina assuming a Socratic role in teaching him about immortality. He deployed this method to the point of allowing himself, in the crafting of the text, to ask confused questions, and even endearingly resist comprehending her arguments for the sake of didactic argument.

In their surprisingly lively teaching exchange, his sister becomes for Gregory a role model and archetype of redeemed humanity, her mystical growth constantly stretching forward (*epektasis*) in sanctity. Her life is shown in his writing demonstrating for Gregory how mankind strives for union with God through a life of prayer and ascetical discipline, and providing an ideal image of the soul's perpetual progress toward the limitlessness of God's goodness.

The concept of *epektasis* is worked out in Gregory's earlier writings, including *On the Making of Man* and *The Life of Moses*. Because the nature of the creature is limited, but the nature of the Creator is limitless, "the soul rises ever higher, and will always make its flight ever higher, by its desire of the heavenly things, straining ahead for what is still to come, as the Apostle says...Activity directed toward virtue causes its capacity to grow through exertion; this kind of activity does not slacken its intensity by the effort, but increases it."[24]

So it is with Macrina: like Moses, with his "great and lofty understanding," Macrina, too: "ever running the course of virtue, never ceased straining toward those things that are still to

---

[23] Silvas, *Macrina the Younger*, p. 48.

[24] Gregory of Nyssa, *The Life of Moses*, Abraham J. Malherbe, Everett Ferguson, trans. (San Francisco: HarperCollins, 2006) II 225-226, p. 113.

come."[25] Thus, if a Christian life like Macrina's can be seen as a journey toward God, then "it is a journey into infinity," as Rowan Williams explains, "not an abstract 'absoluteness,' but an infinity of what Gregory simply calls 'goodness,' an infinite resource of mercy, help and delight. And because of its limitless nature, this journey is always marked by desire, by hope and longing."[26]

Throughout *On the Soul and Resurrection*, Gregory's dialogue is clearly modeled on the Phaedo; yet, Gregory's message reflects distinctly the memory of the voice of his sister. While *epektasis* is not specifically cited, the text illustrates well how Macrina's life can be seen modeling the key facets of the concept. For example, in her long discourse concerning the soul's step-by-step progress toward the divine, Macrina cites Heb. 11:1 to explain that, "faith is the upholding of things hoped for (*elpidzomenon*); love, therefore, is the foremost of all the accomplishments of virtue...love alone somehow preserves within itself the character of the divine blessedness (*tes Theias makariotetos*). The divine life will always be activated through love (*Aei he Theia zoe di' agapes energethese-tai*), and knows no limit to the activity of love."[27]

Note John McGuckin's characterization of Gregory's "complex understanding of the endless 'stretching-out'...of the blessed soul (*epektasis*), alongside the endlessly fathomless being of God, in whose participation it finds itself rendered, though creaturely, in a truly authentic 'illimitability.'"[28] Gregory's metaphysical optimism radiates through his conversation with his sister, as he observes that "we are led to God, being drawn up as by a kind of a hoisting rope (*pros ton anelkomenoi*) from below towards him;" to

---

[25] Gregory of Nyssa, *The Life of Moses*, Prologue 5, p. 29.

[26] Rowan Williams, *The Wound of Knowledge: Christian Spirituality from the New Testament to St. John of the Cross*, revised edition (Boston: Cowley Publications, 2003), p. 65.

[27] An Res 6.31-32, Kr. 90.

[28] John McGuckin, "The Strategic Adaptation of Deification in the Cappadocians," in *Partakers of the Divine Nature: The History and Development of Deification in the Christian Traditions*, Michael J. Christensen, Jeffery A. Wittung, eds (Grand Rapids, MI: Baker Academic, 2008), pp. 110, 114.

which Macrina agrees, "and Hope initiates the forward movement (*to proso kineseos*)."[29]

"I think the Lord teaches us this," Macrina explains, "that especially we who are alive in the flesh must, as far as we can, by a life of virtue (*dia tes areten zoes*), separate and free ourselves somehow from its inclination; so that after death we do not need yet another death (*me palin allou thanatou deometha*) to cleanse us from the residue of this fleshly glue."[30] For as Gregory confirms: "Such is the participation in the divine good (*tou Theiou agathou*): it renders one in whom it comes about greater and more capacious, since it allows the recipient an addition of power and magnitude (*eis dunameos kai megethous*), so that the one being nourished always increases and never ceases to increase."[31]

Macrina provides a teaching analogy which illustrates this progressive expansion of the soul: "Just as in the sprouting of wheat seeds (*to stermati sitos*), the growth toward maturity advances little by little (*aligon he auksesis*); so in the same way in the constitution of the human, the power of the soul reveals itself (*he tes psyches diaphainetai dunamis*), somewhat like the fruit that appears on a plant that has been growing for a while, in a steady progress along with the shooting up of that plant."[32]

Although, in the last days of her life, Macrina no longer appears to Gregory as specifically a woman,[33] this is further evidence of the perpetual progress of her soul toward the divine life modeled on Christ; yet her courage in grief, literally her "manliness (*andreia*),"[34] is not to be construed as gender fluidity; rather, she had been ascending via life-long steps of virtuous discipline toward an "angelic and heavenly life"[35] which transcends gender.

---

[29] An Res 6.10-31, Kr. 82-90.

[30] An Res 6.4, Kr. 80. Here Silvas offers the key to Gregory's mystical theology of *epektasis*: "Perfect spiritual attainment for the human being therefore consists in never finally attaining but always reaching out for the God who is always greater." See Silvas, *Macrina the Younger*, p. 212.

[31] An Res 7.25, Kr. 100.

[32] An Res 9.18, Kr. 122.

[33] VSM 1.3.

[34] VSM 12.5, GNO 381.11.

[35] VSM 18.1.

While there are commentary interpretations to the contrary,[36] Boersma warns that imagining Gregory's writing as postmodern gender fluidity artificially presses the text "through a contemporary grid that does not do justice to the fourth-century social context of Gregory and Macrina. Nyssen is simply not interested in questions of immanent gender reversal."[37]

Rather, the *Life of Macrina* can be seen as "a mystagogical biography that depicts for us Macrina's progress as a virgin mystic toward the angelic life."[38] In fact, for Gregory, "a kind of mystic procession was set in train."[39] Finally, in her closing prayer, Macrina announces her belief that the cosmic battle has been won through the Cross of Jesus Christ, who "opened up for us the way to Resurrection."[40]

On the one hand, we need not take the Cappadocian brother and sister's quoted dialogue at face value as verbatim; yet, the integrity of Gregory's theology invites the reader to consider the essence of Macrina's sanctity and monastic achievement as historically accurate. While Gregory's writing reflects ideals of holiness from his own cultural and spiritual environment, nevertheless both *The Life of Macrina* and *On the Soul and Resurrection* make significant contributions to our knowledge about the development of Christian Asceticism. Furthermore, although our glimpse of Macrina and other Early Christian women is limited by male authorship, we do benefit from the preservation of her memory and voice by her brother quoting his experience of her teaching.

Having experienced breast cancer and prayed for spiritual healing, Macrina was said to have worn around her neck a relic

---

[36] See, for example, Virginia Burrus, "Is Macrina a Woman?: Gregory of Nyssa's *Dialogue on the Soul and Resurrection*," in *The Blackwell Companion to Postmodern Theology*, Graham Ward, ed. (Oxford: Blackwell, 2005), pp. 249-264; and Elizabeth A. Clark, "Holy Women, Holy Words: Early Christian Women, Social History, and the 'Linguistic Turn,'" *Journal of Early Christian Studies* 6 (1998), pp. 424-426.

[37] Hans Boersma, *Embodiment and Virtue in Gregory of Nyssa: An Anagogical Approach* (Oxford: Oxford University Press, 2013), p. 12.

[38] Boersma, *Embodiment and Virtue*, p. 112.

[39] VSM 36.3.

[40] VSM 26.7.

of the True Cross—the *Lignum Crucis*—originally received by Melania the Elder from the Bishop of Jerusalem;[41] yet, as her last days on earth shared with her brother demonstrate, saint and relic can tend to merge in collective memory. Indeed, Gregory reports that in a vision on the road to Annisa, he saw himself carrying saints' relics of a dazzling brilliance and came to interpret them as a precursor of the day Macrina died. Thus, "the resurrected body is both the ascetic who becomes a relic while still alive and the relic that continues after death the changelessness acquired through asceticism."[42]

Finally, Macrina becomes for Gregory and for us "a most unusual figure in patristic writings—as a woman sage who teaches and evangelizes."[43] While, as with most Early Christian women, Macrina is known mostly for the celebrated men she is associated with influencing, it is encouraging that Macrina is beginning to be recognized and acknowledged as the "fourth Cappadocian," on her own merit.

---

[41] See Linda Coon, *Sacred Fictions: Holy Women and Hagiography in Late Antiquity* (Philadelphia: University of Pennsylvania Press, 1997), p. 50.

[42] "The body of Macrina, miraculously healed and made immortal and yet marked by its own particular experience—seems to be what Gregory has in mind when he writes of Resurrection as the reassemblage of the 'identical atoms' we had on earth, 'in the same order as we had before' and yet insists that 'there must be change.'" Caroline Walker Bynam, *The Resurrection of the Body in Western Christianity, 200-1336* (New York: Columbia University Press, 1995), p. 86.

[43] Patricia Wilson-Kastner, "Macrina: Virgin and Teacher," *Andrews University Seminary Studies* 17 (1979), p. 106.

CHAPTER II.4
THE DEACONESS OLYMPIAS: SOULMATE OF ST. JOHN CHRYSOSTOM

The eye of your soul is clean...and by means
of these divine words it looks without hindrance
toward the undefiled Beauty.[1]

During John Chrysostom's earliest days coming to serve as Bishop of Constantinople at the close of the fourth century, he is said to have encountered the Deaconess Olympias; for she was a well-known figure, the frail, aristocratic heiress who "would not budge from the church."[2] As a widow who devoted her life to prayer,

---

[1] Gregory of Nyssa, *Homilies on the Song of Songs*, Prologue10-12, Richard A. Norris, Jr., trans. (Atlanta: Society of Biblical Literature, 2012), p. 3.

[2] Palladius, Bishop of Aspuna, *Dialogue on the Life of St. John Chrysostom*, Robert T. Meyer, trans.; Ancient Christian Writers, no. 45 (New York: Newman Press, 1985), p. 66. Other principle sources for Olympias are: John Chrysostom, *Lettres à Olympias*, Introduction et traduction de Anne-Marie Malingrey; Sources Chrétiennes, v. 13 (Paris: Éditions du CERF, 1947); Gregory of Nyssa: *Homilies on the Song of Songs,* Richard A. Norris, Jr., trans. (Atlanta: Society of Biblical Literature, 2012); Sozomen, "The Ecclesiastical History," Volume IX, The Nicene and Post-Nicene Fathers of the Christian Church, Series II, Philip Schaff, ed. (Edinburgh: T & T Clark, 1997), especially Book VIII; Palladius, Bishop of Aspuna, *The Lausiac History*, Robert T. Meyer, trans. (New York: Paulist Press, 1964), especially No. 56.

"zealous for the road to heaven,"[3] Olympias served as founder and *hegumen* for the monastic foundation she developed on her estate adjacent to the church. Her unparalleled philanthropy and ascetical practice had caused the previous Patriarch to ordain her a Deaconess. More letters from John Chrysostom to Olympias survive than to any other single person. While her share of the correspondence is lost, Gregory of Nyssa is known to have praised "the pure eye of her soul" (*sou kathareuein ton tes psyches ophthalmos*) in his dedicatory preface to her.[4]

Patriarchs corresponded with her, complimented her and rebuked her, even as they enjoyed her generous donations. In the highly patriarchal society of her time, Olympias managed to network and operate among the Bishops of the day, to the extent that *eurgesia* and *megalopsychia* were said to run through her veins like any élite Greek man trained in the finest *paideia*.[5] Furthermore, John Chrysostom's ample and lively correspondence with Olympias, as well as his acknowledgement of her letters, are one indication that the stark lack of extant manuscript evidence authored by Early Christian women is not necessarily a sure measure of their lack of writing productivity.

Although much less is known about Olympias than about several of her celebrated male ecclesiastical associates, a picture of her asceticism and the depth of her Christian relationships can

---

[3] Elizabeth A. Clark, "The Life of Olympias," in *Jerome, Chrysostom, and Friends: Essays and Translations* (New York: Edwin Mellen Press, 1979), p. 128. While the Vita (hereafter noted as Vita with section and page number) is hagiographic in character, the text provides a window into developing fifth-century monasticism, offering examples of spiritual virtues held up as role models for ascetical practice. It has been suggested that the text was written by a writer contemporary to the events who knew Olympias and her community personally—perhaps Heraclides, who was Bishop of Nyssa around 440 AD. Vita, Introduction, p. 108.

[4] Gregory of Nyssa, *Homilies on the Song of Songs*. Prologue 2.10-12.

[5] *Eurgesia* means the urge to do good things; *megalopsychia* is high-minded zest for open-handed gestures of largesse, both attributes considered evidence of a proper Greek philosophical education. Peter Brown, *Power and Persuasion in Late Antiquity: Towards a Christian Empire*; The Curti Lectures (1988) (Madison, WI: University of Wisconsin Press, 1992), p. 83.

be knitted together from the threads of evidence that do survive. An examination of the texts which cite Olympias also offers a useful view into the ascetical ideals operating in the early centuries of the development of monastic practice.

The ascetical life was a burgeoning phenomenon in the Constantinople of Olympias's day, especially in aristocratic circles. A strong showing of élite women dedicated to a Christian life of virginity focused on the prayer of the Church was a feature of the ecclesiastical landscape. During the fourth century, the search for the perfect, philosophical life (*philosophos bios*) came to mean in the Christian sense, "nothing less than a life devoted to the fulfillment of the highest Christian ideals, a life of virginity."[6] By the end of the century, crowds of chanting virgins as a component of Cathedral processions were "an integral part of a Bishop's show of power."[7] Additionally, church widows were a strategic philanthropic resource which no Bishop could ignore. An aristocratic heiress such as Olympias could transform an impoverished urban church into a powerfully successful financial enterprise.

Olympias was born of senatorial Byzantine lineage, probably in 368 C.E.[8] She was the granddaughter of Abblavios, praetorian prefect of Constantine,[9] and the daughter of Count Seleucus, a member of the Order of Imperial Companions to the Emperor.[10] However, even with the advantages of august parentage and several relatives close to the imperial throne, Olympias was orphaned at an early age and her education was relegated to a kinswoman of Gregory of Nazianzus, Theodosia, one of the well-known "cultivated ladies of her time."[11]

---

[6] Susanna Elm, '*Virgins of God:*' *The Making of Asceticism in Late Antiquity* (Oxford: Clarendon Press, 1994), p. 44.

[7] Peter Brown, *The Body and Society*, p. 260. This was later attested by Augustine in Letter 23.3, PL 33:96.

[8] Although a birth date for Olympias of 361 can be calculated according to Libanius (*EP.* 672), more likely a birth date in 368 places her age at eighteen when wedded to Nebridios. Robert Meyer, in his Notes for *Palladius: The Lausaic History*, p. 212.

[9] See Palladius, *The Lausaic History* 56.137.

[10] Vita, notes, p. 143.

[11] Elm, *Virgins of God*, p. 179.

During this formative period, Olympias and her family were in fact well acquainted with Gregory[12] and were instrumental in bringing him to the episcopal throne.[13] Olympias also came in contact with Gregory's Cappadocian companion, Gregory of Nyssa, when he was consecrated Bishop. Gregory Nyssen participated in the Council of Constantinople in 381 and is thought to have initially encountered the pious Olympias then.[14] As a cosmopolitan hostess in the Byzantine capital and a generous benefactor, she had the opportunity to associate with those holding power in the Church "to a greater extent than she could have had in any other role open to a woman."[15]

In 384 or 385, Olympias was given in marriage with her massive estates to Emperor Theodosius's nephew, Nebridios, as a second wife, younger than his son by his first marriage, likely as an imperial perquisite in connection with his appointment in 386 as Prefect of Constantinople.[16] This nuptial arrangement was short-lived, however; when her husband died after only twenty months of marriage, "her later admirers were convinced that she had remained a virgin."[17]

---

[12] Part of the understanding of Olympias's life and relations is generally based on a poem of Gregory Nazianzun written on the occasion of the wedding of Olympias. The thread of her story which has come to be substantiated by this poem, has been challenged recently by current scholars. See Mary Whitby, "'Sugaring the Pill:' Gregory of Nazianzus' Advice to Olympias (Carm. 2.2.6)," *Ramus: Critical Studies in Greek and Roman Literature*, 37:1/2 (2008), pp. 79-98; Neil McLynn, "The Other Olympias: Gregory Nazianzus and the Family of Vitalianus," in *Christian Politics and Religious Culture in Late Antiquity* (Farnham: Ashgate Publishing Ltd., 2009), pp. 227-246.

[13] John Anthony McGuckin, *The Westminster Handbook to Patristic Theology* (Louisville: Westminster John Knox Press, 2004), p. 242.

[14] Gregory of Nyssa: *Homilies*, p. xxi.

[15] Elizabeth A. Clark, "Introduction to The Life of Olympias," in *Jerome, Chrysostom, and Friends: Essays and Translations* (New York: The Edwin Mellen Press, 1979), p. 115.

[16] Clark, "Introduction to The Life of Olympias," p. 110.

[17] Brown, *The Body and Society*, p. 282. See Palladius, *The Lausiac History* 56.137; see also Vita 2.128.

Not surprisingly, the Emperor endeavored to re-align her generous estates into the hands of another of his relatives; but this time she resisted, "leaping like a gazelle over the snare of a second marriage."[18] Instead, "seized with Christ's flame,"[19] Olympias experienced a call to a religious life of charity and renunciation, using Melania the Elder, "that female man of God,"[20] as her role model, in whose steps she "zealously followed."[21] Olympias is recorded responding to the Emperor's demand that she re-marry in words resonant of the Gospel imperative in Mt. 11:29-30: "If my King had desired me to live with a male, He would not have taken away my first husband...He freed me from subjection to a man, while He laid on me the gentle yoke of chastity."[22] As a celibate widow, she adapted ascetic practices modeled on that of Melania the Elder and the monks who had withdrawn into the Egyptian desert.

In retaliation for resisting the emperor's ambitions, Theodosius sequestered Olympias' vast fortune, which included real estate in Thrace, Galatia, Cappadocia and Bithynia, beside her two palaces in the imperial city. A further stipulation, that she not only cease her pious visits to Church but also stop meeting with

---

[18] Palladius, *Dialogue* 17.114.

[19] John Chrysostom, "Homily XIII on Ephesians 4:17-19," NPNF XIII.115.

[20] Melania the Elder (ca. 342-ca. 410), praised by Palladius as "that female man of God" (*Laus. Hist.* 9.43), was, like Olympias, a prominent heiress; when widowed very young, she sold all she had and traveled to the desert hermitages outside Alexandria, "seeking out all the holy men." (*Laus. Hist.* 46.123) Finally, for nearly thirty years, she led the monastic community she founded in Jerusalem. Her grand-daughter, Melania the Younger (ca. 385-438/9) followed her in the ascetical life as a *hegumen* of her own community in Bethlehem. Both Melania the Elder and Melania the Younger made significant contributions to the development of Christian monastic asceticism in the fourth and fifth centuries.

[21] E.D. Hunt, "Palladius of Helenopolis: A Party and its Supporters in the Church of the Late Fourth Century," *Journal of Theological Studies* 24:2 (1973), p. 477. Hunt has suggested that Olympias may have ventured to the Holy Land on pilgrimage and actually encountered her mentor in asceticism, Melania the Elder.

[22] Palladius, *Dialogue* 17.114.

clerics, serves as intriguing evidence of interactions in which she engaged with the clergy of the Great Church, including the Patriarch Nektarios.[23] Palladius confirms that she "addressed priests reverently and honoured bishops."[24]

Finally, however, the emperor "heard of her ascetical lifestyle,"[25] and relented in his imperial displeasure. He allowed Olympias to manage her own property and philanthropic projects again, giving her leave to abandon the demands of her life solely "in preparation for courtly marriage."[26] In fact, not long after that, Patriarch Nektarios, "notwithstanding her youth," had Olympias ordained a Deaconess at only thirty years of age,[27] when it was not customary to ordain Deaconesses until they were sixty.[28] In this, she enjoyed something of the seemingly ambiguous status attained by Macrina, the elder sister of Gregory of Nyssa, of being both widow and virgin. In refusing to marry, widows like Olympias were adapting the one-spouse-only principle of *univira*, "giving it an additional mystical resonance."[29]

On the terrestrial plain, the philanthropic donations of Olympias to the Church were inestimable; among them, she contributed "10,000 pounds of gold, 100,000 pounds of silver, properties scattered all over western Asia Minor, and her family's share of the civic corn dole."[30] It is no surprise why Byzantine bishops courted her; for she "provided their crucial financial base."[31] Palladius even reports that John Chrysostom's future adversary,

---

[23] See Palladius, *Dialogue* 17.114.

[24] Palladius, *The Lausiac History* 56.137.

[25] Palladius, *Dialogue* 17.114.

[26] Mark W. Elliott, *The Song of Songs and Christology in the Early Church: 381-451* (Tübingen: Mohr Siebeck, 2000), p. 24.

[27] Sozomen, *The Ecclesiastical History* 8.9.

[28] Clark, "Introduction to the Life of Olympias," notes, p. 123.

[29] Gillian Cloke, *'This Female Man of God:' Women and Spiritual Power in the Patristic Age, AD 350-450* (London; New York: Routledge, 1995).

[30] Brown, *The Body and Society*, p. 284, Vita 5.130, 7.132.

[31] Nicola Denzey, *The Bone Gatherers: The Lost Worlds of Early Christian Women* (Boston: Beacon Press, 2007), p. 191.

Patriarch Theophilus of Alexandria, "kissed her knees" in polite flattery courting Olympias for church funding.[32]

By the time Nektarios died in 397, Olympias had not only made extensive gifts to the Church, but had also gathered her relatives, household, and a growing number of her followers into a developing ascetical community; her Vita reports that she built a monastery to the south of the Great Church with a pathway leading directly into the narthex. In fact, a neighborhood in Constantinople is even attested from the eighth century as "of the Deaconess," and it is likely that the identity of this area of the city had threads of origin stretching back to Olympias's palace near the Great Church which she transformed to house her growing spiritual community.[33]

John Chrysostom, the new Bishop of Constantinople, hijacked to the capital in haste from his preaching post in Antioch, soon learned of the monastic heiress whose generosity was said to have "maintained" his episcopal predecessor, Nektarios, "to such an extent that he took her advice on ecclesiastical policy as well," as Palladius maintained.[34] Even apart from financial considerations, however, there can be no doubt that John Chrysostom found in Olympias the soul-mate of a lifetime. The friendship he developed with her over time was based on "shared and wholehearted devotion to the service of Christ."[35] Elements in Bishop John's background undoubtedly worked in favor of a good relationship with Olympias, starting with the strong support of his mother. In addition, he admired and respected the ascetical monks he encountered at Antioch, and as a young man had come to join their life in the mountain wilderness outside the city, as soon as his mother died.

---

[32] Clark, "Introduction to the Life of Olympias," p. 115.

[33] Livia Neureiter, "Health and Healing as Recurrent Topics in John Chrysostom's Correspondence with Olympias," *Studia Patristica* XLVII (2010), p. 275. See also Vita 6.131.

[34] Palladius, *Dialogue* 17.115.

[35] C.White, *Christian Friendship in the Fourth Century* (Cambridge: Cambridge University Press, 1992), p. 85.

Also, among Bishop John's relatives to serve as an example was his aunt, the much-respected Deaconess Sabiniana, who was described as "a venerable woman, on intimate terms with God."[36] And in Olympias herself, he encountered a life situation similar to his pious mother. Both women had refused to consider a second marriage after being widowed at an early age; Anthusa had focused instead entirely on the education of her brilliant son.[37] Thus, John could say to each of them, as he did addressing his Letter to a Young Widow, "Your own soul, having once for all torn yourself away from all worldly interests, will display amongst us a heavenly manner of life."[38]

Let us ask, then, as we did with Macrina in the previous chapter, what practical elements of spiritual *askesis* are indicated when the historian Sozomen describes Olympias as "zealously attached to the exercises of monastic philosophy according to the laws of the Church?"[39]—or when Emperor Theodosius learns of "the intensity of her ascetic discipline?"[40] Thus, it is useful to explore here what actually constituted ascetical practice at this very early stage of monastic development. Although textual evidence is scarce, Palladius describes the depth of Olympias's asceticism in this way:

"She disposed of all her goods, giving them to the needy. She took part in no small contests on the behalf of truth...Those who live at Constantinople number her among the Confessors. She died and traveled on to the Lord in her struggles for God."[41] Another witness, her hagiographic Vita, boasts that she practiced hospitality like Abraham, fought for self-control like Joseph, and suffered patiently like Job, and was martyred like Thecla.[42]

---

[36] A. Lucot, *Textes et Documents* 15 (Paris: Picard, 1912); see Aimé Georges Martimort, *Deaconesses: An Historical Study*, K.D. Whitehead, trans. (San Francisco: Ignatius Press, 1986), p. 121.

[37] See John Chrysostom, *On the Priesthood* I.5, NPNF IX.34.

[38] John Chrysostom, "Letter to a Young Widow," NPNF IX.126.

[39] Sozomen, *The Ecclesiastical History*, NPNF IX.404.

[40] Palladius, *Dialogue* 17.114. See Vita 5.130.

[41] Palladius, *The Lausiac History* 56.137.

[42] See Vita 1.127.

Further on in the Vita, the "holy chorus" of the Olympiad sisters, reflecting the piety of their founder, are praised for their monastic virtues; these include: chastity, sleepless vigils, offering praise, charity, and stillness,[43] all similar to ideals expressed by the sayings of the Desert Fathers (*Apophthegmata Patrum*).[44] As Bishop John reminded her congregation of nuns in one of his letters to Olympias,[45] "Although you were married, you now belong to the band of wise virgins, for you were always mindful of the things of God, through almsgiving and patience in suffering, through self-control in eating and sleeping, and in all other things, but especially through modest simplicity in dress. It is in these things that true virginity lies."[46]

Furthermore, the practice of radically limited bathing,[47] which was admired as an element of ascetical practice for both men and women during this period, while perhaps unappealing to contemplate nowadays, was considered an important component of renouncing the pleasures of the world in order to seek divine truth. As John Chrysostom cautioned about the ascetical life, "There are many young women who are strong enough to observe it; but yet they are not prepared to renounce fine clothes."[48]

As Olympias' religious community grew, it drew more than 250 followers to a life of prayer and charity.[49] Like Macrina's

---

[43] Vita 8.132.

[44] Indeed, John Chrysostom acknowledged that women sometimes "outshone men in spiritual warfare and spiritual athletics," which were two of his favorite images for the ascetical life. Homily XIII on Eph. NPNF XIII.115-116.

[45] Throughout this work, the numbering of John Chrysostom's Letters to Olympias follows the standard critical Malingrey edition with, parenthetically, the Migne *Patrologia Graeca* numbering included. John Chrysostom, *Lettres à Olympias*, Anne-Marie Malingrey, ed.; Sources Chrétiennes, v. 13 (Paris: Éditions du CERF, 1947).

[46] Letter VIII (II), Chrysostomus Baur, trans. in *John Chrysostom and his Time*. v. 2; Constantinople (London; Glasgow: Sands & Co., 1960), p. 375.

[47] Palladius, *Dialogue* 17.115.

[48] Letter VIII (II), Baur, *John Chrysostom and his Time*, v. 2, p. 376.

[49] Vita 6.132.

monastic experiment in the Cappadocian community of Annisa, the Olympiad monastic community embraced the holy life of the desert hermits within the setting of a residence; and a "prestige location and noble profile may have shaped it into a female institution like none other."[50] Yet, the world of women's asceticism in the fourth and fifth centuries was "a zone of exceptional fluidity and free choice."[51]

So, although there was great ascetical piety and desire among these aristocratic Christian women to follow the command of Christ and embark on the monastic life, especially within the residential structure of the family; nevertheless, monasticism was still relatively early in its development and significantly flexible in its style. Therefore, the evidence for the piety of Olympias and her fervor for charitable works—even her zeal for launching and organizing spiritual community—had not yet developed to the stage of a formal structure like that of later monasticism, including the use of its terminology. Nevertheless, Hatlie maintains that the community of the Olympiads was, "likely the first, best organized and most prominent of all these endeavors."[52]

In addition to Olympias, Chrysostom "ordained Deacons of the Holy Church three of her relatives, Elisanthia, Martyria, and Palladia, for the monastery. Thus, by the four Diaconal Offices, the established procedure would have been accomplished by them uninterruptedly."[53] In terms of liturgical monastic practice, this arrangement demonstrates that sufficient resources were provided for the offering of a full complement of Daily Office, even including Psalter chanted without interruption.[54]

---

[50] Peter Hatlie, *The Monks and Monasteries of Constantinople, ca. 350-850* (Cambridge: Cambridge University Press, 2007), p. 98.

[51] In the fourth century, "the organization of the ascetic life of any consecrated woman remained remarkably informal." Brown, *The Body and Society*, p. 265.

[52] See Hatlie, *Monks and Monasteries of Constantinople*, pp. 72-74, especially note 34.

[53] Vita.7, trans. Ilaria Ramelli, in "Theosebia: A Presbyter of the Catholic Church," *Journal of Feminist Studies in Religion* 26:2 (2010), p. 98.

[54] However, it is unlikely that Olympias's ascetical community was a monastery of the *akoimetai* or "sleepless" type, offering perpetual psalm-

In his work as Bishop of Constantinople, John Chrysostom was no prince of diplomacy, however; and although the crowds who stood to hear his sermons sometimes interrupted him with applause, his preaching often rankled his fellow Bishops—and the Empress. Eventually, charges were drawn up against him over several issues, and he was exiled. After a reprieve and a second exile, it is likely that Bishop John died on the road, forced by the Empress to evacuate to the farthest reaches of the empire. Olympias, too, came under persecution, and was accused of causing a fire in the Great Church on the night John departed, and she is thought to have died in exile in Nicomedia, probably around 408.[55]

John Chrysostom expresses profound gratitude for the therapeutic consolation of a lady of "such intelligence and wealth of piety (*eulabeias ploutos kai philosophias hypsos*) that her soul has trampled underfoot the pageantry of daily life."[56] Yet, we still have only evidence of John's letters to Olympias; and of those, only examples from the very last years of their long friendship. The letters do provide, though, clear indications of the female voice responding. The fact that their friendship continued with such intensity after Chrysostom was exiled from Constantinople is "evidence for its strength."[57]

For Olympias receiving his correspondence, as for us today when reading John Chrysostom, "you are walking in a paradise

---

chanting day and night. Walter D. Ray, *Tasting Heaven on Earth: Worship in Sixth-Century Constantinople* (Grand Rapids, Mich.: Eerdmans, 2012), p. 11.

[55] A vision of *perigrinatio* surrounded her choice of burial ground: the Metropolitan of Nicodemia dreamed that she appeared to him saying, "Place my remains in a casket, put it in a boat, let the boat go adrift into the stream, and at the place where the boat stops, disembark onto the ground and place me there." The casket landed at Brochthoi and was translated into the Church of St. Thomas there. Vita 11.135.

[56] Letter VIII(II), Malingrey, p. 141.

[57] C.White, *Christian Friendship in the Fourth Century*, p. 86.

of literature, theology and aesthetics;"[58] for considered together
the Letters to Olympias form an effective handbook of pastoral
care, especially for the healing of despondency and *acedia*.
Church historian Philip Schaff has said of them that they "breathe
a noble Christian spirit in a clear brilliant and persuasive style."[59]
On the one hand, Bishop John encourages Olympias to bear her
sufferings bravely, to be even insensible to them; yet on the other
hand, he vividly describes struggling with his own suffering.

Like any good pastor, he works to diffuse his own stress as
well as hers, maintaining that patient fortitude in the face of dis-
comfort is the "evidence of a robust spirit, rich in the fruit of
courage," and "proof of a most finished philosophy."[60] He even
has the confidence to describe his letters as "a salutary medicine
capable of reviving anyone who was stumbling and conducting
one into a healthy state of serenity."[61]

John Chrysostom's Letters to Olympias are richly crafted
with an elaborate infrastructure of metaphorical images; for example, as here, of maritime storms: "While the sea is raging
around you, and the billows are rising to a crest...and everything
is shrouded in the most profound darkness, you, setting the sails
of patience, float on with great serenity, as if it was noonday, and
calm weather, and a favorable breeze wafting you on...such is the
force of virtue as a rudder."[62] His maritime-rich sayings resonate
with a familiarity of the teachings of the desert mother, Amma
Syncletica. While he sees Christ's Passion reflected in his own suffering and the monumental challenges of the Apostles and early
followers mirrored in his "innumerable stumbling blocks,"[63]

---

[58] Archbishop Demetrios, "What is the Bible? The Patristic Doctrine of
Scripture," Keynote Lecture, 3rd Annual Symposium in Honor of Georges
Florovsky, Princeton Seminary, Feb. 16, 2013.
[59] Philip Schaff, "Prolegomena: The Life and Work of St. John Chrysostom," NPNF IX.15.
[60] Letter XII(VI), NPNF IX.297. He uses the term *philosophia* here in the
sense of Christian theological training and moral discipline.
[61] Letter IX(XIV), NPNF IX.301.
[62] Letter XII(VI), NPNF IX.297.
[63] Letter VII(I), NPNF IX.292.

throughout his correspondence, Bishop John's technique is to boast, nevertheless, in his weakness.

In this, he emulates the Apostle Paul, praying that the power of Christ may dwell in him. In his last heart-breaking letter to her, when Olympias resists rallying in spirit, he even wryly proffers a thorn of cheerfulness into the side of her "tyranny of despondency," adding persuasively, "Are you ignorant of how great a reward, even of sickness, awaits one who has a thankful spirit?"[64]

Ultimately, Bishop John is convinced that cheerful endurance releases sin; "it is the greatest means of purification for those who have sinned."[65] He considers that her whole household of Olympiad Deaconesses now have a "higher place assigned to it in Heaven by reason of the suffering which it endures."[66]

Although both John Chrysostom and Olympias espoused radical asceticism as a component of their faith, his letters to her describe how, even more than the remedies and medical art (*tekne*) he received, it was the affection (*sympatheia*) of their friendship which has often helped him to heal from many of his own physical afflictions;[67] therefore, he lavishes vigorous encouragement on Olympias in his letters,[68] exhorting her to work diligently to overcome the strength of her sadness and suffering. She should faithfully endeavor to replace despondency with joy, poetically rendered in the Greek as replacing *athymia* with *euthymia*.[69]

Before any of the letters of John Chrysostom to Olympias were penned, however, Gregory of Nyssa is said to have crafted his *Homilies on the Song of Songs* as a favor for her. Norris maintains that it was "entirely consonant with the character of Olympias, who was much given to study of the Scriptures, that she

---

[64] Letter XVII(IV), NPNF IX.293.

[65] Letter XVII(IV), NPNF IX.295.

[66] Letter XVII(IV), NPNF IX.296.

[67] Letter IV(XII), Malingrey, p. 98.

[68] See, for example, in Letter VIII(II), Malingrey, p. 116.

[69] Letter VIII (II), Malingrey, p. 141. See Livia Neureiter, "Health and Healing," p. 272.

should request of Gregory an interpretation of the Songs of Songs;" and her commission of Gregory is "best assigned to the year 391, or shortly thereafter, when though still in her twenties, she had emerged as a person of significance in her own right."[70] The introductory covering letter of the commentary "to the great ascetic Olympias,"[71] functions as a sort of *apologia* to Gregory's use of allegorical exegesis, since he observes that the Song of Songs is best understood by Olympias as offering secret wisdom, which when uncovered, provides what Norris calls "a glimpse of God's intolerable beauty."[72]

Gregory Nyssen explains that, by using the rhetorical technique of analogy to unfold its inherent mystery, the Songs of Songs is able to illustrate how "lovers of the transcendent Beauty are to relate themselves to the Divine."[73] For even as Gregory of Nyssa praises her for her chaste life (*semnos bios*) and pure soul (*kathara psyche*), Olympias and her community will encounter in the Song of Songs a wisdom (*sophia*) that stands hidden (*egkekrymmene*).[74]

By enclosing and concealing—even protecting—the spiritual sense,[75] the Song of Songs becomes a "teaching that guides those who pay careful heed to it toward knowledge of the mysteries and toward a pure life."[76] Nevertheless, in choosing such inherently explicit Scripture for her chaste sisters, "Olympias can hardly have been oblivious to the paradoxical character of the situation."[77] Yet, as brides themselves espoused to Christ, it was only natural that Olympias reach out to Gregory of Nyssa to

---

[70] Gregory of Nyssa, *Homilies,* Norris, ed. p. xx-xxi.
[71] "Its 'publication' was doubtless attributable to her desire to have a copy of Gregory's observations." R.A. Norris, "The Soul Takes Flight: Gregory of Nyssa and the Song of Songs," *Anglican Theological Review*, 80:4 (1998), p. 518.
[72] Norris, "The Soul Takes Flight," p. 532.
[73] Gregory of Nyssa, Homily 6.183.
[74] Gregory of Nyssa, *Homilies*, Prologue 2.4,14-15.
[75] Gregory of Nyssa, *Homilies*, Introduction, p. xlvii.
[76] Gregory of Nyssa, *Homilies*, Prologue 5.
[77] Hans Boersma, *Embodiment and Virtue in Gregory of Nyssa: An Anagogical Approach* (Oxford: Oxford University Press, 2013), p. 77.

commission a commentary on the Songs of Songs, so that she and her fellow Deaconesses could more fully contemplate their prayerful engagement with the Songs of Songs.

Thus, it is completely fitting that Gregory of Nyssa would craft a commentary on the Song of Songs meant to draw Olympias, with the other virgins in her community, "like a bride toward an incorporeal and spiritual and undefiled marriage with God."[78] In fact, the opening of Homily 1 appears to address the Olympiad Deaconesses directly: "You, who in accordance with the counsel of Paul, have taken off the old humanity with its deeds and lusts like a filthy garment (Col. 3:9) and have clothed yourselves in purity of light in the lightsome raiment of the Lord..."[79]

In conclusion, although it is not possible to know with certainty, a likely monastic profile can be assembled from the textual sources of the ascetical life the Deaconess Olympias shared with her holy sisters in the religious foundation she established within her Constantinopolitan apartments. As virgins consecrated to the Holy Church, who had given away their wealth in charity and almsgiving to follow Christ, psalm-chanting in the Divine Office and in patriarchal Church processions comprised an important component of their liturgical life. Prayer vigils, Scripture study, fasting, limited bathing, chaste dress and stillness as well aligned their lifestyle to that of Melania the Elder and the hermit monks praying in the desert whom she visited.

Olympias' spiritual community represents a pivotal moment in the development of monasticism so early that later terminology, such as "convent," was not yet used. Nevertheless, her ascetical life and philanthropic works, as attested both by contemporary accounts and in later hagiographic memory, witness to a remarkable chapter in the progress of the practice and faith of the Orthodox Church.

---

[78] Gregory of Nyssa, Homily 1.15.
[79] *Ibid.*

CHAPTER II.5
THE HYMNOGRAPHER KASSIA:
CHANTING THE INCARNATION

*The hymns of the Byzantine Church are
Eastern Christianity's most distinctive
contribution to music and poetry.[1]*

Within the realm of Orthodox Liturgy, as well as Byzantine poetry, very few treble-voiced composers have been recognized as
hymnographers; yet, the ninth-century Abbess Kassia (ca. 810-
865 C.E.) is significant among them.[2] Hailed by one Byzantine
chronicler as "a most reverend nun and most noble lady (*mon-
aches eulabeotates kai sebasmias gynaikos*),"[3] she is considered an
Orthodox saint and is venerated on her feast-day of September 7.
A portrait of her emerges from the scant data which can be assembled from Byzantine sources and her impressive *oeuvre* of extant works. Most of what we know about the hymnographer

---

[1] Gustave Reese, *Music in the Middle Ages: With an Introduction on the Music of Ancient Times* (New York: W. W. Norton & Company, Inc., 1968),
p. 78.
[2] There is a great variety of spellings for the ninth-century hymnographer's name evidenced in the literature; among them: Kassiane, Ei-
kasia, Ikasia, Kasia, Casia. The spelling Kassia is used in this work, following two of the three letters addressed to her from St. Theodore the
Stoudite.
[3] The *Patria* of Constantinople, *Scriptores Originum Constantinopolitanarum*
(Leipzig, 1907), p. 276.

Kassia has been gathered from St. Theodore the Studite's three surviving letters to her and several chroniclers of Byzantine history.[4]

Kassia's writing consists of two *kontakia*, a Canon, and about fifty hymns, several of which are included in the authorized Orthodox Liturgy. She also wrote over 250 secular verses crafted in the form of epigrams and iambic *gnomai*, or wise moral verses, probably used as a catechetical device to model ethical ideals for the nuns in her charge in Constantinople.

Like Byzantine hymnography and Byzantium itself, the collection of Kassia's hymns mirror "its very soul, reflecting at once a joyful expectation of Christ's heavenly kingdom and a sorrow at not being worthy of it."[5] Among the best-known hymns of Kassia is the *sticheron doxastikon*,[6] "Lord, the Woman Fallen into Many Sins," chanted as part of Holy Wednesday Vespers, which is sung on Tuesday evening; and also the *sticheron doxastikon* "On the Birth of Christ," often called "When Augustus Reigned," which is chanted during the Vespers service on the Vigil of the Feast of the Nativity. It glorifies the birth of the divine Savior King, with its text reflecting on the parallel rule of the first Roman Emperor Augustus (27 B.C.E.-14 C.E.) and the reign of Jesus Christ. This chapter explores the life of Kassia, and examines her work through the lens of this Christmas hymn, one in which she

---

[4] St. Theodore the Stoudite, Letters 205, 413, 541, PG 99:903-1669. Some of the earliest Byzantine Chroniclers who mention Kassia are from the tenth to the twelfth centuries, including: Symeon the Logothete (tenth century), *Chronographia* (PG 109:685C); George the Monk (eleventh century), *Chronikon* 4.264 (PG 110:1008B); Leo the Grammarian (tenth-eleventh century), *Chronographia* (PG 108:1046A-B); John Zonaris (twelfth century), *Epitome Historiarum* (Book XIII-XVIII, Bonn: Weber, 1897); and Michael Glykas (twelfth century), *Chronographia* (Bonn: Weber, 1836).

[5] Dimitri Conomos, *Byzantine Hymnology and Byzantine Chant* (Brookline, MA: Hellenic College Press, 1984), p. 1.

[6] In Byzantine music, a *sticheron* is a lengthy verse chanted in various parts of the morning and evening Orthodox Office. The term *doxastikon* applies to a *sticheron* which glorifies or commemorates Jesus Christ or a saint.

lyrically contemplates the very moment when the authority of heaven and earth collide.

As a young woman and throughout her life, Kassia had the good fortunate to be deeply associated with St. Theodore the Stoudite (759-826 C.E.) and his Stoudian monks in Constantinople, during the time when they were working to organize and unify the Orthodox Liturgy. It is they who incorporated Kassia's hymns into their liturgical hymn-books, as they were compiling and refining them. Although we do not possess a *vita* detailing Kassia's life story and musical composition achievements, the Stoudian monks recorded her hymns into the Liurgy during the ninth century.

By including her work in the *Menaion*, the monthly liturgical calendar, and in the *Triodion*, the chants for Lent, a few of Kassia's works became authorized for worship throughout the Byzantine Empire. They have assured her memory unto the generations of faithful Orthodox and are sung in Orthodox services to this day.

Kassia crafted her hymns during the imperial reigns of Theophilus (829-842) and also Michael III (842-867).[7] Her aristocratic background is demonstrated by Abbot Theodore addressing his letters to her as *Kassia Kandidatissa*. In her particular case, this probably indicates that she was the daughter of a prominent military officer with connections to the Byzantine court.[8]

Throughout the formative years of Kassia's life, the Iconoclastic Controversy (726-842), in its second phase during the ninth century, swept through the Byzantine Church and State, galvanizing theologians and patriarchs—even emperors and

---

[7] Spyros Panagopoulos reports that Kassia has been historically suggested as the author of the *Akathist Hymn*, but without continuing support. Spyros Panagopoulos, "Kassia: A Female Hymnographer of the 9th Century," in *Proceedings of the 1st International Conference of ASBMH* (1993), p. 115. See also Tillyard, *Byzantine Music and Hymnography* (Charing Cross: The Faith Press, Ltd., 1923) p. 29.

[8] Although the term could indicate that Kassia was married to a military court official, a more likely hypothesis, especially from the evidence of the bride-show tradition described below, is that, in this case, by using *Kandidatissa* in his correspondence, St. Theodore was indicating an officer's daughter, rather than a wife.

regents—to respond with theological reflection, warfare, and compelling verse. The turmoil and creativity of this political and theological environment marked deeply the character of the young Kassia, even before she took the veil; charging her "to personal courage and strong ideals of Christian piety."[9]

Young Byzantine daughters from aristocratic families were expected to be educationally well-equipped no later than their early teens in order to enhance their value as brides on the marriage market. Kassia's youthful education dovetailed with not only the Iconoclastic storm of theological and political ideals, but its persecution as well; she was even said to have undergone the lash as a consequence of her Iconophile opinions and those of the monks she sheltered. Kassia's love of icon veneration is evidenced in her own words in "The Canon for the Remembrance of the Dead," where she cites the veneration of the Theotokos displayed on panels. This is made possible, as the Canon explains, by the infinite presence of God contained in the blessed virgin womb of the Theotokas.[10] Indeed, as a child of her time, caught up in the Iconoclastic Controversy, Kassia has been characterized for her efforts as "a heroine of the Iconophile resistance."[11] At least, she should be glad she was not among her poet contemporaries, the "*graptoi*,"[12] who were made to endure iconoclastic verses inscribed on their foreheads in red hot irons, rather than flogging.

The Iconodule values present in Kassia's writing should come as no surprise since her spiritual father was St. Theodore the

---

[9] Anna Silvas, "Kassia the Nun c. 810-c. 865: an Appreciation," in *Byzantine Women: Varieties of Experience 800-1200*, Lynda Garland, ed. (Burlington, VT: Ashgate Publishing, 2006), p. 19.

[10] Kurt Sherry, *Kassia the Nun in Context: The Religious Thought of a Ninth-Century Byzantine Monastic* (Piscataway, NJ: Gorgias Press, 2011), p. 57.

[11] A. P. Kazhdan, A.-M. Talbot, "Women and Iconoclasm," *Byzantinische Zeitschrift* 84/85 (1991/1992), p. 395.

[12] After the Iconoclastic Controversy subsided, one of them was the soon-to-be Metropolitan Theophanes of Nicaea, who suffered persecution alongside his brother, Theodore. Stephanos Efthymiadis, "Notes on the Correspondence of Theodore the Studite," *Revue des Etudes Byzantines* 53 (1995), p. 142. See also George Ostrogorsky, *History of the Byzantine State* (New Brunswick, NJ: Rutgers University Press, 1969), p. 209.

Stoudite. As demonstrated by the three surviving letters from his correspondence to her, Abbot Theodore had taken Kassia's God-swayed soul under his wing, and his mentoring of her could not help but shape her young Orthodox heart and mind.

It is likely that Theodore the Stoudite is responsible for shep-herding his witty, outspoken spiritual daughter's poetic pen to-ward the writing of hymns, his own hymn-writing being the model. As with Olympias' letters to St. John Chrysostom, de-scribed in the previous chapter, the letters from Kassia to Theo-dore have not survived. We know, however, that the correspond-ence of both women existed; and it is noteworthy that, like Olym-pias, Kassia's letters elicited response from a celebrated Father of the Church.

Theodore's spiritual supervision of Kassia is evidenced by his theology reflected in her hymns. In fact, his influence over her burgeoning monastic vocation, over the outcome and liturgical style of her monastery as it developed, and indeed over monasti-cism in the Eastern Church as a whole during the ninth and the following centuries, cannot be overstated. Kassia's convent was likely developed on the model of his well-established Stoudian Monastery. The existence of Theodore the Stoudite's letters to Kassia lends historical credibility to the figure of the ninth-cen-tury hymnographer.[13]

The popular tradition of Kassia's participation in Empress Euphrosyne's bride show for her stepson, the young Emperor The-ophilos, is mentioned by several historical chroniclers,[14] and it provides evidence of another important form of historical memory. For Kassia is quoted; the well-educated Byzantine poet

---

[13] "Theodore knew and appreciated the budding powers of the most orig-inal and prolific of Byzantine literary women, and that she desired, but was not permitted, to receive from him, authorization for adopting that monastic life to which she aspired in girlhood but—perhaps—only en-tered when disappointed of a seat on the imperial throne." A. Gardner, *Theodore of Studium: His Life and Times* (London: E Arnold, 1905), p. 229.
[14] Among the earlier Byzantine chroniclers, the bride-show tradition is mentioned in a distinctly similar manner by Symeon the Logothete, George the Monk, Leo the Grammarian, and John Zonaris.

is remembered speaking up to the Emperor.[15] In this, she joins the exclusive ranks of women, including the biblical figures, Lydia, the Samaritan Woman—even Mary the God-bearing Theotokas—whose memory has managed to survive over the centuries of patriarchal thought in quoted text.

The royal bride-show episode in Kassia's life supports the persistent memory of an imperial connection for the beloved hymn-writer in the generations after her death. At the time of the Emperor's marriage, Kassia's family was élite enough in its association with the Byzantine court that significant pressure was no doubt exercised upon their young marriageable daughter to embrace the opportunity to ascend the imperial throne as the bride of Theophilos, with the hope of being crowned as *basilissa*. In any case, the incident shows the headstrong character which may reflect Kassia's youthful formation in a military officer's household.

Although Kassia was passed over as a bride for Theophilos, the reported exchange between them still demonstrates a bridal candidate of sound theological education with a good grounding in classical rhetoric. In fact, these external events may have been necessary for Kassia, as an aristocratic daughter in the capitol city, in order to finally establish herself in a much-desired ascetical life. Having failed to procure her a place at court as Empress, Kassia's family likely then chose to provide support for her venture into monasticism by financing the foundation of a nearby monastery in town with their daughter as Abbess. In any case, the hagiographic tradition illustrates that Kassia has survived in popular Byzantine memory, preferring the ascetical nun's veil to an empress's crown and pearled *pendilia*.[16]

---

[15] To the emperor's sly remark, upon encountering Kassia as one of the maidens presented to him during his bride show: *"Ek gynaikós tá cheírō,"* (Through a woman [came forth] the baser [things]), meaning Eve, she is reported to have cleverly quipped, *"Kaí ek gynaikós tá kreíttō."* (Yet through a woman [came forth] the better [things]), meaning Mary the Theotokas. Gibbon deemed it an "affectation of unseasonable wit." E. Gibbon, *The History of the Decline and Fall of the Roman Empire* (London: J. F. Dove, 1821), Book 6, Chap. 48, p. 118.

[16] *Pendilia* are pendents or jewels—often pearls—suspended from either side of crowns or crosses. Byzantine crowns are often displayed on

Later in her life, Kassia saw her beauty as a potential liability, reporting in verse her preference for spiritual over physical beauty:

> One should prefer a drop of luck
> than great beauty.
> It is better to possess grace from the Lord
> than beauty and wealth that does not gain grace.[17]

Because Kassia's faith led her to found a convent on the Seventh Hill of Constantinople, John Zonaras, a twelfth-century chronicler, said of her, "She was allotted a heavenly kingdom instead of an earthly one."[18]

Examination of the *Typikon*, or Rule, established by her spiritual father, Abbot Theodore, for his monastery is useful in reflecting on the structure and nature of Kassia's convent in Constantinople; for the Stoudios *Typikon* undoubtedly influenced hers.[19] In fact, information from these foundational monastic texts is often helpful in discerning details of the unique environment of ninth-century Byzantine monastic community life. In general, the

---

imperial coinage with *pendilia* of large pearls. A good example is a coin depicting Empress Theodora, who Emperor Theophilos chose as his empress over Kassia during his bride show. "Solidus of Theodora as Regent," Mint of Constantinople, 842-843, Arthur M. Sackler Museum, Harvard, in Ioli Kalavrezou, *Byzantine Women and Their World* (New Haven, CT: Yale University Press, 2003), p. 95.

[17] Kassia the Nun, "Beauty," in Antonia Tripolitis, *Kassia: The Legend, the Woman, and her Work* (London: Rutledge, 1992), pp. 120-121. Kassia's epigrams also demonstrate an Orthodox tradition of monastic instruction which was built more on simple reminders about the principles of convent life, rather than on formal synthesized documents or rules. Peter Hatlie, *The Monks and Monasteries of Constantinople, ca. 350-850* (Cambridge: Cambridge University Press, 2007) p. 344.

[18] John Zonaris, *Epitome Historiarum,* Book XIII-XVIII (Bonn: Weber, 1897) pp. 354-355.

[19] "*Stoudios: Rule* of the Monastery of St. John Stoudios in Constantinople," in *Byzantine Monastic Foundation Documents: A Complete Translation of the Surviving Founders' Typika and Testament,* John Thomas and Angela Constantinides Hero, eds (Washington, D.C.: Dumbarton Oaks Research Library and Collection, 2000), pp. 84-119.

Stoudios *Typikon* demonstrates Theodore's efforts to centralize monastic observance into a style emphasizing well-ordered spiritual community over lone ascetical practice. Eventually, monastic communities throughout Byzantium came to treat the Stoudios Monastery *Typikon* as the standard for monasteries, to the point that it was finally regarded as a paradigm of organized, coenobitic monastic life.[20]

As an example, when Theodore took over, the Stoudios monastery was *akoimetoi*—that is, keeping an unending observance of psalm-chanting throughout the night. During his early *hegoumenate*, however, the practice was brought to an end; so, it is probable that Kassia's nearby abbey was coenobitic as well, rather than *akoimetoi*. Honoring her spiritual father, the Abbess Kassia likely stressed the monastic ideal of her nuns remaining in ordered community, rather than eventually separating out into hermitages for a life of unscheduled solitary eremitical prayer.[21]

Kassia's musical compositions and ecclesiastical poetry, written both at her convent and earlier in her life, demonstrate an elevated theological character, with simple dynamic vocabulary, sophisticated play on words, and vibrant imagery. Nearly all Kassia's hymns are *occasional* in character—meaning they are composed for a specific feast-day. "On the Birth of Christ," Kassia's *doxastikon* is an Office hymn composed for the Eve of the Feast of the Nativity.[22] Specifically, the hymn is a *sticheron idiomelon doxastikon* in Mode II.[23]

---

[20] See J.A. McGuckin, "Monasticism" in *Dictionary of Eastern Christianity*, K. Parry, ed. (Oxford: Blackwell, 1999), p. 324. See also McGuckin, "Symeon the New Theologian (d. 1022) and Byzantine Monasticism," in *Mount Athos and Byzantine Monasticism: Papers from the Twenty-eighth Spring Symposium of Byzantine Studies, Birmingham, 1994*, Anthony Beyer and Mary Cunningham, eds (Aldershot, Hampshire: Vaporium, 1996) p. 24.

[21] "*Stoudios: Rule*," *Byzantine Monastic Foundation Documents*, p. 84.

[22] Note that Kassia also wrote eight other *stichera* for the Feast of the Nativity which are not chanted as part of the Orthodox Liturgy currently.

[23] A *sticheron idiomelon* has its own melody composed specifically for a verse, as opposed to a melody which is shared by other *stichera*.

The melody is made up of three phrases, which are each repeated, followed by a fourth and final phrase. This melody structure—a-a-b-b-c-c-d—follows one of the major patterns for the Sequence form.[24] The text is a liturgical poem composed to reflect
upon the St. Luke 2:1-5 Gospel reading which is proclaimed in the
service itself, where Scripture cites both the coming birth of the
Christ Child during the reign of Augustus and the decree demanding that all be registered.

On the Birth of Christ

When Augustus reigned alone upon earth,
the many kingdoms of men came to an end;
and when Thou wast made man of a pure Virgin
the many gods of idolatry were destroyed.
The cities of the world passed under one single rule;
and the nations came to believe
in one sovereign Godhead.

The peoples were enrolled by the decree of Caesar;
and we, the faithful, were enrolled in the name
of the Godhead, when Thou, our God, was made man.
Great is Thy mercy; Glory to Thee.[25]

The hymn chants the praises of the Incarnation, and it reveals the
profound consequences of the birth of the Savior for the order of
the Roman world. Additionally, in the Iconoclastic environment
in which Kassia wrote it, "On the Birth of Christ" would have been
clearly seen as pointing out that the Incarnation justifies the veneration of icons, "not as idols, but as living testimony of the assumption of matter by God."[26] Kassia's technique is able to

---

[24] Note that scholars have observed a connection between the structure
of Kassia's Christmas Eve *sticheron* and one of the Sequence forms which
became popular in the Western Church; to the extent that it has been
suggested that it was brought to the West via the popularity of Kassia's
Nativity *sticheron*. Reese, *Music in the Middle Ages,* p. 81.
[25] Mother Mary and Kallistos Ware, trans., *The Festal Menaion,* vol. 12;
December (London: Faber and Faber, 1969), p. 254.
[26] Niki Tsironis, "The Body and the Senses in the Work of Cassia the
Hymnographer: Literary Trends in the Iconoclastic Period," *Byzantina
Symmeikta* 16 (2014), p. 146.

connect the political situation at the turn of the age for the Roman Empire with the theological dimension of Salvation, weaving in elements pertinent to the critical issues of the day, namely the Iconoclastic Controversy.

This is expressed deploying several pairs of contrasting ideas. There is, in fact, striking use of antithesis in "On the Birth of Christ." For example, Kassia examines ramifications inherent: in Augustus reigning contrasted with God becoming man; the end of polyarchy versus the end of idolatry; the nations under one rule contrasted with the world under one Godhead; and the fact that the people were registered and the faithful were inscribed. Thus, when quoting Kassia's *doxastikon* for the Vespers of the Nativity, Meyendorff claims that she demonstrates a direct connection between the world-wide Byzantine Empire and the "recapitulation" of humanity in Christ. "*Pax Romana* is thus made to coincide with *Pax Christiana.*"[27]

Another key to the meaning of Kassia's Nativity hymn is provided in a lyrical paradox using word-play on two Greek verbs. Here "voice and verse are intimately locked together,"[28] with her well-played comparison of the verbs *apegraphesan*, meaning "register," and *epegraphemen*, meaning "inscribe." Each one uses the root verb *grapheo*, which is also present in the Greek reading from Luke. At the very time that the sole Emperor, Augustus, demanded the population be *registered* and counted as among Caesar, Jesus Christ was coming into the earthly world, and all the faithful were able to be *inscribed* in the name of His divinity and counted among Christ forever. With the alliterative sounds heard when the two verbs are chanted, Kassia reveals a relationship of contrast and dominion set in place by the Incarnation.

See how this compelling word-play contrast is effectively demonstrated in Gheorghita Zugravu's excellent recent contemporary-language translation:

---

[27] See John Meyendorff, *Byzantine Theology: Historical Trends and Doctrinal Themes* (New York: Fordham University Press. 1979), p. 214.
[28] Meyendorff, *Byzantine Theology*, p. 9.

When Augustus reigned alone upon the earth,
the many Kingdoms of men came to an end;
and since You were made man of a pure Virgin
the many gods of idols have been destroyed.

The cities have come under one universal Kingdom
and the nations came to believe
in one divine dominion.

The people were registered by the decree of Caesar;
we, the faithful, have been inscribed in the name of
Your divinity when You our God were made man.
Great is Your mercy, Lord; glory to You.[29]

"On the Birth of Christ" also demonstrates Kassia's support for St. Theodore the Stoudite and his development of the Iconodule concept of the *perigrapton* (circumscribability) of Christ,[30] at a time when he was further defining his Incarnation Theology. This idea is comprehensively worked out in the third of his "Refutations" in *On the Holy Icons*.[31] Christ, while divine, becomes locally present as part of mankind, and is tangible and therefore depictable. For St. Theodore has argued that while, "it is proper to divinity to be incircumscribable...yet, if it is said 'The Lord embodied me'...then if He is tangible, He must also be circumscribable."[32]

Therefore, on the one hand, during the reign of Augustus, all the polyarchy in the known Roman world came to an end for one peaceful chapter of time, identifying everyone under the authority of Caesar; on the other hand, by virtue of the Incarnation made

---

[29] Gheorghita Zugravu, *Kasia the Melodist: And the Making of a Byzantine Hymnographer*, Columbia University Ph.D. dissertation, 2013.

[30] Note that *perigrapton* (circumscribability) is yet another term built upon the root *grapheo*, demonstrating that Kassia's liturgical poem, "On the Birth of Christ," is directly connected to the Incarnation theology of St. Theodore the Stoudite, particularly as it pertains to the circumscribability of Christ.

[31] Theodore the Studite, "Antirhetici Adversus Iconomachos," PG 99. 328-436. For English, see *On the Holy Icons*. Catherine Roth, trans. (Crestwood, NY: St. Vladimir's Seminary Press, 1981).

[32] St. Theodore the Stoudite "Third Refutation of the Iconoclasts," iii.A.4,9,12; *On the Holy Icons*, p. 79.

possible by the birth of Jesus, God is made a visible, describable man, and all the world's faithful are inscribed as Christ's own. "Christ incarnate is revealed within these limitations."[33] Note how this continues to be demonstrated down through the ages in the act of anointing at Baptism.

By mingling and contrasting the authority of Roman rule and the authority of the sphere of Christ, Kassia's Nativity *sticheron doxastikon* acknowledges the action of divine providence at work in this coincidence of events.[34] Kassia "differentiates between the two authorities, relating the emergence of the unified Roman Empire to the political benefits it brought to mankind, and the Incarnation of Christ to the religious ones."[35]

Furthermore, since Kassia's hymn was included by the monks of Stoudios in what would become the authorized liturgical book for the Feast of the Nativity, it can be seen functioning as a piece of effective, nuanced propaganda against Iconoclasm. This was part of "the use of liturgy as a political arena in Byzantium."[36]

On balance, it is fortunate that, by the happy circumstance of the Abbess Kassia's connection to the Stoudios Monastery, through her spiritual father, St. Theodore, her memory has managed to survive in the development of Byzantine hymnography

---

[33] *Ibid.* iii.A.13, p. 82.

[34] In the Lukan commentary from the *Ancient Christian Commentary on Scripture* series, the text of Kassia's "Stickera of the Nativity of the Lord" is listed as one of the Patristic reflections on Luke 2:1-5. The Nun Kassia appears in the company of Chrysostom, Eusebius, Cyril of Alexandria, and Bede; her text is offered as one of the primary source resources, as it were, "from the Fathers." Her chant is acknowledged as lyrically demonstrating that Augustus' triumph pre-figures the triumph of Christ. *Luke,* Arthur A. Just, ed. The Ancient Christian Commentary on Scripture (Downers Grove, IL: InterVarsity Press, 2003), pp. 36-37.

[35] Kosta Simic, "Kassia's Hymnography in the Light of Patristic Sources and Earlier Hymnological Works," *Recueil des Travaux de L'Institut d'Etudes Byzantines* 48 (2001), p. 12.

[36] A. Spanos, "Political Approaches to Byzantine Liturgical Texts," in *Approaches to the Text: From Pre-Gospel to Post-Baroque,* Roy Eriksen, Peter Eriksen, eds (Pisa-Rome: Fabrizio Serra Editore, 2014).

and to be officially recorded in the venerable resources of the Orthodox Liturgy. Kassia's inclusion has enabled her hymns "to sing in harmony with the angelic choirs," in order to "unite earth to heaven in one melodious cosmic hymn of praise to the divine Creator."[37] Additionally, both she and Theodore the Stoudite became part of a trend at that time, when many well-educated men and women were brought to the helm of monastic leadership; and they thereby contributed to the Byzantine Revival developing throughout the next century.

Kassia's leadership and hymnographic contribution were a significant component of what has been deemed "by far the most productive and sophisticated experiment in monastic culture ever to date."[38] Kassia's *sticheron doxastikon* composed for the Vespers service on the Eve of the Feast of the Nativity compares and contrasts the universal power of the sole Roman Emperor with the unifying Advent of Christ, so that the moment of the Incarnation can be seen in its role as part of the trajectory of the Salvation story of the Church. "On the Birth of Christ," as well as her other compositions included in the authorized hymn-books of the Orthodox Liturgy, promise that Kassia's memory will be preserved in the Orthodox Liturgy, praising the Incarnate God of Salvation.

---

[37] E.C. Topping, "Byzantine Hymnography," in Vaporis, ed., *Three Byzantine Sacred Poets* (Brookline, MA: Hellenic College Press, 1979), p. 2.

[38] Hatlie, *Monks and Monasteries of Constantinople,* p. 450.

III.
NEW THEKLAS
AND NEW HELENAS

CHAPTER III.1
EMPRESSES SPEAK OF
PHILANTHROPIA: FOLLOWING
THE COMMAND OF CHRIST

Women in the imperial Byzantine family were taught the virtue of philanthropy by the example of the empresses and princesses who had gone before them, thus becoming the "New Helenas" of their age. Generation after generation, these royal women were brought up and educated in an environment rich with awareness of the *philanthrōpia* of God, the forgiving and patient generosity of God's mercy in loving mankind. Several of those responding in obedience and gratitude to the love of God for mankind leave a record of their patronage in church-building and monastery-founding projects which stands as a tribute to their faith; this chapter explores several of them. The Christian virtue of *philanthrōpia* was preached by Bishops and Patriarchs in the Cathedrals and cited in the traditional Orthodox liturgies of the Church.

After its august beginnings in Attic drama,[1] the term *philanthrōpia* is mentioned only a few times in the New Testament,[2] and

---

[1] Its first use is reported in the Aeschylus tragedy, *Prometheus Bound* (ca. 463 BCE) and again in the Aristophanes comedy *Peace* (ca. 421 BCE); later it appears in Plato's dialogue "Euthyphro" (ca. 399 BCE) and the treatises of Aristotle as well.

[2] Acts 28:2, and 27:3 as an adverb, and Titus 3:4: "But when the goodness and loving kindness (*philanthrōpia*) of God our Savior appeared, he saved us."

in the Septuagint Old Testament as well,[3] but the exhortation to charitable works was established early in the development of Byzantine thought. It is well attested in the patristic teachings of the Church;[4] these time-honored writings assisted in the formation of a God-fearing empress, so that the concept of philanthropy, as it was reflected in its theology and liturgy, was a significant inheritance for the Byzantine Church.

From the treasury of patristic teaching in place even before the establishment of the Byzantine Empire, several texts shed light upon the virtue of *philanthrōpia* and therefore its significance for imperial women, especially where they functuioned as role models for the faithful. Clement of Alexandra (ca.150 C.E.-ca. 215) characterized *philanthrōpia* as the greatest of God's attributes, his love of mankind manifested through the gift of his incarnate Son. The *philanthrōpia* of Christ was seen as deriving from his personal experience of becoming flesh and feeling its weaknesses.

Thus, even a crowned empress could attain to *philanthrōpia* by "becoming poor" and identifying with those in need by way of her philanthropic acts.[5] Therefore, her theological advisors could demonstrate how a wealthy noblewoman might nevertheless become poor in spirit by reciprocating God's love of mankind. "If one is faithful and surveys the magnificence of God's love of

---

[3] Septuagint references to *philanthrōpia*, some as a verb or adjective: II Macc. 4:11, 6:22, 9:27, III Macc. 3:15, 18, 20; IV Macc. 5:12, Esther 8:13, I Esdras 8:10, Wisdom 1:6, 7:23, 12:19.

[4] References to philanthropia in the Fathers of the Church include, but are not exclusive to: Clement of Alexandria, Homily 2.45, Homily 11.10, Homily 12 (6 times), Homily 16.19, *Epistle of Clement* 8, *Protrepticus* 1, 10, *Quis Dives Salvetur*, 3, *Paedagogus* 1.8, 2.18, *Stromateis* 2.9,18; Origen, *Contra Celsum* 1.27, 67, Commentary on Mt. 10:1; Athanasius, *De Incarnatione* 1.3, 4.2,3; 15.2, *Orationes Tres Adversus Arianos* 3.67, 2.51; John Chrysostom, Homily "In Parabolam Debitoris" in Mt. 18.23, Homily 28.1 in Jn., Homily 14.3 in 2 Cor., Homily 3.2 in Philm., Homily 3.6 in Heb., Homily 4.9; Justin Martyr, *Apologiae* 10., *Dialogus cum Tryphone* 47.5, Basil the Great, *Homily VI*, Gregory of Nyssa, *Catechetical Oration*, XV, Gregory Nazianzen, *Oration 14*, Ambrose, "Naboth."

[5] Clement, *Paedagogos* I.VIII.10-11, ANF II.228.

mankind," surely she will "use wealth rightly, so it ministers to righteousness; for if you use it wrongly, it is found to be a minister of wrong."[6]

The theologian Origen (ca.185-ca.254), who also taught in Alexandria, provided encouragement for the philanthropic dimension in religious life by describing Jesus as the *Logos Philanthropos* and teaching that the loving influence of Christ inspires profound transformation in the human character, so that each in turn themselves become humanitarians and philanthropists.[7] Bishop Athanasius of Alexandria (ca. 296-373) wrote that love for mankind is a principle motive of God for the Incarnation, for "our transgression called forth the loving-kindness of the Word that the Lord should both make haste to help us and appear among men."[8] He taught that the loving attitude of God demands that we generously emulate it in our relationships with one another. The commandment of the Lord exhorts the faithful, especially those of substantial means, to humanitarian concern and philanthropy for the poor and needy, and for widows, strangers and orphans.[9]

The wisdom of the Cappadocian Fathers may have been influential to succeeding generations of the Byzantine imperial family as well, particularly the women closest to the throne. Basil the Great (ca.330-ca.379) taught that by philanthropic generosity, "God will welcome thee, angels will laud thee, mankind from the very beginning will call thee blessed. For thy stewardship of these corruptible things thy reward shall be glory everlasting, a crown of righteousness, the heavenly kingdom;" since, after all, "the grace of good works returns to the giver. Thou hast given to the poor, and the gift becomes thine own, and comes back with increase."[10]

---

[6] Clement, "The Rich Man's Salvation" (*Quis Dives Salvetur*) 3, 14, *Clement of Alexandria*, G.W. Butterworth, trans. (London: William Heinemann Ltd., 1968), pp. 277, 299.

[7] Origen, *Contra Celsum* I.67, trans. Henry Chadwick (Cambridge: Cambridge University Press, 1953), p. 62.

[8] Athanasius, *De Incarnatione Verbi Dei* 4:2, NPNF IV.38.

[9] Demetrios J. Constantelos, *Byzantine Philanthropy and Social Welfare* (New Brunswick, NJ: Rutgers University Press, 1968), p. 33.

[10] Basil the Great, Homily VI on Luke xxi.18, *Writings of Basil*, Blomfield Jackson, trans. (Edinburgh: T&T Clark, 1895).

In his *Catechetical Oration*, Gregory of Nyssa (335-394) calls *philanthrōpia* "a special character of the divine nature," and therefore "the cause of the presence of God among men."[11] Thus, he considers it responsible for the Incarnation.[12] Gregory Nazianzen (ca.325-ca.389) in his innovative *Oration 14* "On the Love of the Poor," demonstrated how, by becoming "friends of the poor" (*Philoptochos*), Bishops and laymen, empresses and merchants alike, can learn to emulate the transactional aspect of God's saving love of mankind in generosity to the poor.[13] "Let us share what we have with the poor that we may be rich in the bounty of heaven. Give a portion of your soul, too, not just your body; give a portion to God, too, not just the world; take something from the belly, dedicate it to the Spirit."[14]

By one fortunate enough to be chosen as Empress, Patriarchal teaching could well be taken as cautionary advice as well. Ringing through the "Verses against the Rich" is Gregory's cry for a humanitarian Christian response to the needs of the poor, and as Shewring charmingly renders it:

> Give to the poor; they before God can plead,
> And win, and richly give, the grace we need…
> Honour in him God's handiwork expressed;
> Reverence in it the rites that serve a guest.[15]

Ambrose (339-397), while Bishop of Milan in the Western Church, was influential to Emperor Theodosius I, and his advice may have been familiar to the Theodosian Empresses and noblewomen in court circles, reminding them that "it makes your

---

[11] Gregory of Nyssa, *Catechetical Oration*, XV, NPNF XV.487.

[12] Glanville Downey, "Philanthropia in Religion and Statecraft in the Fourth Century after Christ," in *Historia: Zeitschrift fur Alte Geschichte* 4:2/3 (1955), p. 204.

[13] John A. McGuckin, *St. Gregory of Nazianzus: An Intellectual Biography* (Crestwood, NY: St. Vladimir's Seminary Press, 2001), p. 147.

[14] *Oration 14* in *St. Gregory Nazianzus: Selected Orations*, M. Vinson, trans. (Washington, DC: The Catholic University of America Press, 2003), 22, p. 55.

[15] Gregory Nazianzen, "Verses against the Rich," (Moral Poems, XXVIII), quoted in *Rich and Poor in Christian Tradition*, p. 49.

debtor God the Son, who says 'I was hungry and you gave me to eat. I was thirsty and you gave me to drink, and I was a stranger and you took me in, naked and you clothed me'(Matt. 25:35-36). For he says that whatever was given to any of the least ones was given to him."

Having given birth herself, this message of St. Ambrose may have registered even more deeply with an imperial Byzantine lady than with her husband: "Earth was established in common for all, rich and poor alike. Nature, which begets everyone poor, knows no wealthy for we are not born with clothing or begotten with gold and silver. Naked, it brings us into the light, wanting food, clothing, drink, and naked the earth receives us whom it brought forth, not knowing how to compass our possessions in the tomb."[16]

Closer to home, the Bishop of Constantinople, John Chrysostom (347-407), also vigorously proclaimed the Gospel imperative of Matthew 25, for which he came under criticism from the imperial court and endured temporary exile. While citing it and alluding to it numerous times in his preaching, in Homily 79 on Matt. 25: 31-41, he calls it "this sweetest passage of Scripture" (*tes perikopes tes hedistes*), for "great indeed was Christ's regard for philanthropy and mercy."[17] Poignantly illustrating the theology of philanthropy, he shows that it is Jesus himself—hungry, thirsty, naked, stranger, sick, and imprisoned—whom we encounter among the poor in the streets in need, "for no costly table did He seek, but what was needful only, and His necessary food, and He sought in a suppliant's garb," and he teaches that Christ sees what is offered to the poor as offered to him; "the dignity of the one receiving, for it was God, who was receiving by the poor."

The early fifth-century historian Sozomen describes how *philanthrōpia* is acquired by imitating the prototype, the Heavenly

---

[16] Ambrose, "Naboth," quoted in, Boniface Ramsey, *Ambrose* (London: Routledge, 1997), pp. 138, 118.

[17] Greek translation by Rudulf Brandle, in "This Sweetest Passage: Matthew 25:31-46 and Assistance to the Poor in the Homilies of John Chrysostom," in *Wealth and Poverty in Early Church and Society*, Susan R. Holman, ed. (Grand Rapids, MI: Baker Academic, 2008), p. 132.

King, who is its source. He illustrates how it functions as an imperial virtue by praising Emperor Theodosius II (401-450), to whom the *Ecclesiastical History* is dedicated.[18] Like the emperor, the Christ-loving empress also "promoted the salvation and welfare of the people, placating God of the sake of the empire and emperor."[19] The women in the Imperial Court attending the Liturgy heard the exhortation to *philanthropia* numerous times in each service.

Although the Liturgies of St. Basil and John Chrysostom evolved to their present forms in the eighth and ninth century, and as such have been attended by empresses from those centuries and afterward, *philanthrōpia* is repeated as an attribute of God in the former ten times, and in the latter, twelve times. "The services of Vespers and Orthos, the hymns and prayers of everyday services, reveal that sinful man is redeemed through the *philanthrōpia* of God, which is apophatically described as 'unfathomable,' 'indescribable,' 'immeasurable.'"[20] In times of catastrophe, litanies rang out invoking the *philanthrōpia* of God and galvanizing the humanitarian efforts of, for example, Empress Irene after the earthquake of 740.

These examples illustrate the foundation which was laid down in Christian thought by patristic teaching illuminating the theology of *philanthrōpia*. In reflecting on the relationship between poverty and merit, it showed the way forward for the development of the imperial patron/client relationship as a means of emulating God's love of mankind. The teachings of the Fathers educated imperial women, preparing them for a generous humanitarian response to the needs of the poor, who were to be identified as the image of God, rather than cursed by the gods, as they were seen in Greek society. Because of the love of the Creator, everyone owes generosity to one another, especially those raised to the Imperial throne by birth or marriage. Thus, with the rise of the Byzantine state, and certainly by the fifth and sixth centuries,

---

[18] Sozomen, Introduction, *Ecclesiastical History*, NPNF II.236.

[19] L. James, *Empresses and Power in Early Byzantium* (New York: Leicester University Press, 2001), p. 14.

[20] Constantelos, *Byzantine Philanthropy and Social Welfare*, p. 34.

Christian piety in general and philanthropy in particular were increasingly promoted as a principle of conduct for imperial women, with Helena (ca.49-ca.329), the first Christian empress, offered as the definitive role model.

Eusebius records that Helena built numerous churches in the Holy Land, among her several philanthropic pursuits, many of which resonate with the command of Christ in Matthew 25: "Especially abundant were the gifts she bestowed on the naked and unprotected poor. To some she gave money, to others a supply of clothing; she liberated some from imprisonment, or from the bitter servitude of the mines; others she delivered from unjust oppression, and others again, she restored from exile."[21] While her achievements may be in part legendary, her inspiration to generations of Byzantine imperial women was very real. By their endowment of charitable institutions and other philanthropic actions, several empresses, including Pulcheria, were acclaimed as "new" or "second" or Helenas.

As the royal sister of Theodosius II (401-450) and crowned in her own right after his death, Empress Pulcheria was known to have corresponded with Pope Leo I,[22] and she was responsible for establishing the education of her Imperial brother. Her philanthropic projects reflected pious generosity on a grand scale; ancient sources record that Pulcheria, "possessing great wisdom and a holy mind, educated her brother Theodosios. She gave him a royal training, above all in piety towards God…After building numerous churches, poor-houses, hostels, and monasteries; she endowed all of them with appropriate income in imperial style." She brought her sisterly influence to bear on her imperial brother's philanthropic activities as well: "The pious Theodosius, in imitation of the blessed Pulcheria, sent much money to the Archbishop of Jerusalem for distribution among those in need."[23]

---

[21] Eusebius, *Vita Constantini* III. 44, NPNF I.531.

[22] PG 54.905-908.

[23] Theophanes, the Confessor, *Chronographia: Byzantine and Near Eastern History, AD 284-813*, Cyril Mango, Roger Scott, trans. (Oxford: Clarendon Press, 1997), p. 125.

Thus, Theodosius learned the virtuous habit of philanthropy in part from his pious sister Pulcheria, who was educated enough to have read it and heard it from the Patriarchs themselves. The writings of the court orator, Themistius, may have deepened his understanding of philanthropia as well, for his addresses to the first Theodosius, when he was a new ruler, had taught him that philanthropia is the greatest of the imperial virtues, for by it the soul is fashioned into the image of God.[24]

It was often through philanthropic initiative of imperial women that many of the most important relics of the saints were brought to the Byzantine capitol and reverently housed in churches built specifically for them, which became in turn the location where empresses were crowned and betrothed. Thus, Constantinople grew to be the greatest treasury of relics in Christendom, and this became especially significant after the loss of Jerusalem during the Crusades. The relics "functioned as instruments of power, investiture, and leadership, guaranteeing political authority and displaying divine approval to those who possessed them."[25] When the relics of John Chrysostom were translated from Komana to the capitol, "the blessed Pulcheria placed them in the Church of the Apostles, thus uniting those which had been separated following his deposition from the Church."

Pulcheria also "built a wonderful church for the blessed First Martyr and deposited his holy relics there."[26] By her benefaction, the Chapel of St. Stephen was added to the Daphne Palace complex to house the relic of the Protomartyr's arm brought from Jerusalem and as a treasury for other important relics, such as the precious cross traditionally attributed to Constantine and Helena containing a relic of the True Cross. She was also responsible for

---

[24] Glanville Downey, "Philanthropia in Religion and Statecraft in the Fourth Century after Christ," in *Historia: Zeitschrift fur Alte Geschichte* 4:2/3 (1955), p. 201.

[25] Ioli Kalavrezon, "Helping Hands for the Empire: Imperial Ceremonies and the Cult of Relics at the Byzantine Court," in *Byzantine Court Culture from 829 to 1204*, Henry Maguire, ed. (Washington, DC: Dumbarton Oaks, 1997), p. 55.

[26] Theophanes, the Confessor, *Chronographia*, pp. 135-136,144.

building a church for the much-beloved icon with the Mother of God Hodegitria in the Arsenal area of the capitol.[27]

After the multi-faceted philanthropic projects of Empress Pulcheria, Athenais-Eudokia, the bride chosen for her imperial brother, carried on her pious work, especially later in life when exiled. Athenais was a convert to Orthodoxy from Athens; when she was baptized she took the name Eudokia, and like Helena as well, "carrying out the command of Christ in Matthew 25, she was able to offer service for people—especially for the sick, the hungry, the unclothed, the poor and the neglected."[28]

The imperial sisters-in-law, both hailed as "most-pious" by historians, each offered their robes to the service of the Church to be used as fair linens upon the Altar.[29] Among the many philanthropic institutions that Empress Athenais-Eudokia established was a great poorhouse which was capable of housing 400. She was reported to have worked tirelessly to support the strengthening and building up of the city walls through her patronage of Kyros of Panopolis, whom she influenced her husband to appoint as Prefect of the city. He was said to have built up the walls and "lit up the dark capitol."[30] Her charitable works in Jerusalem were impressive as well.

---

[27] Thomas F. Mathews, *The Byzantine Churches of Istanbul: A Photographic Survey* (University Park, PA: Pennsylvania State University Press, 1976), p. 201.

[28] Demetrios J. Constantelos, "Women and Philanthropy in the History of Hellenism," (available at: https://www.goarch.org/-/women-and-philanthropy-in-the-history-of-hellenism; accessed 1/6/20).

[29] James, *Empresses and Power in Early Byzantium*, p. 154.

[30] "From 439 to 441 there was feverish activity in Byzantium; the best men of the community were working for its welfare. ...Kyros wanted to satisfy Augusta Eudocia, to accomplish her assignment quickly...no poor man was idle in the capital. Out of the generosity of her nature, Eudocia stood by them, rich in her resources....In the few years of his consulship, this poet and builder accomplished miracles. He built the walls. He lit up the dark capitol." Jeanne Tsatsos, *Empress Athenais-Eudocia: A Fifth Century Byzantine Humanist* (Brookline, MA: Holy Cross Orthodox Press, 1977), p. 76.

History has recorded her pilgrimage to Jerusalem in the company of St. Melania the Younger and her relic-collecting projects; after first visiting to set up the foundations, she commissioned designs for churches, a palace and a large inn for pilgrims. "There must be no poor man without help, no old man without care." Her humanitarian generosity, especially toward the end of her life, became renowned: "She spent it all for Christ's work. It is reckoned that in the last seventeen years of her life, she spent for the buildings and for the maintenance of the Holy City more than 20,000 pounds of gold; yet she herself lived in monastic simplicity."[31] The example of Empress Eudokia was undoubtedly an inspiration to the imperial women who came after her, perhaps most explicitly her own great grand-daughter, Princess Anicia Juliana.

Recent archeological exploration uncovered restoration and building expansion which carried on the work of Empress Eudokia into succeeding generations and has brought to light a Byzantine princess who was a significant benefactress of philanthropic projects. In 1960, grading operations around Istanbul's current city-hall at Sarachane in the center of the ancient city uncovered a number of ornately worked cornices and marble blocks. Two of these carried an inscription describing the Byzantine princess Anicia Juliana, praising her royal lineage, and the elaborate church which she had constructed in honour of St. Polyeuktos, replacing a similar one which had been built on the site by Empress Eudocia. The inscription, which adorned the upper periphery of the church, witnesses to the philanthropic generosity of her imperial grand-daughter and her motivation for building.[32]

---

[31] *Ibid.*, p. 96.

[32] It read, in part: "The Empress Eudocia, in her eagerness to honour God, was the first to build a temple to the divinely inspired Polyeuktos...she raised this building from its small original to its present size and form...May the servants of the heavenly King, to whomsoever she gave gifts and to whomsoever she built temples, protect her readily with her son and his daughters. And may the unutterable glory of the most industrious family survive as long as the Sun drives his fiery chariot...What choir is sufficient to sing the work of Juliana, who, after Constantine, after the holy golden light of Theodosius, accomplished in few years a

The Church of St. Polyeuktos, which was built in only three years, was reported by the *Book of Ceremonies* to lie along the imperial processional route from the Theodosian Forum to the Church of the Holy Apostles. It was a remarkable structure to uncover, "a church of such evident grandeur securely dated to the period immediately preceding the accession of Justinian, and some ten years before St. Sophia."[33]

In the company of other more familiar women examined here, it is fascinating to consider this lesser known Byzantine princess who "surpassed the wisdom of renowned Solomon" and raised a temple to receive God. There is an authoritative-looking portrait of her standing between personifications of Magnanimity (*Megalopsychia*) and Prudence (*Sophrosyne*) in the splendidly illuminated medical treatise of Dioscorides, which was said to be produced for her.[34]

Anicia Juliana was born in about 462, and was descended on her mother's side from Emperor Theodosius I. The archeological evidence witnesses to the artistic excellence of the church that she added to her palace, which for ten years was the largest in Constantinople. She spared no expense on its construction and embellishment, which were on a level of quality not seen before in the capitol. As her construction workers finished building the church, probably in 526, "their places on the scaffolding were taken by the decorators—sculptors, mosaicists and workers in revetment and inlay."[35]

Like the Sistine Chapel from the later Renaissance period, the church built by Anicia Juliana attempted to parallel in its dimensions the first Jerusalem Temple: "the sanctuary may have been exactly twenty cubits square, the precise dimensions of the

---

work worthy of her family? She alone has conquered time and surpassed the wisdom of renowned Solomon, raising a temple to receive God, to be the gift of Juliana." Martin Harrison, *A Temple for Byzantium: The Discovery and Excavation of Anicia Juliana's Palace-Church in Istanbul* (Austin, TX: University of Texas Press, 1989), pp. 33-34.

[33] *Ibid.*, p. 35.

[34] The Dioscorides treatise is currently housed in the Vienna Osterreichische Nationalbibliothek.

[35] Harrison, *A Temple for Byzantium*, p. 77.

Holy of Holies in the Temple of Solomon;" and similar to the description in 1 Kgs. 6:29 and Ezek. 41:18, "the Temple included palm trees alternating with pairs of cherubim around the interior...The conclusion that Anicia Juliana was attempting to evoke the Temple is hard to resist."[36] The Church St Polyeuktos now stood as the most sumptuous church in Constantinople, and thus, Justinian's St. Sophia, in its scale, design, and comparative austerity, "is best seen as a deliberate reaction to it."[37]

While philanthropic foundations were erected by Byzantine imperial women primarily to the glory of God, some may also have been established as an atoning gesture. Empress Theodora, the sixth-century wife of Justinian I (483-565), used her own humble origins to good philanthropic affect by establishing the girls school "Of Repentance" (*Metanoia*) for wayward women around 530; Kuleli College now occupies the former site of this charitable foundation. "Girls who had been exploited by greediness and lascivious desires of unscrupulous men found attention, protection, home and food in the philanthropic establishments of Theodora. There, they were prepared to be able to face the difficulties of life, either as wives and mothers or as nuns and social workers."[38]

Thus, the *philanthrōpia* of God was able to absolve sin, provided that prayers and charities were offered on one's behalf. So, for example, Empress Theodora, wife of Theophilos (829-42) asked a group of bishops and monks to pray that her husband be absolved of the sins he had committed through his Iconoclastic policy, and was assured by Symeon of Studios the New Theologian that, relying on the *philanthrōpia* of God, the emperor had indeed been received among the Orthodox with his sins forgiven.[39]

---

[36] *Ibid.*, pp. 138-139. "He carved the walls of the house all around about with carved engravings of cherubim, palm trees, and open flowers." (1 Kgs. 6:29) "It was formed of cherubim and palm trees, a palm tree between cherub and cherub." (Ezek. 41:18)

[37] *Ibid.*, p. 139.

[38] Constantelos, "Women and Philanthropy," p. 4.

[39] Constantelos, *Byzantine Philanthropy and Social Welfare,* p. 38.

Empress Irene, the wife of Emperor Leo IV (750-780) and Regent for Constantine VI (771-797), offers an instance of humanitarian action as a thanksgiving to God for healing. Throughout her life exercising imperial authority, Irene demonstrated an increasingly spiritual sense of the imperial duty to practice philanthropy by patronizing building projects. Particularly after Constantinople was stricken in 740 by a disastrous earthquake, previously mentioned, Irene responded generously by funding restoration to churches and monasteries which were ruined, her generous humanitarian action modeling the litanies offered on the behalf of the "Philanthropos Theos." One example of this restorative work is the Church of the Virgin of the Spring (*tes Peges*), where the source of the water was a spring known for its miraculous healing cures, one in fact marked by a mosaic thank-offering by the empress herself.[40]

It is recorded that around the Church of St. Luke, Empress Irene "built three most important [monuments] for death, life and health. Thus, for death she built the cemeteries for strangers (*xenotaphia*) and for life she built the dining halls (*triklinous*) of Lamias of Pistopeion, and for health she built the hostel (*xenon*) called the Eirene (*ta Eirene*)."[41] Her building projects also included senior center dining halls (*gerotropheia*), soup kitchens and retirement homes. The St. Luke complex came to symbolize her imperial calling to philanthropy. "This extraordinary combination of life, health and death with clearly philanthropic aims and public functions, embodies Irene's concerns for the well-being of the city."[42]

Although the early Byzantine historians have left a narrative record rich with detail, monastic foundation documents (*typika*) also provide an invaluable treasury of textual resources,

---

[40] "Healed at Pege, [she] dedicated gifts to God in thanks—but also so that her healing, this sign of divine favour, would not be forgotten. Religious patronage is a way open to empresses to display their special relationship with God." James, *Empresses and Power in Early Byzantium*, p. 158.

[41] Judith Herrin, *Women in Purple: Rulers of Medieval Byzantium* (Princeton, NJ; Oxford: Princeton University Press, 2001), p. 104.

[42] *Ibid.*

illustrating in greater interior depth the imperial virtue of *philan-thrōpia* lived out by Byzantine empresses. Even allowing for the contributions of editors, typika for monasteries founded by empresses offer insights into the spiritual intent for their philanthropic projects, often in their own words; their Christian response to the love of mankind by the "Philanthropos Kyrios" is richly evident in this material.

Such is the case with Empress Irene Doukaina Komnene, wife of Alexios I Komnenos (1082-1118); her philanthropic work is not only reflected in the *Alexiad* written by her daughter, which is examined in the next chapter; but also, in the typikon of the Convent of the Mother-of-God Kecharitomene in Constantinople which she founded. She was known to have beneficially influenced not only her son the future Emperor John II Komnenos and her daughter, Anna Komnene, but also her sixth child as well; Isaac Komnenos was the founder of the Monastery of the Mother of God Kosmosoteire, and benefactor of the reconstruction and magnificent mosaic work on the Chora monastery still evident to visitors today.

Anna Komnene's mother gave charity to beggars while on military campaign with her husband.[43] She encouraged them not to lose heart or to beg, but exhorted them instead to find active work, suggesting that her philanthropic projects could be "viewed as a way of obtaining God's mercy through giving mercy to the less fortunate."[44]

Beside the Convent of the Theotokos Kecharitomene, Irene Doukaina also jointly founded the male monastery of the Christ Philanthropos, thereby contributing to the reemergence in the twelfth-century of double monasteries. Although now a military depot, it can still be seen in the "colorful façade of its substructures" in the Arsenal-area ruins in Istanbul.[45]

---

[43] *The Alexiad of Anna Comnena*, E.R.A.Sewter, trans. (London: Penguin, 1969) Bk 12, Ch iii, p. 378.

[44] Alice-Mary Talbot, "Byzantine Women, Saints' Lives and Social Welfare," in *Women and Religion Life in Byzantium* (Aldershot: Ashgate Variorum, 2001), p. 11.

[45] Mathews, *The Byzantine Churches of Istanbul*, p. 200.

The Kecharitomene Typikon reflects issues contemporary to the Byzantine Monastic Reform Movement of the twelfth century, among them concern that checks and balances be set in place against financial misconduct. It also demonstrates the philanthropic Christian intentions of a deeply pious empress. The typikon is especially notable in that it begins with an elegantly crafted prayer addressed to the Mother of God Kecharitomene, calling her the "ornament of our race with most saving power," and the "adorned queen standing at the right hand of the Pantokrator," who protects Constantinople, that "the great city entrusted to you be preserved as an ever-flourishing root and ever-flowing font of piety."[46]

Empress Irene credits the Mother of God with leading her to the position of empress, and granting her "much fruitfulness in the Purple" in the blessing of her many children. She is quite specific in stating her philanthropic intention to respond to God's saving love for humanity: "to praise and worship your greatness...and to thank you in a spiritual way for your compassion and mercy towards us; all that I bring to you in return is most fervent love, you who with your First-Born and Only-Begotten maintain the most providential and saving love for humanity."

Acknowledging that the stream of all good things on earth comes from God's love of mankind, so that we "possess nothing of ourselves but are entirely God's...I myself have built for you a holy temple." Thus, the Convent of the Mother of God Kecharitomene is offered; intentionally giving back some of what God has given her, she establishes a nunnery of "solitary singers of praise...dispensing to each of them from your great gifts to me the yearly and daily necessities in accordance with their physical needs." Empress Irene's typikon outlines the parameters of

---

[46] For this and the following, *"Kecharitomene*: *Typikon* of Empress Irene Doukaina Komnene for the Convent of the Mother of God *Kecharitomene* in Constantinople" in *Byzantine Monastic Foundation Documents: A Complete Translation of the Surviving Founders' Typica and Testaments*, John Thomas, Angela Constantinides Hero, eds (Washington, DC: Dumbarton Oaks Research Library and Collection, 2000), pp. 649-724.

monastic life in specific liturgical detail: "I have set up the life of devotion for them cenobitic in everything, establishing and ensuring for this divine company an absence of distraction from all sides in the matter of their holy way of life."

The Divine Office is to order the lives of the nuns, "bowing down...to God seven times a day...rising with David at midnight...lifting holy hands during the night to the Holy of Holies." Irene undergirds the instructions for her earthly support with numerous Scriptural citations and acknowledgement that all good monastic praise and work comes first from God's loving support of mankind, for if "divine help is not present, no good action is easy to accomplish for anyone at all."

Citing Heb. 13:20-21, the typikon ends as it began with prayerful exhortation: "May the God of peace who called us to his eternal glory through his great and unspeakable goodness confirm and strengthen you in his holy will through his only-begotten Son Our Lord and Savior Jesus Christ and the All-Holy Life-Giving Spirit through the intercessions of our Mother of God Kecharitomene," signing herself, "Irene Doukaina in Christ Our God the faithful Empress of the Romans."

Another example of the philanthropy of an empress illustrated in the textual record of the monastic typika is the patronage of Empress Theodora Palaiologina, wife of Michael VIII Palaiologina (1258-1282), whose building activities flowered when she was dowager empress. She restored the convent of Lips in Constantinople, adding the "south" church onto the 300-year-old Church of the Theotokos to house the tombs of her family, since the imperial mausoleum inside the Church of the Holy Apostles had been demolished during the Latin occupation. Of special interest is the benefaction of a twelve-bed women's hospital Empress Theodora built next to the convent, leaving in her typikon careful instructions for the details of its appointment.[47]

This typikon is particularly fascinating in disclosing the spiritual origin of the impulse for the empress to fund the restoration:

---

[47] Alice-Mary Talbot, "The Byzantine Family and the Monastery," in *Women and Religious Life in Byzantium* (Aldershot: Ashgate Variorum, 2001), p. 124.

"the wealth I have received from God I have dedicated to him and to our common Mistress, the Mother of God, in expiation of my sins in this life; may these gifts be found acceptable by God the Almighty, so that he may have mercy on me at the Day of Judgment and give me a share of his blessings...may you mention me constantly in both your common and private prayers to God."[48] For the churches she restored, Empress Theodora received praise in an *enkomion*, asking that God bless "the Pious and Christ-loving empress who out of love for God restored this church and many others which were ruined and who built others from the foundations."[49]

These examples offer a glimpse of the impact imperial women had on Byzantine philanthropy from its earliest centuries. Several generations of patristic teaching helped clarify the connection between poverty and merit before God, and the need for a generous Christian response to the needs of the poor; and, this evidence shows that Byzantine empresses made significant contributions at a time when systems for supplying basic social services were yet under-developed.

In their Greek-influenced culture, in which women were often regarded as invisible components of society and identified with the home front, these examples illustrate how they enhanced the environment around them, especially in times of critical need, such as earthquake, famine, and political catastrophe. In monastic *typika* in particular, imperial women, whose accomplishments may often have been under-reported, were able to make valuable contributions to the textual record. They reveal a more complete picture of several of the Byzantine empresses whose Christian response to the love of God for mankind inspired them to embark upon philanthropic building projects benefiting Byzantine society.

---

[48] "*Lips*: *Typikon* of Theodora Palaiologina for the Convent of Lips in Constantinople" in *Byzantine Monastic Foundation Documents* (Washington, DC: Dumbarton Oaks Research Library and Collection, 2000), p. 1281.
[49] Alice-Mary Talbot, "Old Wine in New Bottles" in *Women and Religious Life in Byzantium,* (Aldershot: Ashgate Variorum, 2001), p. 19.

CHAPTER III.2
ANNA KOMNENE'S *ALEXIAD*: THE VOICE OF THE GOOD DAUGHTER (*KALE THUGATER*)

I wish to recall everything, the achievements before his elevation to the throne and his actions in the service of others.[1]

In exploring significant voices and stories of women contributing to the history of Christianity, we meet in the epic narrative of the *Alexiad* a family from the threshold of twelfth-century Constantinople—the saga of a Byzantine Emperor and Empress described by their imperial daughter. It is the "chief basis of our knowledge of the important period which saw the restoration of Byzantine power and the meeting of Byzantium with the West in the First Crusade."[2] While the *Alexiad* has been examined from the standpoint of social context and genre, it can also be viewed as reflecting one daughter's love, even within the moral and spiritual complexity of this particular Orthodox family as it is played out on the stage of Byzantine Christianity.

The eldest daughter of Emperor Alexios I Komnenos (1057-1118, ruled 1081-1118 C.E.) and Irene Doukaina (1066-1023, or

---

[1] Anna Comnena, *The Alexiad of Anna Comnena*, E.R.A. Sewter, trans. (London: Penguin Books, 1969), Prologue; p. 17; referenced hereafter by book, chapter, and page number. This chapter is dedicated to the memory of Charles Osner and Dorothy June Long.

[2] George Ostrogorsky, *History of the Byzantine State* (New Brunswick, NJ: Rutgers University Press, 1969), p. 351.

1033), Anna Komnene (1083-1153 or 54) is representative of a period in Byzantine history when the power of great aristocratic families became amplified and inter-connected by strategic marriage alliances. Alexios was the first of the Komnenian Byzantine emperors and Irene's family was known to trace its lineage back to the Empress Helena and Constantine the Great; there was a tradition that he had appointed their forbear the Duke of Constantinople, hence the family name Dukas.

Anna Komnene narrates in rich detail the life-panorama of her father in her *opus magnus* which Dölger has called a "work of filial piety…set out to extol the virtues of her father whom she adored and admired above all others."[3] Deemed a "learned work without parallel in the canon of women's writing in Attic history,"[4] the *Alexiad* is the only text written by a woman in the whole of the *Corpus Scriptorum Historiae Byzantinae*. Whatever may be said by the author's critics,[5] in the *Alexiad* Anna Komnene leaves a singular contribution to Byzantine history. "She is one of a small group of medieval women who have not been muted."[6] She has become of late more visible in popular culture; she even finds a place among the names inscribed on the porcelain

---

[3] Franz Dölger, "Byzantine Literature," in *Cambridge Medieval History*; v. 4 *The Byzantine Empire*, edited by J.M. Hussey (Cambridge: Cambridge University Press, 1966-1967), p. 231.

[4] Ellen Quandahl and Susan B. Jarratt, "To Recall Him…Will be a Subject of Lamentation: Anna Comnena as Rhetorical Historiographer," *Rhetorica: A Journal of the History of Rhetoric*, 26:3 (Summer 2008), p. 303.

[5] "The laudatory tendencies in the *Alexaid* and certain other shortcomings, particularly its confused chronology, are more than balanced by the comprehensive mine of information which the authoress was able to provide, due partly to the special faculties afforded by her high position and partly to her own thirst for knowledge." Ostrogorsky, *History of the Byzantine State*, p. 351.

[6] Thalia Gouma-Petersen, "Gender and Power: Passages to the Maternal in Anna Komnene's *Alexiad*," in *Anna Komnene and Her Times*, Thalia Gouma-Petersen, ed. (New York: Garland, 2000), p. 110.

"Heritage Floor" of Judy Chicago's art piece, "The Dinner Party," installed at the Brooklyn Museum.[7] While some interpretations of Anna Komnene bewailing her fate are understandable considering the text, the *Alexiad* and its commentators are examined here for evidence of the author as a faithful daughter expressing loyalty to both of her parents and carrying on scholarly work with the gifts given to her by them and "what God has apportioned to me from above." [Prologue; 17] This chapter looks at Anne Komnene through the lens of filial devotion and asks to what extent the *Alexiad* can be viewed as demonstrating the Byzantine ideal of the good daughter (*kale thugater*) of Alexios I Komnenos.

As a daughter and granddaughter, as wife and sister, Anna Komnene's views of her familial ties are the warp and woof of the fabric of the *Alexiad*; her editorial choices for devoted emphasis and intentional critical omission make up the threads and coloring of its tapestry. From the first, she stresses her royal birth, introducing herself with the defining fact of having emerged from the cradle as a true imperial child "born in the purple," [Prologue; 17] "resembling her father" [VI.viii; 196], two years after he ascended the Byzantine throne; and therefore, she was delivered in the royal birthing room in the palace, a chamber lined with semi-precious purple porphyry stone, designating those born there as *porphyrogenita*.

When still quite young, Anna was betrothed to Constantine, the son of Emperor Michael VII Doukas (c.1050-1078, ruled 1071-1078), in a bid by Alexios I to secure an heir for the Byzantine throne. She was sent off for several years to be brought up within the household of Maria of Alania (ca.1050-ca.1103); and for a time, Anna and her betrothed were named together with the Emperor and the Empress in the official acclamations at court ceremonies.[8] Anna describes this as a happy period of her life, looking up at an impressionable age to the celebrated beauty of her

---

[7] Anna Komnene also appears as a character in the novel, *Count Robert of Paris,* written by Sir Walter Scott in 1832.

[8] Ostrogorsky, *History of the Byzantine State,* p. 376.

intended mother-in-law and rhapsodizing about her captivating fiancé.

Empress Maria was the maternal figure present in her life on the cusp of young womanhood,[9] with Anna treasuring that the Dowager Empress "shared all her secrets with me." [III.i; 105] Later, when a son, John (1087-1143, ruled 1118-1143), was born to Alexios and Irene, this arrangement proved unnecessary and Anna's bright future, at least as an empress, was eclipsed by her infant brother. Expectations of imperial power, however, were indelibly imprinted on her point of view for the rest of her life.

Since the likeliness of her father's dynastic strategy playing out was eradicated by the birth of her brother and the untimely death of her young fiancé as well, Anna was, while still a teenager then married off to Nikephoros Bryennios (1062-ca. 1136-37), a military comrade of her father.[10] Of course, Anna Komnene knew as part of her imperial history the seven women who did manage to rule as Byzantine regents, and two more who even reigned alone. She would have known about the fierce dynastic strategizing of her adoptive mother, Maria of Alania. She knew of the imperial *chrysobull* of Emperor Alexios empowering her grandmother, Anna Dalassene (1025-1102), to control Byzantine administration in her son's absence; she knew it well enough to quote from it in the *Alexiad*.[11] Anna Komnene witnessed a

---

[9] Maria of Alania had caught the eye of Anna's father as well: Alexios Komnenos was "so passionately attached to this beautiful and clever woman that he was ready to sacrifice his own wife Irene for her; he was only saved from this false step, which might have had grave political consequences, by the energetic protests of Patriarch Cosmas who insisted on the crowning of Irene." Ostrogorsky, *History of the Byzantine State*, p. 376.

[10] He was also, it should be noted, a rival emperor during the reigns of both Alexius' predecessors on the throne, Michael VII Doukas and Nikephoros III Botaneiates (1002-1081—ruled 1078-1081).

[11] "I, your emperor, therefore decree explicitly in this present *chrysobull* the following: because of her vast experience of secular affairs (despite the very low value she sets upon such matters), whatever she decrees in writing shall have permanent validity as if I myself, your Serene Emperor, had issued them or after dictating them had had them committed

generation in the sweep of imperial Byzantine history when women's powerful roles at court had been amply evident.

Thus, she could hardly have shared his unalloyed joy when in 1092 her imperial father crowned her little brother *caesar* and celebrated by issuing new coinage containing an "almost pure gold coin, the *hyperpyron.*"[12] Unfortunately, she has also been implicated by many as conspiring with her mother in a bid for the throne after her father died which involved a plot to murder her brother. While her silence about the accomplishments of Emperor John II Komnenos indicates she battled resentment for her brother and his reign, Anna remains adamant in her devotion to her father, faithful to him throughout his lifetime, and present with him in his last hours.

Later, in keeping with the close bond with her father, Anna Komnene wrote admiringly in turn about her husband. [I.v; 40] Notwithstanding her fury that Nikephoros Bryennios would not assist Empress Irene in the assassination plot to wrestle the throne from her brother and assume it himself, she appears on balance to have been happy in her marriage. Nevertheless, when in 1119 the young emperor obtained proof of a conspiracy, he temporarily confiscated their property, and forced both Irene and Anna to retire to a convent, while Bryennius himself remained free. "John, like his father, was alert to his enemies, but merciful to them."[13]

After the death of her mother in 1123 and her husband in 1137, Anna Komnene withdrew further from public life "in order to devote myself to my books and the worship of God," [XIV.vii; 460] and she focused at that time on crafting a grand epic honoring her father's memory, often writing so long into the day that it was "time to light the lamps." [XIII.vi; 411] In reflecting on how

---

to writing. Whatever decisions or orders are made by her, written or unwritten, reasonable or unreasonable, provided that they bear her seal (the Transfiguration and the Assumption), shall be regarded as coming from myself." Book III.vi; 116-117.

[12] Warren Treadgold, *A History of the Byzantine State and Society* (Stanford: Stanford University Press, 1997), p. 618.

[13] Michael Angold, *Church and Society in Byzantium under the Comneni 1081-1261* (Cambridge: Cambridge University Press, 1995), p. 629.

Anna Komnene addressed resolving the difficult case of conscience with her probable guilt in the conspiracy to dethrone
John, her long years in enforced monasticism, with its penitential
components, gave her the prayerful opportunity to come to terms
with her rancor toward her brother.

One of the ways that Anna Komnene authenticates herself as
a historian is by demonstrating her qualifications as an intellectual figure "on a par with any man,"[14] one who "preferred philosophy, the medicine of the soul, to that of the body."[15] She makes
good use of the matchless education of a *porphyrogenita* princess,
speaking with undaunted pride about her imperial upbringing.
Classical education was often described as achievement in a quar-
tet of subject categories favored at the time—Geometry, Arithme-
tic, Astronomy, Music—which were referred to as "the Quadrivium of sciences." [Prologue; 17]

Her scholarly pursuits reflect one of the more admirable arenas in which Anna took after her mother, who cleverly persuaded
her of the wisdom of the Church Fathers. For example, Anna Komnene records her mother teaching her, "I myself do not approach
such books without a tremble. Yet I cannot tear myself away from
them. Wait a little and after a close look at other books, believe
me, you will taste the sweetness of these." [V.ix; 178-179] Empress Irene was often found at table "diligently reading the dog-
matic pronouncements of the Holy Fathers" [V.ix; 178], and was
said to have written the Typikon for the convent she founded, the
Mother of God Kecharitomene.[16]

---

[14] Peter Hatlie, "Images of Motherhood and Self in Byzantine Literature,"
Dumbarton Oaks Papers v. 63 (2003), p. 51.

[15] Georges Tornikios, quoted in Robert Browning, "An Unpublished Funeral Oration on Anna Comnene," in *Aristotle Transformed: The Ancient
Commentators and Their Influence*, Richard Sorabji, ed. (Ithaca, NY: Cornell University Press, 1990), p. 430.

[16] See "*Kecharitomene*: Typikon of Empress Irene Doukaina Komnene for
the Convent of the Mother of God *Kecharitomene* in Constantinople," in
*Byzantine Monastic Foundation Documents: A Complete Translation of the
Surviving Founders' Typika and Testaments*, John Thomas, Angela C. Hero,
eds; Robert Allison *et al*, trans.; commentary by John Thomas

Anna Komnene crafted the *Alexiad* to complete a project inaugurated by her mother; Irene Doukaina had commissioned Anna's husband to write an historical account of the deeds of Alexios after his death. What survives of this effort is the essay "Materials for a History."[17] Anna Komnene composed her own fifteen-volume work during the reign of Manual I, the next emperor after John. Although in all probability she intentionally offered a version of history which passed over her brother's reign in critical silence, John II Komnenos has in fact been regarded by some as the greatest of the Komnenian emperors.[18]

Written in retrospect, the *Alexiad* looks back on memories of her father's life culled from war stories of the emperor's retired comrades-in-arms [XIV.vii; 460], Anna's own eyewitness memories,[19] and conversations between the emperor and his military commander, George Palaiologos, while his niece was present at court.[20] Additionally, the *Alexiad* provides the only known full Byzantine historical account of the First Crusade, and "no study of that enterprise is complete without an analysis of the information she supplies."[21] It is perhaps a high compliment that Anna Komnene's history is consulted as often as it is, and that her

(Washington, D.C.: Dumbarton Oaks Research Library and Collection, 2000), pp. 649-726.

[17] Nicephoros Bryennios, "Materials for a History," Henri Gregoire, trans. *Byzantion* 23 (1953), pp. 469-530; and *Byzantion* 25-27 (1955-57), pp. 881-925.

[18] John Birkenmeier, *The Development of the Komnenian Army: 1081–1180* (Leiden: Brill, 2002), p. 85.

[19] "She listened attentively to those who gave displays of their wisdom every day before her father the Emperor and was roused to emulation by them." Tornikios, quoted in Browning, "An Unpublished Funeral Oration on Anna Comnene," p. 405.

[20] "From all these materials the whole fabric of my history—my true history—has been woven." Book XIV.vvi; 461.

[21] Paul Stephenson, "Anna Comnene's *Alexiad* as a Source for the Second Crusade?" *Journal for Medieval History* 29 (2003), p. 41.

strategic military accounts are comprehensive enough that her authorship as a woman has even been doubted.[22]

Writing in first-person was emerging noticeably in the eleventh and twelfth centuries, and Anna includes descriptions of her own formation and accomplishments in the *Alexiad*; the loyal daughter is unapologetically present as part of her father's story. Another example of this trend is Michael Psellus (1018-1078), who knit his own character into *The Chronographia*[23] and, like Anna, included his education and achievements, personally intervening in his account to heighten the drama of events by emotionally responding to them.[24]

So, as a faithful daughter who is present in her own work, Anna Komnene was an innovative child of her time. When compared with the terminology and language of the histories of Michael Psellos or Niketas Choniates, Anna speaks "not as a woman in an *écriture feminine*, but in the same full-blown atticising form of Greek favoured by the dominant élite of eleventh- and twelfth-century Byzantium."[25] The *Alexiad* is often criticized, but it is more often referenced as a source of history, and it provides a unique window into the imperial epicenter of Komnenian Byzantium. Alexios I, "that master of strategy" [I.vii; 48], and his family are all viewed at work and at prayer, receiving friend and foe at court, and strategizing Byzantine survival in precarious times.

---

[22] "Howard-Johnston's idea that detailed and lively battle narratives cannot have been written by a woman and must therefore derive from lost Breyennios dossiers rather than having been written by Anna Komnene has fortunately not found many adherents." Dion C. Smythe, "Middle Byzantine Family Values and Anna Komnene's Alexiad" in *Byzantine Women: Varieties of Experience 800-1200*, Lynda Garland, ed. (Aldershot: Ashgate, 2006), p. 130. For James Howard-Johnson's evaluation of Anna Komnene's authorial integrity, see "Anna Komnene and the Alexiad," in *Alexios I Komnenos: Papers*, Margaret Mullett and Dion Smythe, eds (Belfast: Belfast Byzantine Texts and Translations, 1996).

[23] See Michael Psellus, *The Chronographia*, E. R. A. Sewter, trans. (London: Routledge & K. Paul, 1953).

[24] Quandahl and Jarratt, "To Recall Him," p. 317.

[25] D. C. Smythe, "Women as Outsiders," in *Women, Men and Eunuchs*, Liz James, ed. (London: Rutledge, 1997), p. 156.

Although the title suggests an heroic prose epic praising the life and exploits of Alexios I Komnenos, the *Alexiad* presents "no stock panegyric" of the father Anna loved, but rather, expounds virtues he actually possessed and "dramatizes events that were in fact dramatic."[26] Emperor Alexios inherited an empire in financial shambles and a disintegrating imperial frontier with daunting foes pressing in on all sides. While still a young general, he proved himself to be a successful and politically savvy warrior; yet after early military successes, Alexios mounted several campaigns only to be repeatedly vanquished.

Therefore, in his rise toward the Byzantine throne, he came to rely on the powerful relatives of, first, his mother, Anna Dalassene; then of his adoptive mother, Maria of Alania;[27] and of his wife, Irene Doukaina. Since he was often away on military campaigns more comprehensively narrated by other Byzantine historians, Anna may at times have seldom seen her father; but when she did, her memories were vivid and detailed.

Alexios and his family "did much to promote the new wave of monastic piety," as founders and re-founders of monasteries and convents.[28] Empress Irene was "deeply pious and became the patron of monks and holy men;"[29] Alexios, however, was often on bad terms with the Church. Hardly a paragon of wholesomeness, considering his dynastic machinations, he was condemned by Patriarch Cosmas as deserving of public penitential rebuke.

Through Anna's eyes, Alexios is seen seeking the counsel of the Patriarch on the advice of his mother, and asking repentance for allowing his supporters to sack Constantinople during the course of his coup to overtake the throne.[30] He and the members

---

[26] Treadgold, *A History of the Byzantine State,* p. 693.

[27] Since Maria of Alania was only about seven years older than Irene's son, this double-team mothering of Alexios for the sake of dynastic strategy created a dove-tailing of the generations which was unusual, to say the least.

[28] Angold, *Church and Society in Byzantium,* p. 69.

[29] *Ibid.,* p. 45.

[30] Additionally, the fact that he confiscated Church treasures to pay for his military campaigns is evidenced by his *chrysobull* promising to make

of his family were forced to submit to penances prescribed by the Patriarch. Anna Komnene's description of the joy with which they each acquitted their allotted share does not quite disguise the humiliation it was. [III.vi; 115] In fact, eventually Alexios retaliated by forcing Patriarch Cosmas to resign.[31]

In the *Alexiad*, Anna Komnene consciously positions herself "within an august genealogy through her allusions to and imitation of classical historians,"[32] demonstrating that her ways of writing and thinking were formed by the complex fabric of Greek *paideia*. Thus, the *Alexiad* was crafted for an audience which could be assumed to possess a rich knowledge of Homeric influences and citations.[33] "A modern and most noble Hercules" in Anna's eyes [I.x; 52], Alexios and even his enemies, are depicted as sharing in "an heroic struggle in the style of Greeks versus Trojans."[34] Anna Komnene's pen crafting an epic hero who stood tall in a world already populated by heroes of mythic strength and beauty rather than simply by men and women has been considered a step forward in Byzantine historiography.[35]

Even when she was not an eyewitness, she manages to fill the page with jeweled scenes of the imperial court and graphic images of the mechanics of warfare, [XIII.iii; 402] but also with endearing true-to-life details and startling episodes she knew firsthand from the remarkable characters in her family.[36] In her highly

---

amends and never do it again. Angold, *Church and Society in Byzantium*, p. 47.

[31] Angold, *Church and Society in Byzantium*, p. 69.

[32] Quandahl and Jarratt, "To Recall Him," p. 324.

[33] "Evoking ancient writers, orators, and mythical figures is both a display of Anna's erudition and acquaintance with works of antiquity and a frame for her own writing in a comparable elevated, lively manner." Carolyn L. Connor, *Women of Byzantium* (New Haven: Yale University Press, 2004), p. 246.

[34] Connor, *Women of Byzantium*, p. 247.

[35] Jakov Ljubarskij, "Why is the *Alexiad* a Masterpiece of Byzantine Literature?" in *Anna Komnene and her Times*, Thalia Gouma-Peterson, ed. (New York; London: Garland Publishing, Inc, 2000), p. 175.

[36] For example, Anna Dalassene demanding sanctuary in Hagia Sophia during her son's coup d'état by clasping the sacred doors at the entrance

visual literary style, Anna Komnene depicts her father in the midst of it all as the operational centerpiece: analyzing maneuvers, issuing orders, and campaigning to retrieve the four corners of the empire. At once both congenial father figure and warrior-emperor, she describes him as respected by subjects and foes alike, driving the reins of the empire.[37]

Anna Komnene also looked up to the strong women in her family and she describes the reins of the empire being driven by one of them as well.[38] Anna Dalassene is one of three impressive maternal figures at play in the make-up of Anna Komnene's family life. Like many young girls, Anna adored her grandmother and characterized her as courageous and assertive, the "mother of the Komneni," [II.iv; 85] a phrase which Anna Dalassene herself adopted as a semi-official title during her years in power; a seal survives inscribed with the phrase.[39]

Anna also offers the reader appreciative descriptions of her mother, Irene Doukaina, comparing her lovely hands to carved ivory. [III.iii; 110-111] She highlights her own relationship of filial devotion with a miraculous occurrence in connection with her birth: since her father was away on campaign, Empress Irene is said to have made the sign of the cross upon her belly, charging her unborn child to stay the onset of labor until his return. [VI.viii; 196] In this, Anna was compliant.

---

and crying out, "Unless my hands are cut off, I will not leave this holy place, except on one condition: that I receive the Emperor's cross as guarantee of safety." Book II.v; 85. Another remarkable action-film-worthy image depicts the warrior-prowess of her father, who suddenly struck at the enemy; "his hand, together with the sword in it, was at once hurled to the ground." Book I.viii; 50.

[37] Connor, *Women of Byzantium*, p. 248.

[38] "He yielded her precedence in everything, relinquishing the reins of government, as it were, and running alongside as she drove the imperial chariot...She governed with him, sometimes even grasping the reins and alone driving the chariot of power—without accident or error." Book III.vi; 116.

[39] Barbara Hill, *Imperial Women in Byzantium 1025-1204: Power, Patronage and Ideology* (New York: Longman, 1999), p. 117.

Thus, she paints a picture of the rounds of her pious imperial family life with scheduled times for Scripture to be read and Psalms to be offered, where "it was natural that men of culture should attend the palace when the devoted pair (my parents, I mean) were themselves laboring so hard night and day in searching the Holy Scriptures." [V.ix; 178] Later, after her childbearing years, Empress Irene accompanied her husband on campaign,[40] and was known for her generosity and good counsel to the poor. [XII.iii; 377-378] Maria of Alania as well comes in for admiration and praise in Anna Komnene's description.[41]

Anna Dalassene, Irene Doukaina, and Maria of Alania each figure significantly in Anna's family life and that of her father, Alexios I. All three women "deal with the individual crises they face with courage and vision."[42] Both Anna Komnene's mother and her grandmother retired to the convents they founded, Irene Doukaina to the Kecharitomene, and Anna Dalassene to the Pantepoptes. Anna followed in turn, also retiring to the Kecharitomene convent, "where she interacted with educated men who flocked there to read, write, and recite."[43]

Note that only when her mother's efforts to put Nikephoros Bryennios on the throne failed did Anna Komnene "throw in her hand and seek consolation in learning,"[44] and it was in her forced convent retirement "overlooking the tranquil waters of the Golden Horn,"[45] that she wrote the *Alexiad*.[46] In the portraits of

---

[40] "By night she was the unsleeping eye, by day his most conspicuous guardian." Book XII.iii; 376.

[41] Maria of Alania is described as "tall, like a cypress tree; her skin was snow-white...eyebrows flame-colored, arched above eyes of light blue...a living work of art, an object of desire to lovers of beauty." Book III.ii; 107.

[42] Barbara Hill, "Anna Komnene," in *Women and Gender in Medieval Europe*, Margaret Schaus, ed. (New York: Routledge, Taylor & Francis, 2006), p. 444.

[43] Hill, "Anna Komnene," p. 444.

[44] Ostrogorsky, *History of the Byzantine State*, p. 377.

[45] Browning, "An Unpublished Funeral Oration on Anna Comnene," p. 401.

[46] Also, Browning suggests that, from the Convent of the Mother of God Kecharitomene, Anna Komnene "played a role in the revival of

her grandmother and her mother, maternal imagery is mobilized to "argue for an aristocratic woman's right of access to both a full intellectual life and real political power."[47] Furthermore, in Anna Komnene's use of the theme of parental relationships, she reveals and defines herself in a manner consistent with the mother-son portraits of authors such as Gregory of Nazianzus, Theodore of Stoudios, and Michael Psellos.[48]

Although in his history of the middle centuries of the Byzantine state[49] written in the next generation after Anna Komnene, Niketas Choniates blames Empress Irene for inciting Anna's husband to seize the throne and names Anna as an instigator of the plot, the historian Zonaras does not in fact represent Anna as in any way a conspirator against her brother the emperor:

> The secondary literature, eliding Zonaras and Choniates, has frequently constructed a biography in which Anna and her mother at this time together attempt to wrest the crown from John. When this plot fails, Anna is exiled to the convent, where, embittered, she remains for the rest of her life. As we will see, generations of scholars have created this story, using familiar topoi about women's psychology to craft a picture of Anna as a woman with a vexed relationship to imperial power.[50]

More recently, in fact, commentators including Robert Browning and Barbara Hill have been more cautionary in their estimation of Anna's responsibility in plans to overthrow the throne.[51]

Aristotelian scholarship in the Byzantine world" with her philosophical circle "numbering among its members Michael of Ephesus and probably Eustratios of Nicaea." Robert Browning, "An Unpublished Funeral Oration on Anna Comnene," pp. 400-401.

[47] Hatlie, "Images of Motherhood and Self in Byzantine Literature," p. 51.

[48] *Ibid.*, p. 52.

[49] See Niketas Choniates, *O City of Byzantium: Annals of Niketas Choniatēs,* translated by Harry J. Magoulias (Detroit: Wayne State University Press, 1984).

[50] Quandahl and Jarratt, "To Recall Him," p. 306.

[51] Browning, "An Unpublished Funeral Oration on Anna Comnena," p. 5; Hill, *Imperial Women in Byzantium 1025-1204,* p. 34.

While frustration over unfulfilled imperial ambition likely spear-headed Anna Komnene's efforts to favor her father over her brother in describing her family circumstances, the *Alexiad* was nevertheless an unprecedented achievement. Treadgold hails it as "the finest work of historical art since Procopius' *Wars*. Anna set a high standard for the Byzantine historians to come."[52] In fact, the extent to which she was successful is evident if we ask: What would be known about the First Crusade in general and Anna Komnene in particular, if she had not crafted the *Alexiad*?[53] It is a "multi-dimensional history, one that demands attention to its learned ways of representing and performing the past in relation to both individual and socio-political experience."[54]

Anna Komnene commits herself again and again to impartiality; however, considering her proximity to the events, she protests too much. As a useful historical resource for the First Crusade, it must be admitted that she describes it within the narrow focus of her father's point of view, not delving into details of its origin. Judged as world history, it is plainly found wanting. Yet, although the text was never explicitly intended as such, the *Alexiad* remains a significant source for the First Crusade from the Byzantine perspective;[55] and with its elaborate web of strategic eyewitness military details, it may indeed, as he states, have awakened Gibbon's jealousy.[56] Indeed, in recent scholarship, Anna Komnene's historical work in the *Alexiad* has often been accepted as "an official authorial voice."[57]

---

[52] Treadgold, *A History of the Byzantine State and Society*, p. 693.

[53] Gouma-Petersen, "Gender and Power: Passages to the Maternal in Anna Komnene's *Alexiad*," p. 112.

[54] Quandahl and Jarratt, "To Recall Him," p. 335.

[55] Stephenson, "Anna Comnene's *Alexiad* as a Source for the Second Crusade?" p. 41.

[56] "The perpetual strain of panegyric and apology awakens our jealousy to question the veracity of the author." Edward Gibbon, *The History of the Decline and Fall of the Roman Empire* (New York: Harper & Bros., 1880), v. 4, p. 619.

[57] Gouma-Petersen, "Gender and Power: Passages to the Maternal in Anna Komnene's *Alexiad*," p. 110.

By writing an epic life of her father, Anna Komnene has, on balance, contributed to the story of Byzantium as we know it. Even with the bitter disappointment of her relationship with her brother starkly unreconciled, the *Alexiad* can be considered an act of devotion by the good daughter (*kale thugater*) and an example of the complexities of love in action within the Orthodox family, one which has left us a lasting record of twelfth-century Byzantium. It can be viewed as an aspect of her role in the family that Anna seems content with an arranged marriage and presupposes that love and affection will be found within it; yet she considered herself to be an imperial Komnene all her life. Her husband, while he appears in her history, does not fill her life in the way that her father did.[58]

Anna retained such an effective dynastic connection with her family that her seal bears the name Komnene and not Bryennisa, her name by marriage. Her own daughter, Irene, preferred to identify herself through the line of her grandmother, styling her name as Irene Doukaina, rather than using her father's name; thus, the criterion for choosing her surname was "prestige, not paternity." And, in fact, none of her children took their father's name.[59] In aristocratic families where several of the women were quite as powerful as their husbands, it appears that often "power, property, and prestige traveled down the female line."[60]

The *topos* of the faithful daughter is also reflected in Anna's description of her father's creation of the orphanage of St. Peter and St. Paul on the acropolis of Constantinople, thus praising him for the imperial virtue of *philanthrōpia*; "Rather daringly, perhaps, I would say that the emperor's work could be compared with my Savior's miracle." [Book XV.vii.; 491] Its mission was to "care for the needs of the poor and refugees whose presence on the streets of the capitol contributed to the instability of Constantinopolitan

---

[58] Hill, *Imperial Women in Byzantium 1025-1204*, pp. 125-128.

[59] *Ibid.*, p. 137.

[60] Anjeliki E. Laiou, "Women in the History of Byzantium," in *Byzantine Women and Their World*, Ioli Kalavrezou, ed. (Cambridge, MA: Harvard University Art Museums, 2003), p. 29.

society."[61] Her esteemed regard for her mother is evidenced in Anna's intellectual prowess, her pious askesis, and the fact that she carefully and consistently cites both of her parents when acknowledging her imperial genealogy. [Prologue; 17]

Anna Komnene's account of the family gathered around the deathbed of Emperor Alexios includes her own presence there as his dutiful daughter, compassionately preparing nourishment for him in his last days and placing herself between her grieving mother and the sight of her father as he was suffering *in extremis.* In the text, she clearly identifies her younger brother as the emperor's successor, and reports that in imminent anticipation of imperial accession, he moved "to the house set apart for him" in the Great Palace. [XV.vi, 512] As death approached, the emperor "was slow to reject his wife's irresponsible proposal to disinherit his son in favor of the Caesar Nikephoros Bryennios. According to John himself, whose word was accepted, Alexios decided for his son just before dying in August."[62]

As an eye witness, Anna Komnene describes in frank medical detail her dying father's painful symptoms and in response the loving ministrations of her sister and mother in grief, as well as her own, holding her father's hand to the end. In his funeral oration for her, Tornikes praises Anna in this moment, "who according to those who say anything was her brother's rival, although she knew that her father had just left this world, forgot the imperial title and joined with her mother in mourning, as they sat alone on the floor with bared heads."[63]

Finally, the *Alexiad* can be seen as a unique examination of several of the relationships within her imperial family. While she may not have fulfilled her dream of exercising influence over the empire as empress, Anna Komnene was able to advance the memory and renown of her beloved father by the crafting of an epic narrative describing his achievements. Thus, as the pious

---

[61] Angold, *Church and Society in Byzantium under the Comneni 1081-1261,* p. 69.

[62] *Ibid.,* p. 628.

[63] Georges Tornikios, quoted in Browning, "An Unpublished Funeral Oration on Anna Comnene," p. 404.

daughter of Emperor Alexios I Komnenos, she has left an enduring legacy in Byzantine history from the educated gifts, personal devotion, and experience of her own voice.

BIBLIOGRAPHY

PRINCIPAL ORIGINAL RESOURCES AND CRITICAL EDITIONS

For Lydia:

Novum Testamentum Graece, Eberhard and Erwin Nestle [*et al*], 27th rev. edition (Stuttgart: Deutsche Bibelstiftung, 1995). For English: *The New Oxford Annotated Bible: New Revised Standard Version: with the Apocrypha*; 4th edition/ Michael D. Coogan, ed. (Oxford; New York: Oxford University Press, 2010).

For Thekla and Tryphaena:

"Praxeis Paulou kai Thekles" in *Acta Apostolorum*, R.A. Lipsius, M. Bonnet, eds (Hildesheim: Georg Olms, 1958), pp. 235-272. For English, "The Acts of Paul," in *New Testament Apocrypha*, revised ed., W. Schneemelcher, ed., R. McL. Wilson, trans. (Louisville, KY: Westminster/John Knox Press, 1992), pp. 2:213-270. See also Jeremy W. Barrier, *The Acts of Paul and Thecla: A Critical Introduction and Commentary* (Tübingen: Mohr Siebeck, 2009).

"Thaumata tes Hagias kai Proto-martyros Theklas," in *Vie et miracles de Sainte Thecle: Texte Grec, Tradution et Commentaire*, Gilbert Dragon, Maria Dupré La Tour, trans. (Bruxelles: Société des Bollandistes, 1978). For selected English translation, see: Scott F. Johnson, *The Life and Miracles of Thekla: A Literary Study* (Washington, D.C.: Center for Hellenic Studies, 2006). See also "The Miracles of Saint Thekla," in *Miracle Tales from Byzantium*), Alice-Mary Talbot, Scott Fitzgerald

Johnson, trans. (Cambridge, MA: Harvard University Press, 2012), pp. 1-202.

For Perpetua:

Passion de Perpétue et de Félicité suivi des Actes, J. Amat, ed. "Sources Chrétiennes," no. 417 (Paris: Les Éditions du Cerf, 1996); for English, Thomas J. Heffernan, *The Passion of Perpetua and Felicity* (Oxford: Oxford University Press, 2012). See also: J. Armitage Robison, *The Passion of S. Perpetua* (Cambridge: Cambridge University Press, 1981); Walter H. Shewring, ed., *The Passion of Perpetua and Felicity: A New Edition and Translation of the Latin Text Together with the Sermons of St. Augustine upon These Saints* (London: Sheed and Ward, 1931).

For Helena:

Eusebius, *Vita Constantinii*, PG 20.909-1232; for English, Averil Cameron, Stuart G. Hall, *Eusebius: Life of Constantine* (Oxford: Clarendon Press, 1999).

For Syncletica:

"Vita et Gesta Sanctae Seataeque Magistrate Syncleticae," PG 28.1487-1558; for English:
Pseudo-Athanasius, *The Life and Regimen of the Blessed and Holy Syncletica: Part One: The Translation*, Elizabeth Bongie, trans. (Toronto: Peregrina Publishing Co., 2003).
Sayings of Syncletica, "Apophthegmata Patrum Graecorum" (Alphabetical Collection) PG 65.71-412; supplemented by J.-C. Guy, *Recherches sur la Tradition Grecque des Apophthegmata Patrum*, Subsidia Hagiographica 36 (Brussels: 1962); for English: *Give Me a Word: The Alphabetical Sayings of the Desert Fathers*, John Wortley, trans. (Crestwood, NY: St. Vladimir's Seminary Press, 2014).

For Macrina:

S. Gregorii Episcopi Nysseni, De Anima et Resurrectione cum Sorore Sua Macrina Dialogus, J. G. Krabinger, ed. (Leipzig: Gustav Wittig, 1837); for English, Anna M. Silvas, *Macrina the*

Younger, Philosopher of God (Turnhout, Belgium: Brepols Publishers, 2008).

S. *Gregorii Episcopi Nysseni, Vita Sanctae Macrinae*, Virginia Woods Calahan, ed., in *Ascetica*, VIII,1, *Gregorii Nysseni Opera*, Werner Jaeger, gen. ed. (Leiden: Brill, 1958-1996); for English, Anna M. Silvas, *Macrina the Younger, Philosopher of God* (Turnhout, Belgium: Brepols Publishers, 2008).

For Olympias:

John Chrysostom, *Lettres à Olympias*, Anne-Marie Malingrey, trans.; Sources Chrétiennes, v. 13 (Paris: Éditions du CERF, 1947); for English, "Letters of St. Chrysostom to Olympias," in *Saint Chrysostom: On the Priesthood; Ascetic Treatises; Select Homilies and Letters; Homilies on the Statues*; NPNF IX.284-304.

Palladius, Bishop of Aspuna, *Dialogue on the Life of St. John Chrysostom*, Robert T. Meter, trans. (New York: Newman Press, 1985).

"Vita Sanctae Olympiadis," Hippolyte Delehaye, ed. *Analecta Bollandiana* 15 (1896), pp. 400-423; for English, Elizabeth A. Clark, "The Life of Olympias," in *Jerome, Chrysostom, and Friends: Essays and Translations* (New York: Edwin Mellen Press, 1979), pp. 127-142.

For Kassia:

Kassia the Nun. "When Augustus Reigned," in Mother Mary and Kallistos Ware, trans., *The Festal Menaion*, vol. 12, December (London: Faber and Faber, 1969), p. 254.

Theodore the Studite, Letters 205, 413, 541, PG 99.903-1669.

Patria of Constantinople, *Scriptores Originum Constantinopolitanarum* 276 (Leipzig, 1907); John Zonaris, *Epitome Historiarum*, Book XIII-XVIII (Bonn: Weber, 1897); Michael Glykas, *Chronographia* (Bonn: Weber, 1836); Symeon the Logothete, *Chronographia*, PG 109; George the Monk, *Chronikon*, PG 110; Leo the Grammarian, *Chronographia*, PG 108.

For Anna Komnene:

Alexiad, PG 131.39-1244; for English, Anna Comnena, *The Alexiad of Anna Comnena*, E.R.A. Sewter, trans. (London: Penguin

Books, 1969). See also Anna Comnena, *The Alexiad of the Princess Anna Comnena: being the History of the Reign of her Father, Alexius I, Emperor of the Romans, 1081-1118 A.D.*, Elizabeth A.S. Dawes, trans. (London: K. Paul, Trench, Trubner & Co., 1928).

OTHER PRIMARY SOURCES

Ancrene Riwle, M.B. Salu, trans. (Notre Dame, IN: University of Notre Dame Press, 1955.)

Augustine, Sermons 280, 281, 282 (On the Anniversary of the Martyrs Perpetua and Felicity) in Sermons III/8 (273-305A) *On the Saints*, Edmund Hill, trans. (Hyde Park, NY: New City Press, 1994), pp. 72-82.

Basil the Great, Homily VI on Luke xxi.18, *Writings of Basil*, Blomfield Jackson, trans. (Edinburgh: T&T Clark, 1895).

Byzantine Monastic Foundation Documents: A Complete Translation of the Surviving Founders' Typika and Testaments, John Thomas, Angela Constantinides Hero, eds (Washington, DC: Dumbarton Oaks Research Library and Collection, 2000).

Choniates, Niketas, *O City of Byzantium: Annals of Niketas Choniatēs*, Harry J. Magoulias, trans. (Detroit: Wayne State University Press, 1984).

Clement of Alexandria, "The Rich Man's Salvation" (*Quis Dives Salvetur*), *Clement of Alexandria*, G.W. Butterworth, trans. (London: William Heinemann Ltd., 1968).

Egeria's Travels, John Wilkinson, trans. (Warminster: Aris & Phillips Ltd., 2002).

Ephraim the Monk, *Ephraimii Monachi Imperatorum et Patriarchum Recensus Intrerete* (Bonnaie: Bekker, 1840).

Evagrius Ponticus, *The Praktikos & Chapters on Prayer*, John Eudes Bamberger, trans. (Kalamazoo, MI: Cistercian Publications, 1981.

French Bernard Flusin and Joseph Paramelle, "De Syncletica in Deserto Jordanis," *Analecta Bollandiana* 100 (1982), pp. 291-317; for English: Tim Vivian, "Syncletica of Palestine: A Sixth-Century Female Anchorite," *Vox Benedictina: A Journal of Translations from Monastic Sources* 10/1 (1993), pp. 9-37.

Kallistos, Nikephoros, *Ecclesiasticae Historicae*, PG 145-147.

Gregory Nazianzus, "De Vita Sua," in *Three Poems*, D.M. Meehan, trans. (Washington, DC: The Catholic University of America Press, 1987), pp. 75-130.

Gregory Nazianzus, Oration 14 in *St. Gregory Nazianzus: Selected Orations*, M. Vinson, trans. (Washington, DC: The Catholic University of America Press, 2003).

Gregorii Nysseni Opera, v. 6, *In Canticum Canticorum* (Leiden: E.J. Brill, 1960); for English, Gregory of Nyssa: *Homilies on the Song of Songs*, Richard A. Norris, Jr., trans. (Atlanta: Society of Biblical Literature, 2012).

Gregory of Nyssa, *Catechetical Oration*, NPNF 5.473-509.

Gregory of Nyssa, *From Glory to Glory: Texts from Gregory of Nyssa's Mystical Writings*, Herbert Musurillo, trans. (Yonkers, NY: St. Vladimir's Press, 1979).

Gregory of Nyssa: The Letters, Anna M. Silvas, ed. (Leiden; Boston: Brill, 2007).

Gregory of Nyssa, *The Life of Saint Macrina*, Kevin Corrigan, trans. (London: Peregrina Publishing Co., 2005).

Gregory of Nyssa, *On the Soul and the Resurrection*, Catherine P. Roth, trans. (Crestwood, NY: St Vladimir's Seminary Press, 1993).

Matericon: Instructions of Abba Isaiah to the Honorable Nun Theodora (Safford, AZ: St. Paisius Serbian Orthodox Monastery, 2001).

Musurillo, Herbert A., *The Acts of the Christian Martyrs* (Oxford: Clarendon Press, 1972).

New Documents Illustrating Early Christianity: A Review of the Greek Inscriptions and Papyri, G.H.R. Horsley, S.R. Llewelyn, eds (North Ryde, N.S.W.: Ancient History Documentary Research Centre, Macquarie University, 1981-1995).

Palladius, Bishop of Aspuna, *The Lausiac History*, Robert T. Meyer, trans. (New York: Paulist Press, 1964).

Papyrus Oxyrynchus XII.1467, "Petition for Ius Tres Liberorum," B. P. Grenfell and A. S. Hunt, eds. Available at: http://www.papyrology.ox.ac.uk/POxy/ (accessed 1/6/2020).

The Paradise of the Fathers: Being the Histories and Sayings of the Monks and Ascetics of the Egyptian Desert, Vol. 1, E.A. Wallis Budge, trans. (translation of Syriac Sayings of the Fathers) (London: Chatto & Windus, 1970).

Pliny the Elder, *Natural History*, H. Rackham, trans. (Cambridge, MA: Harvard University Press, 1938-1963).

Psellus, Michael, *The Chronographia*, E.R.A. Sewter, trans. (London: Routledge & K. Paul, 1953).

Rader, Rosemary, "The Martyrdom of Perpetua: A Protest Account of Third-Century Christianity," in *A Lost Tradition: Women Writers of the Early Church,* Patricia Wilson Kastner, ed. (Lanham, MD: University Press of America, 1981), pp. 1-17.

Seventh Ecumenical Council, *Acta* (Florence: *Sacrorum Conciliorum Nova et Amplissima*, 1758-1798).

Sozomen, *Ecclesiastical History*, NPNF II. 179-427.

Tertullian, *Homily on Baptism*, Ernest Evans, trans. (London: SPCK, 1964).

Tertullian, "On the Veiling of Virgins," available at: http://www.newadvent.org/fathers/0403.htm (accessed 1/6/20)

St. Theodore the Studite, *Antirhetici Adversus Iconomachos*, PG 99.327-436; for English, *On the Holy Icons,* Catherine Roth, trans. (Crestwood, NY: St. Vladimir's Seminary Press, 1981).

Theophanes, the Confessor, *Chronographia: Byzantine and Near Eastern History, AD 284-813* Cyril Mango and Roger Scott, trans. (Oxford: Clarendon Press; New York: Oxford University Press, 1997).

Verba Seniorum, excerpted in *The Desert Fathers*, Helen Waddell, trans. (London: Constable & Co., Ltd., 1936).

Vitae Patrum, Pelagius and John, in PL 73.855-1022; for English: "The Saying of the Fathers (*Verba Seniorum*)" in Owen Chadwick, *Western Asceticism: Selected Translations with Introductions and Notes* (Philadelphia: The Westminster Press, 1958), pp. 33-189.

Secondary Resources

Allen, Pauline, and Wendy Mayer, "John Chrysostom," in *The Early Christian World*, Philip F. Esler, ed. (London; New York: Routledge, 2000), pp.1128-1150.

Angert-Quilter, Theresa, *A Commentary on the Shorter Text of the Acts of Thecla and its New Testament Parallels* (North Sydney: Australian Catholic University, 2014).

Angold, Michael, *Church and Society in Byzantium Under the Com-neni, 1081-1261*, (Cambridge: Cambridge University Press, 1995).

Ascough, Richard S., *Lydia: Paul's Cosmopolitan Hostess* (Collegeville, MN: Liturgical Press, 2008).

Barnes, Timothy D., *Constantine and Eusebius* (Cambridge, MA: Harvard University Press, 1981).

Baur, Chrysostomus, *John Chrysostom and his Time* (London; Glasgow: Sands & Co., 1960).

Bergmann, Bettina, Wendy M. Watson, *The Moon and the Stars: Afterlife of a Roman Empress* (South Hadley, MA: Mount Holyoke College Art Museum, 1999).

Boersma, Hans, *Embodiment and Virtue in Gregory of Nyssa: An Anagogical Approach* (Oxford: Oxford University Press, 2013).

Bouyer, Louis, *The Spirituality of the New Testament and the Fathers* (New York: The Seabury Press, 1963).

Bowersock, Glen W., *Martyrdom and Rome* (Wiles Lectures) (Cambridge: Cambridge University Press, 1995).

Bralewski, Slawomir, "The Pious Life of Empress Helena, Constantine the Great's Mother: In the Light of Socrates and Sozomen," *Studia Ceranea* 7 (2017), pp. 27-39.

Branick, Vincent, *The House Church in the Writings of Paul* (Wilmington, DE: Michael Glazier, 1989).

Bremmer, Jan N., Marco Formisano, eds, *Perpetua's Passions: Multidisciplinary Approaches to the Passio Perpetuae et Felicitatis* (Oxford: Oxford University Press, 2012).

Bremmer, Jan N., *The Rise and Fall of the Afterlife: The 1995 Read-Tuckwell Lectures at the University of Bristol* (London: Routledge, 2002).

Brennois, Nikephoros, "Materials for a History," Henri Gregoire, trans. *Byzantion* 23 (1953), pp. 469-530; and *Byzantion* 25-27 (1955-57), pp. 881-925.

Brown, Peter, *The Body and Society: Men, Women and Sexual Renunciation in Early Christianity* (New York: Columbia University Press, 1988).

Brown, Peter, *Power and Persuasion in Late Antiquity: Towards a Christian Empire*; The Curti Lectures (1988) (Madison, WI: University of Wisconsin Press, 1992).

Brown, Raymond E., *An Introduction to the New Testament* (New York: Doubleday, 1997).

Browning, Robert, "An Unpublished Funeral Oration on Anna Comnena," in *Aristotle Transformed: The Ancient Commentators and Their Influence*, Richard Sorabji, ed. (Ithaca, NY: Cornell University Press, 1990), pp. 393-406.

Brubaker, Leslie, "Memories of Helena: Patterns in Imperial Female Matronage in the Fourth and Fifth Centuries," in *Women, Men, and Eunuchs: Gender in Byzantium*, Liz James, ed. (London: Routledge, 1997), pp. 52-75.

Brubaker, Leslie, Helen Tobler, "The Gender of Money: Byzantine Empresses on Coins (324-802)," *Gender & Money* 12:3 (Nov 2000), pp. 572-594.

Bruun, Patrick M., *The Roman Imperial Coinage, VII, Constantine and Licinius A.D. 313-337*, C.H.V. Sutherland, R.A.G. Carson, gen. eds (London: Spink and Son Ltd, 1966).

Burras, Virginia, *Chastity as Autonomy: Women in the Stories of the Apocryphal Acts* (Queenston, ON: Mellon, 1987).

Burton-Christie, Douglas, The *Word in the Desert: Scripture and the Quest for Holiness in Early Christian Monasticism* (New York: Oxford Press, 1993).

Cahill, J. B., "The Date and Setting of Gregory of Nyssa's Commentary on the Song of Songs," *Journal of Theological Studies* (1981), pp. 447-460.

Cartlidge, David R., J. Keith Elliott, *Art and the Christian Apocrypha* (London: Routledge, 2001).

Castelli, Elizabeth A., *Martyrdom and Memory: Early Christian Culture Making* (New York: Columbia University Press, 2004).

Chryssavgis, John, "The Desert and the World: Learning from the Desert Fathers and Mothers," *Greek Orthodox Theological Review* 53 (2008), pp.141-154.

Chryssavgis, John, *In the Heart of the Desert: The Spirituality of the Desert Fathers and Mothers* (Bloomington, IN: World Wisdom, 2003).

Clark, Elizabeth, "Early Church Women: Sources and Interpretation," in *That Gentle Strength: Historical Perspectives on Women in Christianity*, Lynda Coon, ed. (Charlottesville, VA: University Press of Virginia, 1990).

Cloke, Gillian, 'This Female Man of God:' Women and Spiritual Power in the Patristic Age, AD 350-450 (London; New York: Routledge, 1995).

Cohick, Lynn H., Women in the World of the Earliest Christians: Illuminating Ancient Ways of Life (Grand Rapids. MI: Baker Academic, 2009).

Cohick, Lynn H., Amy Brown Hughes, Christian Women in the Patristic World: Their Influence, Authority, and Legacy in the Second through Fifth Centuries (Grand Rapids, MI: Baker Academic, 2017).

Connor, Carolyn L., Women of Byzantium (New Haven; London: Yale University Press, 2004).

Conomos, Dimitri, Byzantine Hymnology and Byzantine Chant (Brookline, MA: Hellenic College Press, 1984).

Constantelos, Demetrios J., Byzantine Philanthropy and Social Welfare (New Brunswick, NJ: Rutgers University Press, 1968).

Coon, Linda, Sacred Fictions: Holy Women and Hagiography in Late Antiquity (Philadelphia: University of Pennsylvania Press, 1997).

Corrigan, Kevin, "Syncletica and Macrina: Two Early Lives of Women Saints" Vox Benedictina: A Journal of Translations from Monastic Sources 6:3 (July 1989), pp. 241-257.

Cotter, Wendy, "Women's Authority Roles in Paul's Churches: Countercultural or Conventional?" Novum Testamentum 36:4 (1994), pp. 350-372.

Cotter-Lynch, Margaret, Saint Perpetua across the Middle Ages: Mother, Gladiator, Saint (New York: Palgrave Macmillan, 2016).

Davies, Stevan L., The Revolt of the Widows: The Social World of the Apocryphal Acts (Carbonville, IL: Southern Illinois University Press, 1980).

Davis, Stephen J., The Cult of St. Thecla: A Tradition of Women's Piety in Late Antiquity (Oxford: Oxford University Press, 2001).

Denzey, Nicola, The Bone Gatherers: The Lost Worlds of Early Christian Women (Boston: Beacon Press, 2007).

Dodds, E.R., Pagan and Christian in the Age of Anxiety (Cambridge: Cambridge University Press, 1965).

Doran, Robert, "Thecla and the Governor: Who Clothes Whom?" in *A Most Reliable Witness: Essays in Honor of Ross Shephard Kraemer*, Susan Ashbrook Harvey et al, eds (Providence, RI: Brown University, 2015), pp. 17-25.

Downey, Glanville, "*Philanthropia* in Religion and Statecraft in the Fourth Century after Christ," in *Historia: Zeitschrift fur Alte Geschichte* 4:2/3 (1955), pp. 199-208.

Drake, H.A., "Eusebius on the True Cross," *Journal of Ecclesiastical History* 36:1 (Jan. 1985), pp. 1-22.

Drijvers, Jan Willem, "Helena Augusta: Exemplary Christian Empress," *Studia Patristica* XXIV (1993), pp. 500-506.

Drijvers, Jan Willem, "Helena Augusta, the Cross, and the Myth: Some New Reflections," *Jahrbuch zu Kultur und Geschichte des Ersten Jahrtausends n. Chr., Millennium* 8 (2011), pp. 125-174.

Drijvers, Jan Willem, *Helena Augusta: The Mother of Constantine the Great and the Legend of Her Finding the True Cross* (Leiden: Brill, 1992).

Drijvers, Jan Willem, "Promoting Jerusalem: Cyril and the True Cross," in *Portraits of Spiritual Authority: Religious Power in Early Christianity, Byzantium, and the Christian Orient*, Jan Willem Drijvers, John W. Watt., eds (Leiden: Brill, 1999), pp. 78-95.

Dronke, Peter, *Women Writers of the Middle Ages: A Critical Study of Texts from Perpetua to Marguerite Porete* (Cambridge: Cambridge University Press, 1984).

Dunn, James D.G., *The Acts of the Apostles* (Valley Forge, PA: Trinity Press International, 1996).

Dunn, James D.G., *Beginning from Jerusalem* (Grand Rapids, MI: William B. Eerdmans Pub. Co., 2009).

Dunn, Shannon, "The Female Martyr and the Politics of Death: An Examination of the Martyr Discourses of Vibia Perpetua and Wafa Idris," *Journal of the American Academy of Religion* 78:1 (March 2010), pp. 202-225.

Efthymiadis, Stephanos, "Notes on the Correspondence of Theodore the Studite," *Revue des Études Byzantines* 53 (1995), pp. 141-163.

Elm, Susanna, '*Virgins of God:' The Making of Asceticism in Late Antiquity* (Oxford: Clarendon Press, 1994).

Ferguson, Everett, *Baptism in the Early Church: History, Theology, and Liturgy in the First Five Centuries* (Grand Rapids, MI: William B. Eerdmans Pub. Co., 2009).

Ferguson, Everett, *Backgrounds of Early Christianity* (Grand Rapids, MI: William B. Eerdmans Publishing Company, 2003).

Finn, Thomas M., *Early Christian Baptism and the Catechumenate: West and East* (Collegeville, MN: Liturgical Press, 1992).

Fitzmyer, Joseph A., *The Acts of the Apostles: A New Translation with Introduction and Commentary* (New York: Doubleday, 1998).

Forman, Mary, "Amma Syncletica: A Spirituality of Experience," *Vox Benedictina* 10:2 (Winter 1993), pp. 199-237.

Forman, Mary, "Purity of Heart in the Life and Works of Amma Syncletica," in *Purity of Heart in Early Ascetic and Monastic Literature: Essays in Honor of Juana Raasch, O.S.B.*, H.A. Luckman, L. Kulzer, eds (Collegeville, MN: Liturgical Press, 1999), pp. 161-174.

Frankopan, Peter, "Pereception and Projection: Anna Comnene, the *Alexiad* and the First Crusade," in *Gendering the Crusades*, Susan B. Edgington, Sarah Lambert, eds (New York: Columbia University Press, 2002), pp. 59-76.

Frend, W.H.C., *Martyrdom and Persecution in the Early Church: A Study of a Conflict from the Maccabees to Donatus* (Oxford: Basil Blackwell, 1965).

Gaddis, Michael, *There is No Crime for Those Who Have Christ* (Berkeley, CA: University of California Press, 2005).

Gardner, Alice, *Theodore of Studium: His Life and Times* (London: Edward Arnold, 1905).

Gehring, Roger W., *House Church and Mission: The Importance of Household Structures in Early Christianity* (Peabody, MA: Hendrickson Publishers, 2004).

Georgiou, Andriani, "Helena: The Subversive Persona of an Ideal Christian Empress in Early Byzantium," *Journal of Early Christian Studies* 21:4 (Winter 2013), pp. 597-624.

Gillman, Florence M., *Women who Knew Paul* (Collegeville, MN: The Liturgical Press, 1992).

Gold, Barbara K., "Gender Fluidity and Closure in Perpetua's Prison Diary," *Journal on Gender Studies in Antiquity* No. 1 (2011), pp. 237-251.

Goodspeed, Edgar Johnson, "The Book of Thekla," *American Journal of Semitic Languages and Literatures* 17 (1901), pp. 65-95.

Gould, Graham, "A Note on the *Apophthegmata Patrum*," *Journal of Theological Studies* 37 (1986), pp. 133-139.

Gould, Graham, *The Desert Fathers on Monastic Community* (Oxford: Clarendon Press, 1993).

Gouma-Petersen, Thalia, ed. *Anna Komnene and Her Times* (New York: Garland, 2000).

Gryson, Roger, *The Ministry of Women in the Early Church*, Jean Laprote, Mary Louise Hall, trans. (Collegeville, MN: Liturgical Press, 1976).

Gunderson, Erik, "The Ideology of the Arena," *Classical Antiquity* 15:1 (Apr. 1996), pp. 113-151.

Haenchen, Ernst, *The Acts of the Apostles: A Commentary* (Philadelphia: Westminster Press, 1971).

Harbus, Antonina, *Helena of Britain in Medieval Legend* (Suffolk: D.S. Brewer, 2002).

Harmless, William, *Desert Christians: An Introduction to the Literature of Early Monasticism* (Oxford: Oxford University Press, 2004).

Harrison, Martin, *A Temple for Byzantium: The Discovery and Excavation of Anicia Juliana's Palace-Church in Istanbul* (Austin, TX: University of Texas Press, 1989).

Hatlie, Peter, "Images of Motherhood and Self in Byzantine Literature," *Dumbarton Oaks Papers* 63 (2003), pp. 41-57.

Hatlie, Peter, *The Monks and Monasteries of Constantinople, ca. 350-850* (Cambridge: Cambridge University Press, 2007).

Heffernan, Thomas J., "*Ius Conubii* or *Concubina*: The Marital and Social Class of Perpetua in the *Passio Sanctarum Perpetuae et Felicitatis*," *Analecta Bollandiana* 136 (2018), pp. 14-42.

Heffernan, Thomas J., "Nomen Sacrum: God's Name as Shield and Weapon in the Acts of the Christian Martyrs," in *Scripture and Pluralism*, Thomas J. Heffernan, ed. (Leiden: Brill, 2005), pp. 10-28.

Herrin, Judith, "Late Antique Origins of the 'Imperial Feminine:' Western and Eastern Empresses Compared," *Byzantinoslavica* 74 (2016), pp. 5-25.

Hill, Barbara, "Alexios I and the Imperial Women," in *Alexios I Komnenos: Papers,* Margaret Mullett and Dion Smythe, eds, pp. 37-54. (Belfast: Belfast Byzantine Texts and Translations, 1996).

Hill, Barbara, *Imperial Women in Byzantium 1025-1204: Power, Patronage and Ideology* (New York: Longman, 1999).

Hoek, van den, Annewies, John J. Herrmann, Jr., "Thecla the Beast Fighter: A Female Emblem of Deliverance in Early Christian Popular Art," *The Studia Philonica Annual: Studies in Hellenistic Judaism* 13 (2001), pp. 212-249.

Holman, S. R., ed., *Wealth and Poverty in Early Church and Society,* (Grand Rapids, MI: Baker Academic, 2008).

Holum, Kenneth, "Hadrian and St. Helena: Imperial Travel and the Origins of Christian Holy Land Pilgrimage," in *The Blessings of Pilgrimage,* Robert G. Ousterhout, ed. (Urbana, IL: University of Illinois Press, 1990), pp. 68-81.

Holum, Kenneth, *Theodosian Empresses: Women and Imperial Dominion in Late Antiquity* (Berkeley, CA: University of California Press, 1982).

Horowitz, Maryanne Cline, "The Image of God in Man: Is Woman Included?" *The Harvard Theological Review* 72: 3/4 (1979), pp. 175-206.

Hunt, Edward D., *Holy Land Pilgrimage in the Later Roman Empire, A.D. 312-460* (Oxford: Clarendon Press, 1982).

Hunt, Edward D., "Palladius of Helenopolis: A Party and its Supporters in the Church of the Late Fourth Century," *Journal of Theological Studies* 24 (1973), pp. 456-480.

Hylen, Susan E., *A Modest Apostle: Thecla and the History of Women in the Early Church* (New York: Oxford University Press, 2015).

James, Liz, *Empresses and Power in Early Byzantium* (New York: Leicester University Press, 2001).

Jewett, Robert, *A Chronology of Paul's Life* (Philadelphia: Fortress Press, 1979).

Joubert, Stephen J. "Paul as *Paterfamilias* of the Christian House-hold Group in Corinth," in *Modeling Early Christianity: Social-Scientific Studies of the New Testament in its Context* (London; New York: Routledge, 1995), pp. 213-223.

Kadel, Andrew, *Matrology* (New York: Continuum, 1995).

Kadel, Andrew, "Writing of the Mothers: Women Authors of the Eastern Church before the Fifteenth Century," in *Women in the Orthodox Church: Past Roles Future Paradigms*, J.M. Lasser, ed. (New York: Theotokos Press, 2008).

Kalavrezou, Ioli, *Byzantine Women and Their World* (New Haven and London: Yale University Press, 2003).

Kalavrezon, Ioli, "Helping Hands for the Empire: Imperial Cere-monies and the Cult of Relics at the Byzantine Court," in *Byzantine Court Culture from 829 to 1204*, Henry Maguire, ed. (Washington, DC: Dumbarton Oaks, 1997), pp. 53-79.

Kazhdan, A.P., A.-M. Talbot, "Women and Iconoclasm," *Byzantinische Zeitschrift* 84/85 (1991/1992), pp. 391-408.

Kazhdan, A.P., "'*Constantin Imaginaire*:' Byzantine Legends of the Ninth Century about Constantine the Great," *Byzantion* 57 (1987), pp. 195-250.

Kee, Robert Clark, "The Transformation of the Synagogue after 70 AD CE: Its Importance for Early Christianity," *New Testament Studies* 36 (1990), pp. 1-24.

Kelly, J. N. D., *Golden Mouth: The Story of John Chrysostom—Ascetic, Preacher, Bishop* (London: Gerald Duckworth & Co. Ltd., 1995).

King, Margot H., "The Desert Mothers: A Survey of the Feminine Anchoretic Tradition in Western Europe." Reprinted from Peregrina Publishing Co. Available at: www.hermitary.com/ articles/mothers.html (accessed 1/6/2020)

Kitzler, Petr, "*Passio Perpetuae* and *Acta Perpetuae*: Between Tradition and Innovation," *Listy Filologicke* 100:1-2 (2007), pp. 1-19.

Klawiter, Frederick C., "The Role of Martyrdom and Persecution in Developing the Priestly Authority of Women in Early Christianity: A Case Study of Montanism," *Church History* 49:3 (Sept. 1980), pp. 251-261.

Koenig, John, *Charismata: God's Gifts for God's People* (Philadelphia: The Westminster Press, 1978).

Koenig, John, *The Feast of the World's Redemption: Eucharistic Origins and Christian Mission* (Harrisburg, PA: Trinity Press International, 2000).

Koenig, John, *New Testament Hospitality: Partnership with Strangers as Promise and Mission* (Philadelphia: Fortress Press, 1985).

Koenig, John, *Soul Banquets: How Meals Became Mission in the Local Congregation* (Harrisburg, PA: Morehouse Publishing, 2007).

Kostenberger, Andreas J., "Women in the Pauline Mission," in *The Gospel to the Nations: Perspectives on Paul's Mission* (Leicester: Apollos, 2000), pp. 221-247.

Kraemer, Ross Shepard, *Unreliable Witnesses: Religion, Gender, and History in the Greco-Roman Mediterranean* (Oxford: Oxford University Press, 2011).

Kristensen, Troels Myrup, "The Landscape, Space, and Presence in the Cult of Thekla at Meriamlik," *Journal of Early Christian Studies* 24:2 (Summer 2016), pp. 229-263.

Krueger, Derek, *Writing and Holiness: The Practice of Authorship in the Early Christian East* (Philadelphia: University of Pennsylvania Press, Inc. 2011).

Larsen, Lillian, "The *Apophthegmata Patrum* and the Classical Rhetorical Tradition;" *Studia Patristica* XXXIX (Leuven: Peeters, 2006), pp. 409-415.

Lavin, I., "The Ceiling Frescoes in Trier and Illusionism in Constantinian Painting," *Dumbarton Oaks Papers* 21 (1967), pp. 99-113.

Lensky, Noel, "Empresses in the Holy Land: The Creation of a Christian Utopia in Late Antique Palestine," in *Travel, Communication, and Geography in Late Antiquity: Sacred and Profane*, Linda Ellis, Frank Kiner, eds (San Francisco: San Francisco State University, 2004), pp. 113-124.

Liebeschuetz, J. H., *Barbarians and Bishops: Army, Church, and State in the Age of Arcadius and Chrysostom* (Oxford: Clarendon Press, 1990).

Lipsett, B. Diane, *Desiring Conversion: Hermas, Thecla, Aseneth* (Oxford: Oxford University Press, 2011).

Ljubarskij, Jakov, "Why is the *Alexiad* a Masterpiece of Byzantine Literature?" in *Anna Komnene and her Times*, Thalia Gouma-Peterson, ed. (New York; London: Garland Publishing, Inc, 2000), pp. 169-186.

MacDonald, Dennis Ronald, *The Legend and the Apostle: The Battle for Paul in Story and Canon* (Philadelphia: Westminster Press, 1983).

MacDonald, Margaret Y., "Was Celsus Right?: The Role of Women in the Expansion of Early Christianity," in *Early Christian Families in Context: An Interdisciplinary Dialogue,* David L. Balch, Carolyn Oziak, eds (Grand Rapids, MI: Eerdmans, 2003), pp. 157-184.

MacDonald, Margaret Y., "Rereading Paul: Early Interpreters of Paul on Women and Gender," in Ross Shepard Kraemer, Mary Rose D'Angelo, eds, *Women and Christian Origins* (New York: Oxford Press, 1999), pp. 236-253.

Mainstone, Rowland J., *Hagia Sophia: Architecture, Structure and Liturgy of Justinian's Great Church* (London: Thames & Hudson, 1988).

Malherbe, Abraham J., *Social Aspects of Early Christianity*, (Philadelphia, PA: The Fortress Press, 1983).

Marshall, I. Howard, "Luke's Portrait of the Pauline Mission," in *The Gospel to the Nations: Perspectives on Paul's Mission* (Leicester: Apollos, 2000), pp. 99-113.

Martimort, Aimé Georges, *Deaconesses: An Historical Study*, K.D. Whitehead, trans. (San Francisco: Ignatius Press, 1986).

Mathews, Thomas F., *The Byzantine Churches of Istanbul: A Photographic Survey* (University Park, PA: Pennsylvania State University Press, 1976).

Matthews, Shelly, *First Converts: Rich Pagan Women and the Rhetoric of Mission in Early Judaism and Christianity* (Stanford, CA: Stanford University Press, 2001).

McClanan, Anne, *Representations of Early Byzantine Empresses: Image and Empire* (New York: Palgrave Macmillan, 2002).

McGuckin, John Anthony, *The Path of Christianity: The First Thousand Years* (Downers Grove, IL: IVP Academic, 2017).

McGuckin, John Anthony, "The Strategic Adaptation of Deification in the Cappadocians," in *Partakers of the Divine Nature:*

The History and Development of Deification in the Christian Traditions, Michael Christenson, J.A. Wittung, eds (Grand Rapids, MI: Baker Academic, 2008), pp. 95-114.

McGuckin, John Anthony, "Symeon the New Theologian (d. 1022) and Byzantine Monasticism," in *Mount Athos and Byzantine Monasticism: Papers from the Twenty-eighth Spring Symposium of Byzantine Studies, Birmingham, 1994*, Anthony Bryer, Mary Cunningham, eds (Aldershot, Hampshire: Vaporium, 1996), pp. 17-35.

McLynn, Neil, "The Other Olympias: Gregory Nazianzus and the Family of Vitalianus," in *Christian Politics and Religious Culture in Late Antiquity* (Farnham, Surrey: Ashgate Publishing Ltd., 2009), pp. 227-246.

McNamara, Jo Ann, "Muffled Voices: The Lives of Consecrated Women in the Fourth Century," in *Distant Echoes: Medieval Religious Women*. John A. Nichols, Lilian T. Shank. eds, (Kalamazoo, MI: Cistercian Publications, Inc., 1984), pp.11-29.

Meeks, Wayne A., *The First Urban Christians: The Social World of the Apostle Paul* (New Haven, CT: Yale University Press, 2003).

Meyendorff, John, *Byzantine Theology: Historical Trends and Doctrinal Themes* (New York: Fordham University Press, 1979).

Morris, Colin, *The Sepulchre of Christ and the West: From the Beginning to 1660* (Oxford: Oxford University Press, 2005).

Murphy-O'Connor, Jerome, *St. Paul: A Critical Life,* (Oxford: Clarendon Press, 1996).

Misset-van de Weg, Magda, "Answers to the Plights of an Ascetic Woman Named Thecla," in *A Feminist Companion to the New Testament Apocrypha*, Amy-Jill Levine, ed. (London: T & T Clark International, 2006), pp. 146-162.

Neureiter, Livia, "Health and Healing as Recurrent Topics in John Chrysostom's Correspondence with Olympias," *Studia Patristica* XLVII (2010), pp. 267-272.

Neyrey, Jerome H., ed.,*The Social World of Luke/Acts: Models for Interpretation*, (Peabody, MA: Hendrickson Publishers, 1991).

Norris, Richard A., "The Soul Takes Flight: Gregory of Nyssa and the Song of Songs," *Anglican Theological Review* 80: 4 (1998), pp. 517-561.

Oden, Amy G., *And You Welcomed Me: A Sourcebook on Hospitality in Early Christianity* (Nashville, TN: Abingdon Press, 2001).

Ostrogorsky, George, *History of the Byzantine State*, revised edition (New Brunswick, NJ: Rutgers University Press, 1969).

Panagopoulos, Spyros, "Kassia: A Female Hymnographer of the 9th Century," in *Proceedings of the 1st International Conference of ASBMH* (1993), pp. 111-123.

Parker, A.S.E., "The *Vita Syncleticae*: Its Manuscripts, Ascetical Teachings and its Use in Monastic Sources;" *Studia Patristica* XXX (1997), pp. 231-234.

Pelikan, Jaroslav, *Acts* (Grand Rapids, MI: Brazos, 2005).

Pelikan, Jaroslav, *Christianity and Classical Culture: The Metamorphosis of Natural Theology in the Christian Encounter with Hellenism* (New Haven, CT: Yale University Press, 1993).

Perkins, Judith, *The Suffering Self: Pain and Narrative Representation in the Early Christian Era* (London: Rutledge, 1995).

Pervo, Richard I., *Acts: A Commentary* (Minneapolis, MN: Fortress Press, 2009).

Petersen, Joan M., *Handmaids of the Lord: Holy Women in Late Antiquity and the Early Middle Ages* (Kalamazoo, MI: Cistercian Publications, Inc., 1996).

Pettersen, Alvyn, "Prison of Conscience," *Vigiliae Christianae* 41:2 (June 1987), pp. 139-153.

Petroff, Elizabeth Alvilda, *Medieval Women's Visionary Literature* (New York: Oxford University Press, 1986).

Polaski, Sandra Hack, "Paul and Real Women," *Word & World*, 30:4 (Fall 2010), pp. 391-398.

Quandahl, Ellen, Susan B. Jarratt, "To Recall Him...Will be a Subject of Lamentation: Anna Comnena as Rhetorical Historiographer," *Rhetorica: A Journal of the History of Rhetoric* 26:3 (Summer 2008), pp. 301-335.

Ramsey, William M., "The Acta of Paul and Thekla," in *The Church in the Roman Empire Before A.D. 170* (New York: G.P. Putnam, 1893), pp. 390-410.

Rapp, Claudia, "Figures of Female Sanctity: Byzantine Edifying Manuscripts and Their Audience," *Dumbarton Oaks Papers* 50 (Washington, DC: Dumbarton Oaks Center for Byzantine Studies, 1996), pp. 313-44.

Reese, Gustave, *Music in the Middle Ages: With an Introduction on the Music of Ancient Times* (New York: W. W. Norton & Company, Inc., 1968).

Ray, Walter D., *Tasting Heaven on Earth: Worship in Sixth-Century Constantinople* (Grand Rapids, MI: Eerdmans, 2012).

Salisbury, Joyce E., *The Blood of Martyrs: Unintended Consequences of Ancient Violence* (New York: Routledge, 2004).

Salisbury, Joyce E., *Perpetua's Passion: The Death and Memory of a Young Roman Woman* (New York: Routledge, 1997).

Schroeder, Caroline T., "Women in Anchoritic and Semi-Anchoritic Monasticism in Egypt: Rethinking the Landscape," *Church History* 83:1 (March 2014), pp. 1-17.

Schottroff, Luise, *Lydia's Impatient Sisters: A Feminist History of Early Christianity* (Louisville, KY: Westminster John Knox Press, 1995).

Schüssler Fiorenza, Elisabeth, *In Memory of Her: A Feminist Theological Reconstruction of Christian Origins* (New York: Crossroad, 1992).

Shaw, Brent D., "The Passion of Perpetua," *Past & Present* 139:1 (May 1993), pp. 3-45.

Sherry, Kurt, *Kassia the Nun in Context: The Religious Thought of a Ninth-Century Byzantine Monastic* (Piscataway, NJ: Gorgias Press, 2011).

Silvas, Anna M., "Kassia the Nun c. 810-c. 865: an Appreciation," in *Byzantine Women: Varieties of Experience 800-1200*, Lynda Garland, ed. (Burlington, VT: Ashgate Publishing, 2006), pp. 17-39.

Simic, Kosta, "Kassia's Hymnography in the Light of Patristic Sources and Earlier Hymnological Works," *Recueil des Travaux de L'Institut d'Etudes Byzantines* 48 (2001), pp. 7-37.

Smythe, Dion C., "Middle Byzantine Family Values and Anna Komnene's *Alexiad*" in *Byzantine Women: Varieties of Experience 800-1200*, Lynda Garland, ed. (Aldershot: Ashgate, 2006), pp. 125-139.

Spanos, Apostolos, "Political Approaches to Byzantine Liturgical Texts," in Roy Eriksen and Peter Young, *Approaches to the Text: From Pre-Gospel to Post-Baroque* (Pisa-Rome: Fabrizio Serra Editore, 2014), pp. 63-81.

Stephenson, Paul, "Anna Comnene's *Alexiad* as a Source for the Second Crusade?" *Journal for Medieval History* 29 (2003), pp. 41-54.

Streete, Gail Corrington, *Redeemed Bodies: Women Martyrs in Early Christianity* (Louisville, KY: Westminster John Knox Press, 2009).

Talbot, Alice-Mary, *Women and Religious Life in Byzantium* (Aldershot: Ashgate Variorum, 2001).

Tilley, Maureen, "The Ascetic Body and the (Un)making of the World of the Martyr," *Journal of the American Academy of Religion* 59:3 (Autumn 1991), pp. 467-479.

Tillyard, H.J.W., *Byzantine Music and Hymnography* (Charing Cross: The Faith Press, Ltd., 1923).

Topping, Katafygiotou Eva, "Byzantine Hymnography," in *Three Byzantine Sacred Poets*, Nomikos Michael Vaporis, ed. (Brookline, MA: Hellenic College Press, 1979), pp. 1-11.

Topping, Katafygiotou Eva, *Holy Mothers of Orthodoxy* (Minneapolis, MN: Light & Life Publishing, 1987).

Topping, Katafygiotou Eva, "Kassiane the Nun and the Sinful Woman," *Greek Orthodox Theological Review* 26 (1981), pp. 201-209.

Touliatos-Banker, Diane, "Women Composers of Medieval Byzantine Chant," *Journal of College Music Society, College Music Symposium* 24:1 (St. Louis, MO: University of St. Louis, 1984), pp. 62-80.

Treadgold, Warren, *A History of the Byzantine State and Society* (Stanford: Stanford University Press, 1997).

Tripolitis, Antonia, *Kassia: The Legend, the Woman, and her Work* (London: Rutledge, 1992).

Tsarsos, Jeanne, *Empress Athenais-Eudocia: A Fifth Century Byzantine Humanist* (Brookline, MA: Holy Cross Orthodox Press, 1977).

Tsironis, Niki, "The Body and the Senses in the Work of Cassia the Hymnographer: Literary Trends in the Iconoclastic Period," *Byzantina Symmeikta* 16 (2014), pp. 138-159.

Tubbernee, William, "Initiation/Baptism in the Montanist Movement," in David Hellholm, ed., *Ablution, Initiation, and*

Baptism: Late Antiquity, Early Judaism, and Early Christianity (Berlin: De Gruyter, 2010-2011), pp. 917-946.

Tucker, J. Brian, "God-fearers: Literary Foil or Historical Reality in the Book of Arts," *Journal of Biblical Studies* 5:1 (Jan. 2005), pp. 21-39.

Vogt, Joseph, "Pagans and Christians in the Family of Constantine the Great," in *The Conflict between Paganism and Christianity in the Fourth Century*, Arnaldo Momigliano, ed. (Oxford: Clarendon Press, 1963), pp. 38-54.

Whitby, Mary, "'Sugaring the Pill:' Gregory of Nazianzus' Advice to Olympias (Carm. 2.2.6)," *Ramus: Critical Studies in Greek and Roman Literature* 37:1/2 (2008), pp. 79-98.

White, Caroline, *Christian Friendship in the Fourth Century* (Cambridge: Cambridge University Press, 1992).

Williams, Rowan, "Macrina's Deathbed Revisited: Gregory of Nyssa on Mind and Passion," in *Christian Faith and Greek Philosophy in Late Antiquity* (Leiden: E.J. Brill, 1993), pp. 228-246.

Wilson-Kastner, Patricia, "Macrina: Virgin and Teacher," *Andrews University Seminary Studies* 17 (1979), pp.105-117.

Witherington, Ben, *The Acts of the Apostles: A Socio-Rhetorical Commentary* (Grand Rapids, MI: William B. Eerdmans Publishing Company, 1998).

Witherington, Ben, *Women in the Earliest Churches* (Cambridge: Cambridge University Press, 1988).

Zugrava, Gheorghita, *Kasia the Melodist: And the Making of a Byzantine Hymnographer*, Columbia University Ph.D, dissertation (2013).

INDICES

INDEX OF SUBJECTS

Porphyrogenita, "born in the Purple," 94, 173, 179, 182

Prayer, see also *Askesis*, 30, 60, 63-64, 75-77, 108-113, 115-125, 127-141, 170-175, 187-188

Purple fabric dealer, see also *Porphuropolis*, 2, 14, 30-31, 33, 37

Perigrapton, Circumscribability, 153-155

Quadrivium of Sciences, classical education, 182

Resurrection, 9-10, 46, 61, 64, 79, 115, 122, 124-125

Rule, monastic, see also *Typika*, 10, 14, 149, 171-175, 182

Sebomene ton Theon, see also God-fearer, 27, 31, 37-38

Secvritas Repvblice, Security of the Nation, personification of, 91

Sequence, liturgical, Western Church, 151

Sine manu, type of arranged marriage, 26, 71

Sophrosyne, Prudence, personification of, 169

Sticheron, Byzantine hymn, 12, 144, 149, 151, 154-155

Toga virilis, assumption of, coming of age, 70

Triodion, Orthodox chants for Lent, 12, 145

True Cross, see also Holy Cross, 7, 86-101, 125, 166

Typika, monastic Rule, 10, 14, 149, 171-175, 182

Vademecum, hand-book, 112

Virginity, see also Celibacy, 4, 45-46, 53, 61-62, 65-66, 116, 118, 120-121

Verba Seniorum, 104

"We sections" in Acts, 28-29, 39

"When Augustus Reigned," see "On the Birth of Christ," 12, 144, 149, 150-155

Widows, Order of, 43

Visions, of the presence of God, 7, 47, 60-61, 67-81, 94, 125, 137

INDEX OF NAMES

Alexios I Komene, Emperor, 172, 177-193

Alexander the Great, 29

Ambrose, Bishop of Milan, 5, 92-93, 160, 162-163

Anicia Juliana, Princess, 168-170

Anthusa, mother of John Chrysostom, 134

Antony the Great, 104, 108